Individual, School, and National Factors Impacting Teachers' Workplace Learning

By drawing on observation and detailed discourse analysis from interviews with teachers in Lithuanian and North American schools, this text identifies individual, school-specific, and national factors which impact teachers' informal professional learning.

Addressing multiple layers of teacher learning, this text illustrates how factors including socio-economic status, individual learning style, cultural attitudes to education, and political histories support or impede workplace learning. Drawing on three fields of research—teacher education, cultural anthropology, and comparative international—the book posits teacher learning as a multidimensional socio-cultural process. Finally, combining a typology of informal learners with other policy-driven factors, the text indicates how practices at school, district, and national levels might stimulate workplace learning.

Offering methodological innovations including unique research design and creative ways of using discourse analysis, this book will be of particular use to researchers and doctoral students in education, organizational and educational psychology, cultural anthropology, management, and beyond.

Elena Jurasaite-O'Keefe is Associate Professor of Curriculum and Instruction at St. John's University, New York, USA.

Routledge Research in Teacher Education

The Routledge Research in Teacher Education series presents the latest research on Teacher Education and also provides a forum to discuss the latest practices and challenges in the field.

Professional Learning and Identities in Teaching
International Narratives of Successful Teachers
Edited by A. Cendel Karaman and Silvia Edling

Teacher Quality and Education Policy in India
Understanding the Relationship between Teacher Education, Teacher Effectiveness, and Student Outcomes
Preeti Kumar and Alexander W. Wiseman

Teacher Educators and their Professional Development
Learning from the Past, Looking to the Future
Edited by Ruben Vanderlinde, Kari Smith, Mieke Lunenberg, and Jean Murray

Individual, School, and National Factors Impacting Teachers' Workplace Learning
Discourses of Informal Learning in North America and Lithuania
Elena Jurasaite-O'Keefe

Teacher Education in Russia
Past, Present and Future
Edited by Ian Menter

For more information about this series, please visit: https://www.routledge.com/Routledge-Research-in-Teacher-Education/book-series/RRTE

Individual, School, and National Factors Impacting Teachers' Workplace Learning

Discourses of Informal Learning in North America and Lithuania

Elena Jurasaite-O'Keefe

Routledge
Taylor & Francis Group
NEW YORK AND LONDON

First published 2022
by Routledge
605 Third Avenue, New York, NY 10158

and by Routledge
2 Park Square, Milton Park, Abingdon, Oxon, OX14 4RN

Routledge is an imprint of the Taylor & Francis Group, an informa business

Library of Congress Cataloging-in-Publication Data
Names: Jurasaite-O'Keefe, Elena, author.
Title: Individual, school, and national factors impacting teachers'
workplace learning : discourses of informal learning in North America and Lithuania / Elena Jurasaite-O'Keefe.
Description: New York, NY : Routledge, 2021. | Series: Routledge research in teacher education | Includes bibliographical references and index. | Identifiers: LCCN 2021006635 (print) | LCCN 2021006636 (ebook) | ISBN 9780367418564 (hardback) | ISBN 9781032048321 (paperback) | ISBN 9780367816605 (ebook)
Subjects: LCSH: Teachers--In-service training--North America. | Teachers--In-service training--Lithuania. | Teachers--Language. | Discourse analysis.
Classification: LCC LB1731 .J87 2021 (print) | LCC LB1731 (ebook) | DDC 370.71/1--dc23
LC record available at https://lccn.loc.gov/2021006635
LC ebook record available at https://lccn.loc.gov/2021006636

ISBN: 978-0-367-41856-4 (hbk)
ISBN: 978-1-032-04832-1 (pbk)
ISBN: 978-0-367-81660-5 (ebk)

Typeset in Galliard
by SPi Technologies India Pvt Ltd (Straive)

This book was written in the turbulent times: They will be remembered by a raging corona virus pandemic and social unrest in the United States in addition to significant personal events. I dedicate this book to my grandchildren Dziazy, Yuri, and Sergio: Keep reaching for the stars in spite of any obstacles that pop up on your way.

Contents

Figures

Tables

Acknowledgements

I would compare working on a book to an ascent to the peak of a mountain—a route that starts wide and open, and later becomes narrower and steeper, until it reaches the highest point from which other peaks call and new horizons open. To undertake this journey alone is impossible. I am deeply indebted to those people who have supported me on this route. They have shared their time, their ideas, their energy, and their encouragement; they have made my journey not only possible but also exciting and enjoyable. In addition to the teachers at the three participating schools to whom I am immensely grateful, I wish to acknowledge and thank my family, the Harbisons and the O'Keefes, my colleagues at the University of Michigan, Hofstra University, and St. John's University, and my friends for their interest in my work and their patience.

I am indebted to my parents late Lydia Kutuzova and Jonas Jurasas, and my late grandmother, Marija Vasiutinskaja for immersing me in an atmosphere of creativity and continuous learning, for teaching me to be curious, for inspiring me to do the best I can in every endeavor, and for always supporting me in the pursuit of my dreams.

My special thanks to my professors Lesley Rex and Jeff Mirel for their inspiration and invaluable contribution to both my intellectual growth and my current work. From the very first moment I met Lesley in the Educational Studies doctoral program at the University of Michigan, she has been the perfect mentor, knowing how to inspire and challenge, and when to provide a suggestion or to let me find ways for resolving my dilemmas on my own. From her, I learned to be my own best critic. My alignment with Lesley's approaches to research created opportunities for our collaboration on scholarly publications.

Prof. Jeff Mirel's invaluable advice helped me apply my knowledge of Eastern European education and find ways of taking it to another level. Prof. Magdalene Lampert has been my guru since my first semester at the University of Michigan. Her scientific curiosity and perception of education as a complex and ever-changing system encouraged me to apply different lenses in exploring educational phenomena. I also wish to acknowledge other teachers and scholars who have supported me along the way. I am grateful to Profs. Virginia Richardson and Gary Fenstermacher for captivating my scientific curiosity with the idea of tacit knowledge. I thank Deborah Ball, Jay Lemke, Elizabeth Moje, and Pamela Moss, all of whom have been both influential in and supportive of my intellectual work. I would also like to thank the University of Michigan Center for Russian and Eastern European Studies for providing me with the opportunity for conducting my research over several summers in Lithuania. My affiliation with this Center has been both rewarding and stimulating. In addition, I wish to thank the international team of educators in the Open Society Institutes and Egmont Foundation in Denmark, who contributed immensely to shaping my stance in education in the earlier years.

I am immensely grateful to AnnMarie Dull, a doctoral student from St. John's University, Department of Curriculum and Instruction, who was the first reader of the full manuscript and whose comments, suggestions, and additions made this narrative flow much better. Especially important is her contribution to Parts II and IV, in which she provided specific information in regards to American education policy and its relation to the state of professional development. This book greatly benefitted from her outstanding talent as a writer and editor.

And finally, I wish to thank my anonymous reviewers for their insightful comments and suggestions and my dear friends, colleagues, and doctoral students who keep inspiring me to do my best work. Among them, my special thanks to Prof. Sandra Abrams for sharing her wisdom in publishing. In addition, I would like to acknowledge Dr. Andra Miletta for helping me think about applying my ideas and recommending me a wonderful place at which to do that.

Abbreviations

ELA	English Language Arts
EU	European Union
IDEA	Individuals with Disabilities Education Act
NAEP	National Assessment of Educational Progress
NCLB	No Child Left Behind
OECD	Organization for Economic Co-operation and Development
PD	Professional Development
PTO	Parent Teacher Organization

Introduction

Overview of This Chapter

The Introduction tells the story of how this book was conceived with the idea of researching tacit knowledge and finding ways of doing it. It gives a short overview of the problem of informal learning in general and teacher informal workplace learning in particular arguing that informal workplace learning was not given enough credit as a way of professional growth. Further, this piece reasons for a multilayered approach for researching teacher workplace learning. Then, it describes the author's background and qualifications, and concludes with the overview of the structure of the book, providing short descriptions for each part and chapters.

My 40 years of experience in education in Lithuania, Russia, the United States, and over a dozen other countries has acquainted me with many teachers. Every time I encountered brilliant educators, I wondered what impelled them to learn the intricacies of teaching and how to apply them with such mastery. Even though they studied in college, many would admit that after graduation they still did not know how to teach. While teaching, these educators actively pursued professional development (further PD), though they would point out that they had not received from workshops what they needed. So then, how did they turn from "ugly ducklings" into beautiful "swans"? Much has been written suggesting effective models for teacher education, mentoring, and induction, yet many questions about how, when, and where teachers learn remain unanswered. Traditional teacher PD has been examined vastly, including its effectiveness, but issues around its effectiveness persist. Given that, how do teachers compensate for what they cannot obtain in workshops? How else do they learn? I had a hunch, but I wanted to ask teachers if that hunch made any sense.

Over a decade ago, I was supervising student teachers in an elementary school in Midwestern United States. On the playground, a group of excellent teachers with whom I had collaborated before, were talking and I asked them if they thought their PD helped them resolve their everyday teaching challenges. Their answer was simple—"no". My next question was about what they did when and if PD was not helpful. They began describing many strategies they used every day, including discussing their challenges with each other, looking for solutions on websites, reading professional journals, trying out different approaches to discover what worked. "So, you learn every day in your workplace informally!" I exclaimed with amazement that my hunch was confirmed. "Yes, that's exactly how we learn!" said one of the teachers, and the others nodded. It was this conversation that inspired my research of teachers' informal learning that eventually led to this book.

About teacher learning, Aichele and Coxford (1994) wrote that "[b]ecoming a learner again makes them better teachers" (p. vii). Decades of research on different aspects of teacher learning, including looking at it from different perspectives, has confirmed this conclusion. For the most part, the contexts of these investigations are the wide range of pre-service and in-service events and examination of teachers' own classroom practice; however, the vast literature on PD and teacher learning have left me wondering about the role everyday learning plays in teachers' professional growth. So far, only a few studies examine distinctive contexts for teacher informal learning (e.g., Becher, 1999; Jurasaite-Harbison & Rex, 2010; Knight, 2002a, 2002b; Lave & Wenger, 1991) such as their interactions before and after classes, during co-planning sessions, their lunch and coffee breaks as well as other in-school activities. This kind of learning falls under the category of workplace learning the study of which, not necessarily teacher workplace learning per se, increased rapidly in the last decade (Dochy, Gijbels, Segers, & van den Bossche, 2011; Ellinson, & Noe, 2017; Ifenthaler, 2018; Illeris, 2011; Jurasaite-Harbison, 2012; Kyndt, Gijbels, Grosemans, & Donche, 2016; Malloch, & Cairns, 2014; Marsick, & Watkins, 2016; Messmann, Segers, & Dochy, 2018; Misko, 2008; Rowden, 2006).

With this book, I join the growing stream of research and explore the domain of learning that has been unfairly overlooked earlier but that merits the attention of other researchers and educators: informal teacher learning in the workplace. I view teacher learning as a cultural practice (Hodkinson, Biesta, & James, 2004; Hodkinson & Bloomer, 2000), a process of professional growth (Clarke & Hollingsworth, 2002) that encompasses different kinds of learning (Knight & Murray, 1999; Knight, 2002b) and occurs in various contexts throughout teachers' professional preparation and practice. I acknowledge that because informal learning occurs at any time and place, my challenge as a researcher is to circumscribe an area of study that would serve well as an entry point into the subject. For this research, I have chosen to focus my investigation of learning that happens in teachers' workplace—that is, at school. This point of entry is imperative to respond to the perceived need in teacher education to understand how teacher learning over a professional career can be supported and sustained. In addition, my experiences as an educator in multiple school settings—a teacher, a school principal, a coordinator of a large international child development project, a teacher educator, and an educational researcher—bring on a unique perspective of this theme, both as an insider and as an outsider.

As research in the area of school-based informal teacher learning is still rather scarce, my project is an exploratory study. By exploring this topic, I aim to contribute to re-conceptualization of professional development to include and accredit informal learning, which happens every day in settings that are not necessarily designed for such learning. If teacher educators, researchers, and policymakers recognize that such learning is important for teachers' professional growth, then there is a need to look for ways to help teachers recognize and take advantage of informal learning opportunities. To do that, we need to understand how informal workplace learning happens, how educational systems perceive such learning, and which features of school culture could stimulate, discourage, or stifle it.

To present informal learning as complex multilayered cultural practice, I organize this book into four parts that explore informal teacher learning at individual, institutional and district/national levels. In doing so, I agree with Jon Prosser (1999) who argues that "using a single framework to understand the immense complexity of schools is [...] limiting" (p. xii). Thus, these parts employ three different analytical frameworks that emerge from the analysis of three kinds of relationships: learners' interactions with self and others; learners' interactions with organizational systems; and learners' interactions with national systems. In the next section, I introduce these three contexts in more detail and describe the design of the study that underlies this book, its participants, the data set, and research approaches.

Study Design, Participants, Data, and Research Approaches

The brief summary that follows provides an overview of the research design, participants, and approaches. The study design emerged from my perception of the three cultural layers as embedded within each other and deeply interrelated, which reminded me of a nesting doll called "matrioshka" in Russian. To illuminate special characteristics and patterns of each cultural layer, I invited teachers from three schools across two countries (Lithuania and the United States) to join me on my exploratory journey. This design made it possible to identify patterns that most likely would not be readily visible within a single culture without comparing it to others. These patterns describe cultural webs of meanings (Anderson-Levitt, 2002) that position teachers as learners in culturally specific ways. They are visible in teachers' interactions with school administrators, colleagues, parents, and with me as a researcher, as well as in other instances of everyday life in the schools such as co-planning sessions, lunches, coffee breaks, and so forth. In addition, I bring into the discussion national educational policies, evident in documents such as laws, resolutions, agreements, and school websites to examine how the participating teachers as learners interpret and interact with these policies.

The theoretical framework for this comparative design combines theories of learning and culture to represent teachers as learners in informal settings. This framework made it possible for me to pursue the following questions to construct a cohesive view of teacher informal workplace learning:

- What are elementary teachers' learning patterns in the USA and Lithuania, and how are they similar and different?
- In what ways do teachers position themselves as learners in informal situations within individual school and national cultures?
- How does culture (on national, institutional, and individual levels) relate to teacher learning in informal settings?

Pursuing these questions requires close investigation of teachers' learning contexts, which appeared to be culturally specific. Such contexts seem to possess both cross-cultural and intracultural similarities and differences.

Because of my interest in focusing on these contexts and their close connections to culture, I chose to conduct my research in Lithuania and the United States. My linguistic fluency and cultural embeddedness in both countries as well as close relationship with different ethnic groups in Lithuania gave me a natural proximity that provided me with finely tuned cultural and educational knowledge. It also gave me the social awareness to explore complex contexts and processes of teacher informal learning that may have not presented themselves as clearly to someone without that proximity. While this did serve as an asset to the research, I was also keenly aware from the outset that my long history as a Lithuanian educator (I used to work in the school with Russian language of instruction as a beginning teacher of English as a foreign language in the 1980s and trained teachers from the school with Lithuanian language of instruction in the 1990s as part of a large international project) made it necessary for me to observe, examine, and reflect on my own biases and predispositions throughout this project.

Having worked as a teacher educator in both countries, I understand the professional learning cultures of each and hypothesized that features of informal learning could be better illuminated through their comparison in settings that are culturally different due to their histories and socioeconomic factors. Recently, these countries have become more culturally similar due to globalizing trends in social and educational values and practices. Nevertheless, both countries' diverse multicultural social structures pose challenges to the investigation of the cultural processes. As such, this research design permitted me to explore similarities and differences of teacher informal learning contexts among schools serving ethnic minorities and the dominant population in Lithuania. Unfortunately, time constraints did not allow me to mirror this selection in the United States; only one suburban public school took part in this project, yet the difference in the demographic make-up of the students in the two Lithuanian schools still yielded surprising themes. All three schools were in high regard in their communities: the American school had an excellent reputation for serving its community, and both schools in Lithuania attracted students from all over the city because of their unique curriculum that included the study of English as a foreign language from the second grade. The two Lithuanian schools each used different languages of instruction: one enrolled students from Russian-speaking families and the other served Lithuanian families, which made it possible to compare ethnically different schools within a single nation. Finally, I focused my exploration on elementary education teachers because most of my professional experience is in this area, adding yet another layer of proximity to the contexts I wished to investigate.

In each school, upon my written request to interview three or four elementary teachers from different grade levels, the principals were the ones who introduced me to the potential participants. They were: four teachers from the second, fourth, fifth grades, and the reading specialist in the US Midwestern school; four teachers from the first, third, and fourth grades in one Lithuanian school; and three Lithuanian-born teachers of Russian decent from the first, second and fourth grades in the second Lithuanian school (with the Russian language of instruction).

To explore the patterns of these teachers' informal learning, I identified and analyzed written and oral representations. To discern meanings that teachers attributed to the contexts of their informal learning, I employed ethnographic and sociolinguistic methods in collecting, transcribing and analyzing data. The body of data collected over a 2-year period included one-on-one, group, and "elite" interviews (Marshall & Rossman, 1999) with teachers and administrators (seventy-eight hours of interviews), teachers' reflective journals, artifacts and documents, photographs, and video images of the school and classrooms, observational field notes, and secondary sources such as educational laws and other documents that represent national policies.

The Structure of the Book

The book draws on three fields of research: teacher education, comparative and international education, and cultural anthropology, and includes four parts in which I address multiple layers of teacher learning. Throughout the book, I discuss the relationships among the nature of informal learning, its content, and its contexts by focusing on how teachers constructed and acted upon an important part of their professional identities—themselves as professional learners. In the "Final Thoughts" chapter, I revisit the conclusions drawn in each part and reflect on the findings. Throughout the book, I apply different analytical frameworks to illuminate various aspects of teacher learning. In a metacognitive mode,

I step back and reflect on how different methods of inquiry revealed specific aspects of informal learning in the research. In addition, I apply an international comparative perspective to investigate how cultural aspects of teachers' informal learning in their workplace are similar and different in the two countries and three school cultures. Such cross-cultural comparison sanctions further investigation of features in teacher learning that are similar within and across cultures, even when cultural and national contexts differ.

Part I consists of three chapters and discusses the multilayered design that I call a "nesting doll" design and introduces the participants of the study by presenting their short professional portraits.

The five chapters comprising Part II focus on the individual participants in the study. Drawing upon scholarship in teacher education, I present a framework for analyzing individual teacher learning that includes five informal learning categories: dispositions, focus, sources, processes and reactions. These categories emerged (Strauss & Cobrin, 1998) from applying discourse analytic tools, which are detailed in the chapter, to examine teachers' reflective journals. I then discuss how individual teachers in the Lithuanian and American schools construct their learning in informal settings at their workplaces. Through a cognitive discourse analysis of the teachers' journal entries and interviews, how they position themselves as learners in their everyday practice is revealed. The cognitive discourse analysis illuminates specific patterns that are characteristic of the five informal learning categories and highlights the variations within each of them. This five-category structure represents teacher informal learning as a complex phenomenon in which various combinations of multiple dimensions of the teachers' engagement in informal learning assume different patterns suggesting a possible typology of informal learning. This structure also serves as a framework for hypothesizing cultural patterns of teacher learning within school and national educational settings. The findings of these five chapters call for further in-depth exploration of cultural similarities and differences in teacher learning within an international comparative perspective.

In Part III, I explore the institutional cultures of the participating Lithuanian and American schools through analyzing the learning environments created by the school cultures. I discuss ways the teachers relate to their school culture and ways they position themselves as learners in their workplace environments. Building on the assertion that teacher learning does not occur in isolation, literature from the fields of cultural anthropology and educational leadership informed this analysis (in addition to literature on teacher education). This literature reveals that teachers co-construct their understandings of innovations by collaborating and learning from each other (e.g., Clark, Moss, Goering, Herter, & Lamar, 1996; Thomas, Wineburg, Grossman, Myhre, & Woolworth, 1998), and through reflection on their experience (e.g., Korthagen & Wubbels, 1995; Van Manen, 1995). To illustrate how such knowledge develops, I present three school cases in three large chapters that describe how teachers interact with and within each school culture in the process of their workplace professional learning. With the goal of undertaking a systematic analysis of informal teacher learning, this chapter investigates an unexplored link between organizational (school) culture and professional informal workplace learning of the organization's members (teachers). To examine the interactional nature of learning opportunities that construe the schools' cultural webs, the cultural lens in this part is shaped by the perspective of interactional ethnography (e.g., Green & Dixon, 1993; Rex, 2006) that provides a pathway to investigate interactional manifestations of teachers' learning in their workplace.

Part IV, in addition to teacher education and cultural anthropology, draws upon comparative and international education scholarship to discuss relationships between broader (district, national) education cultures in Lithuania and the United States and informal teacher learning. The four chapters in Part IV illuminate teachers' identities as learners within national contexts. By examining two education systems through synchronic (within the moment) and diachronic (over time) lenses, I employ discourse analysis to interpret meanings that elementary teachers assigned to their interactions with those systems. Similarities and differences found in teachers' professional learning were found to be related to national processes of educational reforms and transnational processes of globalization. Though teachers from both countries considered informal learning in the workplace as an essential part of their professional learning, I found that education systems did not officially recognize it as a form of professional development. In order to create diverse learning opportunities, I suggest that national and international education communities need to re-conceptualize teachers' PD to include informal professional learning as a legitimate part. Applying linguistic anthropology (Hymes, 1972), I move between an etic and an emic perspectives and examine how teachers in different schools perceive themselves as learners and how national cultures create opportunities for their everyday informal professional development.

In the Final Thoughts chapter, I reflect on how my findings illuminated by the fields of teacher education, comparative and international education, and educational anthropology inform the investigation of teachers' informal workplace learning. In my final discussion, I not only assert important implications of the results of this study for the educational research, policy and practice, but also call for a conversation about re-conceptualizing teacher professional development to the recognize alternative yet impactful ways teachers learn.

In sum, this book takes an initial step toward building the knowledge of how teachers learn informally every day by documenting and analyzing opportunities for such learning on the individual, school, and national levels. Representing ways elementary teachers respond and employ these opportunities for professional growth may inform teacher educators and administrators about ways to support teachers in becoming critical and reflective professionals who continuously improve their practice. This book also illuminates the value of informal learning for PD and considers its place in policy and teacher education by encouraging educators in these areas to emphasize the role of informal opportunities in learning. Readers will also witness that though cultural differences may exist among schools and their teachers, the cultures of teacher learning are becoming more analogous as perceptions of what constitutes as learning change. Finally, the frameworks discussed in this book could be applicable for studying informal learning of professionals in other areas.

References

Aichele, D. B., & Coxford, A. F. (1994). *Professional development for teachers of mathematics*. Reston, VA: National Council of Teachers of Mathematics.

Anderson-Levitt, K. M. (2002). *Teaching cultures: Knowledge for teaching first grade in France and the United States*. Cresskill, NJ: Hampton Press, Inc.

Becher, N. (1999). *Professional practices: Commitment and capability in a changing environment*. New Brunswick, NJ: Transaction Publishers.

Clark, C., Moss, P. A., Goering, S., Herter, R. J., & Lamar, B. (1996). Collaboration as dialogue: Teachers and researchers engaged in conversation and professional development. *American Educational Research Journal*, *33*(1), 193–231.

Clarke, D., & Hollingsworth, H. (2002). Elaborating a model of teacher professional growth. *Teaching and Teacher Education*, *18*(8), 947–967.

Dochy, F., Gijbels, D., Segers, M., & van den Bossche, P. (2011). *Theories of learning for the workplace: Building blocks for training and professional development programs*. London: Routledge.

Ellinson, J., & Noe, R. A. (2017). *Autonomous learning in the workplace*. New York: Routledge.

Green, J., & Dixon, C. (1993). Introduction to "Talking knowledge into being: Discursive and social practices in classrooms". *Linguistics and Education*, *5*, 231–239.

Hodkinson, P., Biesta, G., & James, D. (2004). *Towards a cultural theory of collegebased learning* [Paper]. Manchester: The Annual Conference of the British Educational Research Association.

Hodkinson, P., & Bloomer, M. (2000). Stokingham Six Form College: Institutional culture and dispositions to learning. *British Journal of Sociology of Education*, *21*(2), 187–202.

Hymes, D. H. (1972). Models of the interaction of language and social life. In J. J. Gumperz & D. H. Hymes (Eds.), *Directions in sociolinguistics: The ethnography of communication* (pp. 35–71). New York: Holt, Rinehart, and Winston.

Ifenthaler, D. (2018). *Digital workplace learning: Bridging formal and informal learning with digital technologies* (1st ed.). Cham: Springer.

Illeris, K. (2011). *The fundamentals of workplace learning: Understanding how people learn in working life*. London/New Yok: Routledge.

Jurasaite-Harbison, E. (2012). Workplace learning in informal contexts: Transnational comparison of teacher professional growth in Lithuania and the

United States. In M. Ginsburg (Ed.), *Preparation, practice, and politics of educators: Problems and prospects in comparative perspective.* Rotterdam, Netherlands: Sense Publishers.

Jurasaite-Harbison, E., & Rex, L. A. (2010). School cultures as contexts for informal teacher learning. *Teaching and Teacher Education, 26*, 267–277.

Knight, P., & Murray, S. (1999). Understanding teachers' professional culture through interview: A constructivist approach. *Evaluation and Research in Education, 13*(3), 144–156.

Knight, P. T. (2002a). Learning from schools. *Higher Education, 44*, 283–298.

Knight, P. T. (2002b). A systematic approach to professional development: Learning as practice. *Teaching and Teacher Education, 18*(3), 229–241.

Korthagen, F. A. J., & Wubbels, T. (1995). Characteristics of reflective practitioners: Towards an operationalization of the concept of reflection. *Teachers and Teaching, 1*(1), 51–72.

Kyndt, E., Gijbels, D., Grosemans, I., & Donche, V. (2016). Teachers' everyday professional development: Mapping informal learning activities, antecedents, and learning outcomes. *Review of Educational Research, 86*(4), 1111–1150.

Lave, J., & Wenger, E. (1991). *Situated learning: Legitimate peripheral participation.* Cambridge: Cambridge University Press.

Malloch, B., & Cairns, L. (2014). *The SAGE handbook of workplace learning.* New York: SAGE.

Marshall, C., & Rossman, G. B. (1999). *Designing qualitative research* (3rd ed.). Thousand Oaks, CA: SAGE.

Marsick, V. J., & Watkins, K. (2016). *Informal and incidental learning in the workplace.* London: Routledge.

Messmann, G., Segers, M., & Dochy, F. (2018). *Informal learning at work* (1st ed.). London/New York: Routledge.

Misko, J. (2008). *Combining formal, non-formal and informal learning for workplace skill development.* Australia: Australian Industry Group.

Prosser, J. (1999). *School culture.* London: Paul Chapman.

Rex, L. A. (Ed.). (2006). *Discourse of opportunity: How talk in learning situations creates and constrains.* Cresskill, NJ: Hampton Press, Inc.

Rowden, R. W. (2006). *Workplace learning: Principles and practice.* Malabar, FL: Krieger Publishing Company.

Strauss, A., & Cobrin, J. (1998). *Basics of qualitative research: Techniques and processes for developing grounded theory* (2nd ed.). Thousand Oaks, CA: SAGE.

Thomas, G., Wineburg, S. S., Grossman, P. L., Myhre, O., & Woolworth, S. (1998). In the company of teachers: An interim report on the development of a community of teacher learners. *Teaching and Teacher Education, 14*(1), 21–32.

Van Manen, M. (1995). On epistemology of reflective practice. *Teachers and Teaching, 1*(1), 33–50.

Part I

Multiple Layers of Workplace Learning

Part I

Multiple Layers of Workplace Learning

Overview of This Chapter

Part I introduction focuses on discussing multiple layers of workplace learning demonstrating the difference between formal, informal and incidental learning. Different definitions of informal workplace learning are discussed including Marsick's and Kyndt's accounts of informal learning characteristics and dimensions with the idea that the outcomes of workplace learning should be considered holistically. Workplace learning is described as in-context, hands-on, and experiential that is cyclic in nature. The questions that frame this part focus on investigating how teachers learn in informal settings. Further, the contribution of the three chapters to the main picture of the complexity and multilayerdness of learning that comprise this part are separately defined.

Learning is a complex, multifaceted process that occurs in a specific time and space, involves different levels of support, and the use of various resources. Learning is driven by intentionality in gaining certain knowledge and skills. Though formal and informal learning are often conceptualized and defined as dichotomous, together with Eraut (2004) and Kyndt (2016), I maintain that these two forms of learning represent a continuum ranging from organized learning in a setting intentionally designed for it to spontaneous learning that could be part of any experience. Workplace learning is considered a place where these learning forms uniquely intersect in the processes of negotiation between individual and organizational interests and ideas and ever-improving practice (Boud, 1998; Manuti et al., 2015). Stern and Sommerlad (1999) proposed to re-interpret the term "workplace learning", focusing on its "elasticity" by claiming that "learning" and "work" have a complex relationship that is represented by three broad approaches: "the workplace as a site for learning; the workplace as a learning environment; and learning and working as inextricably linked" (p. 2). Interpreting these approaches, Sambrook (2005) offered an important clarification of the meaning of workplace learning by distinguishing between learning *at* work (formal learning) and learning *in* work (informal and incidental learning).

Marsick (1987) drew a distinction between education/training and learning by pointing out a teaching component that formalizes learning. She defined education and training as organized and controlled delivery systems, while distinguishing learning as

> "a way in which individuals or groups acquire, interpret, re-organize, change or assimilate a related cluster of information, skills and feelings. It is also primary to the way in which people construct meaning in their personal or shared organizational lives"
>
> (p. 4).

Furthermore, by adopting McLagan's (1983) model, Marsick and Watkins (2001) demonstrated that the relationship of formal to informal and incidental learning in terms of time and money spent equals approximately to 17:83 percent respectively. Thus, it is crucially important to study informal and incidental learning, which, on average, occupy an overwhelmingly larger amount of time in professional learning.

Informal workplace learning, though interrelated with formal learning, has its own distinctive features. Marsick and Volpe (1999) characterized informal workplace learning as follows:

- It is integrated with daily routines.
- It is triggered by an internal or external jolt.
- It is not highly conscious.
- It is haphazard and influenced by chance.
- It is an inductive process of reflection and action.
- It is linked to learning of others.

(p. 5)

Argyris and Schön's (1974) perspective adds several important dimensions to Marsick's definition of informal and incidental learning. They suggested that informal learning happens as a surprise, under non-routine circumstances that require amplified attention in defining the nature of the problem, and experimentation with possible solutions. They also pointed out that critical reflection is necessary for reframing the situation that has been problematized. Finally, they pointed out that professionals in the workplace learn more than technical rules of the job; they learn to "think like an…" architect, doctor, teacher, etc.; they learn the criteria and exercise judgment when they encounter new experiences. Much of their perceptions are shaped in the contexts through learning informally.

The later definitions of informal learning have congealed previous findings with empirical research in different professional practices. For example, Kyndt et al. (2014) provided a detailed account of specific characteristics of informal learning:

> Informal learning is characterized by a low degree of planning and organizing in terms of learning context, learning support, learning time, and learning objectives. Informal learning opportunities are not restricted to certain environments. The learning results from engagement in daily work-related activities in which learning is not the primary goal. Informal learning is undertaken autonomously, either individually or collectively, but without an instructor. It often happens spontaneously and unconsciously. From the learner's perspective, it is unintentional. Finally, informal learning outcomes are unpredictable. (pp. 2393–2394)

Marsick and Volpe (1999) define incidental learning as "a by-product of some other activity, such as accomplishment, interpersonal interaction, sensing the organizational culture, or trial-and-error experimentation" (p. 7), which is serendipitous, always tacit, and often obscured in the context of other activities. Further, the authors converge with Argyris and Schön's (1974) stance that informal and incidental learning could be "enhanced by proactivity, critical reflectivity, and creativity. [Thus, informal learning occurs] through a dialectical process of action and reflection" (p. 8). Situated outside formally designed activities, both informal and incidental learning processes "often take place under non-routine conditions, that is, when the procedures and responses that people normally use fail" (Marsick & Volpe, 1999, p. 6). Puzzled by the failure of their previously used approaches, professionals become more critical toward their taken-for-granted assumptions, become more reflective and innovative, and start looking for creative solutions. While doing this, they may re-define the problem that they are facing and come up with original solutions right in the moment, or they turn to resources that might help them come up with new ideas. Based on this premise, informal learning could be an intentional, planned, self-directed process that differs from incidental learning, which is never planned or intentional.

Learning outcomes do not seem to correlate directly with the degrees of formality seen with informal workplace learning. Though following Doyle, Reid, and Young (2008) and Matthews (1999), Kyndt et al. (2016) defined learning outcomes "as sustainable changes in knowledge, skills, and attitudes as a result of engaging in learning activities (p. 1114), others (e.g., Marsick & Watkins, 2001) observed that learning might result in changes visible in a new behavior, or it could be a minor invisible shift in a viewpoint. Since informal workplace learning often occurs while solving specific work-related challenges, outcomes of such learning are highly contextualized and integrated with the work processes and, according to Eraut (2004), should be regarded holistically. In these contexts, learning outcomes could become visible in the solutions to the immediate workplace problems along with similar problems in the future, or they can reveal themselves much later as they are applied in different contexts.

The defining features of informal learning are learning in context, hands-on, and from experience. Oscar Wilde is believed to have said, "experience is the hardest kind of teacher. It gives you the test first and the lesson afterward" summarize the relationship of informal learning to experience: "the test" reveals what needs to be learned and sets off the process of informal learning. Kolb's (1984) investigation of learning through experience that draws on Dewey, Lewin's *Gestalt* psychology, Piaget's developmental psychology, clinical psychotherapists and psychologists (Jung, Erikson, Rogers, Perls, and Maslow) and the "radical educators", especially Freire and Illich, make an important contribution toward a better understanding of informal learning. Kolb held that people gain and transform their experiences differently: Some gain access to understanding the experience through concrete experience (CE), while others through abstract conceptualization (AC). Some transform their experiences through reflective observation (RO), others through active experimentation (AE). The latter of these two of Kolb's dimensions interrelate, resulting in both a typology of learning styles of experiential learning (Boyatzis & Kolb, 1995) and an experiential learning cycle (Kolb et al., 2001) that moves from experiencing, to observing, to conceptualizing, to experimenting and back to experiencing in the process of transforming experience into knowledge. The learning typology in experiential learning theory describes how one prefers to learn in general pointing to, but also taking into consideration, the adaptive flexibility that allows learners to be successful in different learning contexts (Passareli & Kolb, 2012).

This quick summary of the complexities of informal workplace learning demonstrates the roots of the questions that I ponder, some of which I will attempt to answer in this book, while others require more investigation. I wonder if learners' experiences in informal settings are different from formal learning situations and, if so, in what ways. How do learners use their adaptive flexibility in informal settings? Do they learn in an "autopilot" mode? Does the learning process differ in informal settings? These are some of those guiding questions that inspired me to perform a systematic investigation into informal workplace learning.

About This Part

This Part discusses the multilayered approach that leads to what I call a "nesting doll" design, which I applied in studying informal workplace learning of elementary teachers in two countries. The "nesting doll" approach is derived from the complexity of learning in general as well as informal learning specifically, that is discussed in Chapter 1. The "nesting doll" design is highlighted in Chapter 2, which I use to explain different layers of the study and how they build upon each other. Another way to think about this design in motion is to imagine going through a vortex that swipes and intermixes different particles in a spinning pattern heading to a new place. Our thought could take this route following the trajectories that teachers as learners take in the workplace. Thus, Chapter 3 introduces the participating teachers by describing their journey into teaching that frames their professional portraits' sketches.

References

Argyris, C., & Schön, D. A. (1974). *Theory in practice: Increasing professional effectiveness*. San Francisco, CA: Jossey-Bass.

Boud, D. (Ed.). (1998). *Current issues and new agendas in workplace learning*. Adelaide: National Centre for Vocational Education Research.

Boyatzis, R. E., & Kolb, D. A. (1995). From learning styles to learning skills: The executive skills profile. *Journal of Managerial Psychology*, 10(5), 3–17.

Doyle, W., Reid, J. G., & Young, J. D. (2008). Barriers to and facilitators of managers' workplace learning in small and large knowledge-based firms. *Small Business Institute Research Review*, *35*, 79–93.

Eraut, M. (2004). Informal learning in the workplace. *Studies in Continuing Education*, *26*, 247–273. doi:10.1080/158037042000225245

Kolb, D. A. 1984. *Experiential Learning: Experience as the Source of Learning and Development*. Englewood Cliffs, New Jersey: Prentice-Hall.

Kolb, D. A., Boyatzis, R. E., & Mainemelis, C. (2001). Experiential learning theory: Previous research and new directions. *Perspectives on Thinking, Learning, and Cognitive Styles*, *1*(8), 227–247.

Kyndt, E., Gijbels, D., Grosemans, I., & Donche, V. (2016). Teachers' everyday professional development: Mapping informal learning activities, antecedents, and learning outcomes. *Review of Educational Research*, *86*(4), 1111–1150.

Kyndt, E., Govaerts, N., Verbeek, E., & Dochy, F. (2014). Development and validation of a questionnaire on informal workplace learning outcomes: A study among socioeducational care workers. *British Journal of Social Work*, *44*, 2391–2410. doi:10.1093/bjsw/bct056

Manuti, A., Pastore, S., Scardigno, A. F., Giancaspro, M. L., & Morciano, D. (2015). Formal and informal learning in the workplace: A research review. *International Journal of Training and Development*, *19*(1), 1–17.

Marsick, V. J. (1987). New paradigms for learning in the workplace. *Learning in the Workplace*, *16*(2), 11–30.

Marsick, V. J., & Volpe, M. (1999). The nature and need for informal learning. *Advances in Developing Human Resources*, *1*(3), 1–9.

Marsick, V. J., & Watkins, K. E. (2001). Informal and incidental learning. *New Directions for Adult and Continuing Education*, *2001*(89), 25–34.

Matthews, P. (1999). Workplace learning: Developing a holistic model. *Learning Organization*, *6*, 18–29.

McLagan, P. A. (1983). *Models for excellence: The conclusions and recommendations of the ASTD training and development competency study*. Alexandria, VA: American Society for Training and Development.

Passarelli, A. M., & Kolb, D. A. (2012). Using experiential learning theory to promote student learning and development in programs of education abroad. *Student learning abroad: What our students are learning, what they're not, and what we can do about it*, 137–161.

Sambrook, S. (2005). Factors influencing the context and process of work-related learning: Synthesizing findings from two research projects. *Human Resource Development International*, 8, 101–119.

Stern, E., & Sommerlad, E. (1999). *Workplace learning, culture and performance.* London: Institute of Personnel and Development.

1 The Complexity of Teacher Learning

Overview of This Chapter

This chapter discusses the complexity of studying teacher learning, which is often encountered as an entwined combination or a fusion of formal, informal, non-formal, and incidental kinds that could be challenging to separate. It presents a review of research on approaches to teacher learning including cognitive, narrative, situated, and organizational perspectives, offering a definition of teacher learning used in the book that perceives teacher learning as professional growth and as a cultural practice that encompasses different varieties of learning deeply situated in the context.

Approaches to Teacher Learning

Different approaches have been used to investigate teacher learning, and over time, the focus of the research has shifted to include aspects of informal learning. Cognitive perspectives focus upon teachers' behavior in the classroom, assuming that it is directed by teachers' rational thinking (e.g., Clark & Peterson, 1986). More recent studies depart from this point of view to include a focus on both the conscious and less conscious aspects of learning (e.g., Hoekstra, Beijaard, Brekelmans, & Korthagen, 2007; Knight, 2002a, 2002b). For example, through stories teachers tell about their experiences in the process of reflecting upon them, the narrative perspective (e.g., Clandinin, 1992) studies the meanings learners attribute to informal learning in the workplace. Investigation of learning from this perspective provides an insider's view into the beliefs, personal philosophies and meanings that teachers ascribe to their actions and the lessons they learn from reflecting on those actions. On the other hand, research from the organizational perspective on teacher learning (e.g., Fullan, 1991; Handy & Aitken, 1986; Hargreaves, 1994, 1999), investigates teacher learning and professional development as the means for school improvement and refers to contexts for such development as school cultures. Those researchers argue that most school cultures include a variety of managerial arrangements and relationships, and, thus, could be characterized by several cultural types. School typologies they have developed provide diagnostics of the character about school cultures in order to develop policies for school improvement.

Another approach, which I adopt in this study is a socio-cultural perspective, that conceives teacher learning as a social practice that is inherently personified (Jurasaite-Harbison & Rex, 2005, 2010). Teachers are agents of learning who do so through actively constructing their knowledge rather than acquiring it. Following Pierre Bourdieu and his co-authors (1990, 1992), I perceive learning as cultural and relational in which the distinction between formal and informal learning becomes untenable (Hodkinson, Biesta, & James, 2004). I distinguish it only for analytic purposes to deepen our understanding of informal learning in which teachers (and let me hypothesize that we all) engage every day (Eraut, 2004). Opposing views that regard informal learning as inferior seem to lack clear understanding of the complexity of the process or act of learning itself. A few scholars attest to the superiority of informal learning, claiming that it matters even more than formal situations (Engstrom, 1991; Lave & Wenger, 1991). I posit that a combination of both types makes professional learning effective and meaningful, though in this study, I focus exclusively on informal learning as a way to elevate its importance in studies of teacher learning and professional development.

The complexity of teacher learning is reflected in the vast variety of the different aspects that are investigated in the overall body of educational research. Investigations span from delineating the acquisition of content knowledge (e.g., Bauer, 2013; Şendağ & Odabaşı, 2009; Shulman, 1986, 1987), to pedagogical knowledge (e.g., Gatbonton, 2008; König et al., 2011; Morine-Dershimer & Kent, 1999), to identifying the mechanisms and conditions of learning (e.g., Carter, 1990; Leinhardt, 2001), to analyzing the ways in which knowledge is held and assessed (e.g., Fenstermacher, 1994; Fenstermacher & Richardson, 2005), and with its latest investigation into teacher study groups (Firestone, Cruz, & Rodl, 2020), to illuminating the processes of how professional knowledge develops in practice and informs it (e.g., Clandinin & Connelly, 1996; Cochran-Smith & Lytle, 1999; Florio-Ruane, 2000; Korthagen, 2001; Lieberman & Miller, 2008; Pennell & Firestone, 1998; Thomas et al., 1998; Zeichner, 1998).

I view teacher learning as a cultural practice (Hodkinson & Bloomer, 2000; Hodkinson et al., 2004), a process of professional growth (Clarke & Hollingsworth, 2002) that encompasses different varieties of learning (Knight & Murray, 1999; Knight, 2002a, 2002b) that, in its turn leads to the development of professional knowledge (pedagogical and content) and identity. In other words, professional learning is viewed as "an orchestration" of different kinds of knowledge that develop in and through interaction with others, texts and environments (Leont'ev, 1981/1974). I emphasize the interactive nature of informal learning because it can occur for a teacher at any time and place stimulated by interactions with and in social contexts. My challenge as a researcher is to circumscribe an area of study that would serve well as an entry point into this complex subject. While all areas and aspects of teacher learning are important to explore, for this study, I have chosen to focus my investigation only on learning that happens in teacher's workplace—at the school. In particular, I examine how teachers learn informally in their everyday workplace contexts such as: their interactions with students, school administrators, colleagues, and parents; and in their planning and co-planning sessions, during their lunches, coffee breaks, preparation times, and other occurrences.

References

Bauer, W. I. (2013). The acquisition of musical technological pedagogical and content knowledge. *Journal of Music Teacher Education*, *22*(2), 51–64.

Bourdieu, P., & Passerson, J.-C. (1990). *Reproduction in education, society and culture* (2nd ed.). London: SAGE.

Bourdieu, P., & Wacquant, L. J. D. (1992). *An invitation to reflexive sociology*. Chicago, IL: The University of Chicago Press.

Carter, K. (1990). Teachers' knowledge and learning to teach. In W. R. Houston, M. Haberman, & J. Silkula (Eds.), *Handbook of research on teacher education* (Vol. 2, pp. 291–310). New York: MacMillan.

Clandinin, J. D. (1992). Narrative and story in teacher education. In T. Russell & H. Munby (Eds.), *Teachers and teaching: From classroom to reflection* (pp. 124–137). London: Falmer Press.

Clandinin, D. J., & Connelly, F. M. (1996). Teachers' professional knowledge landscapes: Teacher stories—stories of teachers—school stories—stories of schools. *Educational Researcher*, *25*(3), 24–30.

Clark, C., & Peterson, P. (1986). Teachers' thought processes. In M. C. Wittrock (Ed.), *Handbook of research on teaching* (3rd ed., pp. 255–296). New York: Teachers College Press.

Clarke, D., & Hollingsworth, H. (2002). Elaborating a model of teacher professional growth. *Teaching and Teacher Education*, *18*(8), 947–967.

Cochran-Smith, M., & Lytle, S. L. (1999). The teacher research movement: A decade later. *Educational Researcher*, *28*(7), 15–29.

Engstrom, Y. (1991). *Learning, working and imagining: Twelve studies in activity theory*. Helsinki: Orienta-Konsutit Oy.

Eraut, M. (2004). Informal learning in the workplace. *Studies in Continuing Education*, *26*, 247–273.

Fenstermacher, G. D. (1994). The knower and the known: The nature of knowledge in research on teaching. In L. Darling Hammond (Ed.), *Review of research in education* (p. 20). Washington, DC: American Educational Research Association.

Fenstermacher, G. D., & Richardson, V. (2005). On making determinations of quality in teaching. *Teachers College Record*, *107*(1), 186–213.

Firestone, A. R., Cruz, R. A., & Rodl, J. E. (2020). Teacher study groups: An integrative literature synthesis. *Review of Educational Research*, *90*(5), 675–709.

Florio-Ruane, S. (2000). *Teacher education and the cultural imagination: Autobiography, conversation, and narrative.* Mahwah, NJ: Lawrence Erlbaum Associates.

Fullan, M. (1991). *The new meaning of educational change* (2nd ed.). New York: Teacher College Press.

Gatbonton, E. (2008). Looking beyond teachers' classroom behaviour: Novice and experienced ESL teachers' pedagogical knowledge. *Language Teaching Research, 12*(2), 161–182.

Handy, C., & Aitken, R. (1986). *Understanding schools as organizations.* London: Penguin Books.

Hargreaves, A. (1994). *Changing teachers, changing times: Teachers' work and culture in the postmodern age.* London: Cassell.

Hargreaves, D. H. (1999). The knowledge-creating school. *British Journal of Educational Studies, 47*(2), 122–144.

Hodkinson, P., & Bloomer, M. (2000). Stokingham Six Form College: Institutional culture and dispositions to learning. *British Journal of Sociology of Education, 21*(2), 187–202.

Hodkinson, P., Biesta, G., & James, D. (2004). *Towards a cultural theory of college-based learning* (paper). Manchester: The Annual Conference of the British Educational Research Association.

Hoekstra, A., Beijaard, D., Brekelmans, M., & Korthagen, F. (2007). Experienced teachers' informal learning from classroom teaching. *Teachers and Teaching, 13*(2), 189–206.

Jurasaite-Harbison, E., & Rex, L. A. (2005). Taking on a researcher's identity: Teacher learning in and through research participation. *Linguistics and Education, 16*, 425–454.

Jurasaite-Harbison, E., & Rex, L. A. (2010). School cultures as contexts for informal teacher learning. *Teaching and Teacher Education, 26*, 267–277.

Knight, P. T. (2002a). A systematic approach to professional development: Learning as practice. *Teaching and Teacher Education, 18*(3), 229–241.

Knight, P. T. (2002b). Learning from schools. *Higher Education, 44*, 283–298.

Knight, P. T., & Murray, S. (1999). Understanding teachers' professional culture through interview: A constructivist approach. *Evaluation and Research in Education, 13*(3), 144–156.

König, J., Blömeke, S., Paine, L., Schmidt, W. H., & Hsieh, F. J. (2011). General pedagogical knowledge of future middle school teachers: On the complex ecology of teacher education in the United States, Germany, and Taiwan. *Journal of Teacher Education, 62*(2), 188–201.

Korthagen, F. (2001). *Linking practice and theory: The pedagogy of realistic teacher education.* Mahway, NJ: Lawrence Erlbaum Associates.

Lave, J., & Wenger, E. (1991). *Situated learning: Legitimate peripheral participation.* Cambridge: Cambridge University Press.

Leinhardt, G. (2001). Instructional explanations: A commonplace for teaching and location for contrast. In V. Richardson (Ed.), *Handbook of research on teaching* (4th ed., pp. 333–357). Washington, DC: American Educational Research Association.

Leont'ev, A. N. (1981/1974). The problem of activity in psychology. In J. V. Wertsch (Ed.), *The concept of activity in Soviet psychology.* Armonk, NY: M.E. Sharpe.

Lieberman, A., & Miller, L. (2008). *Teachers in professional communities: Improving teaching and learning*. New York, NY: Columbia University.

Morine-Dershimer, G., & Kent, T. (1999). The complex nature and sources of teachers' pedagogical knowledge. In J. Gess-Newsome & N.G. Lederman (Eds). *Examining pedagogical content knowledge* (pp. 21–50). Science & Technology Education Library, Vol. 6. Dordrecht: Springer. https://doi.org/10.1007/0-306-47217-1_2

Pennell, J. R., & Firestone, W. A. (1998). Teacher-to-teacher professional development through state-sponsored networks. *Phi Delta Kappan*, *79*(5), 354.

Şendağ, S., & Odabaşı, H. F. (2009). Effects of an online problem based learning course on content knowledge acquisition and critical thinking skills. *Computers & Education*, *53*(1), 132–141.

Shulman, L. (1986). Those who understand: Knowledge growth in teaching. *Educational Researcher*, *15*(7), 4–14.

Shulman, L. (1987). Knowledge and teaching: Foundations of the new reform. *Harvard Educational Review*, *57*(1), 1–22.

Thomas, G., Wineburg, S. S., Grossman, P. L., Myhre, O., & Woolworth, S. (1998). In the company of teachers: An interim report on the development of a community of teacher learners. *Teaching and Teacher Education*, *14*(1), 21–32.

Zeichner, K. M. (1998, June 2–4). *The role of practitioner research in personal, educational, and social reconstruction*. Paper presented at the *Conference on Action Research (Aksjonforskining)*, University of Tromso, Norway.

2 Researching Informal Teacher Learning

Overview of This Chapter

This chapter discusses ways of researching informal teacher learning within the socio-cultural framework and explains the "nesting doll" design used in this project. The study hypothesizes about the cultural mediation of relationships between the nature of informal learning itself and how opportunities for it arise in different educational cultures and contexts. It explores how teachers construct and act upon an important part of their professional identities—teachers as learners. The research design combines an emic and etic analytical frameworks for comparing the cultural features of teachers' informal learning practices. The three layers of analysis, the "nesting doll" approach, enable the reader to follow the trail of teachers' professional growth from identifying individual learning patterns, to teachers learning in the contexts of their schools' cultures, and finally, to their learning in the cultural contexts of broader educational (district, national) systems and examine opportunities that these contexts afford.

Vignette

> Quite a few years ago in a doctoral class taught by Prof. Virginia Richardson, we discussed the concept of tacit knowledge (introduced by Michael Polanyi in 1958/2015). This concept fascinated me so much that I decided to put it at the center of my research. Later, in a private conversation with Prof. Richardson in which I shared my drive to research tacit knowledge, she asked me a very good question: "If you want to analyze the concept, you need to make it visible for examination. Then, it will not be tacit anymore. So, how would you research tacit knowledge?" This question posed an inspiring methodological challenge, which led me to look for ways to access tacit learning processes and make them explicit.

A socio-cultural perspective, which I adopt in this study, conceives teacher learning as a social practice that is viewed as cultural and relational (Bourdieu & Passerson, 1990; Bourdieu & Wacquant, 1992; Jurasaite-Harbison & Rex, 2010, 2013). Teachers as agents learn through their interactions where they construct their knowledge rather than acquire it. This approach transpires over the course of this book through the detailed discussion of the following three themes as contexts of learning: teachers as learners, school cultures as contexts for learning, and professional learning within broader educational cultures. While each of the three themes require the use of a slightly different analytical framework, each remains under the "umbrella" of the same socio-cultural perspective that is addressed in Parts II, III, and IV of this book.

This approach offers a holistic perspective on the analysis of informal workplace teacher learning that positions teachers' voices within immediate and broader contexts, which I conceive as being similar to a nesting doll in which a smaller individual doll appears from a larger one that, in turn, is immersed in an even larger one. The metaphor of a nesting doll reflects this approach accurately because while each of the dolls can stand on its own, only when they are stacked within each other and become one do they become a cultural symbol, an educational toy (*matrioshka*, in Russian) and a useful metaphor to represent the complexity of the phenomenon of interest.

Taking a journey through multiple layers at which teacher informal learning happens, this approach enables us to examine each "doll" that represents a separate but immersed layer of analysis. An image of concentric circles might come to mind to represent the model that this study follows; however, flat circles would fail to emphasize the complexities of the relationships among the different factors, including the multidimensionality of informal workplace learning and multilayered embeddedness of research participants (teachers), as well as relationships between the different layers, where the next size stratum embraces the smaller ones and embeds them into broader contexts. The subjective experiences of teachers in their everyday practice are thereby immersed in an ethnographic examination of their school cultures, as both also reflect larger cultures, including district and national cultures. Each participating teacher's voice comprises multiple voices that feature different identities, representing a dialogic nature of learning, and reflects what Bakhtin (1981) called heteroglossia.

In order to explore these complexities, I designed an exploratory study that enabled me to gather different data representative of teacher's informal workplace learning to analyze through these frameworks. Because studies of informal teacher learning, especially international studies, are so few, this exploratory study was designed to generate and try out conceptual frameworks and methods for future research. Consequently, the design limits the number of locations and participants, and utilizes a variety of data sources and analytical tools, so as to pursue several themes: teachers as adult learners; professional identity (co)construction in informal settings; relationship between institutional and personal culture in the process of learning; and teachers' perceptions of relationship of their informal learning to broader (district, national) educational systems. Throughout the analysis, the examination of the situated language use that carries symbolic representations of learning culture allows us to participate in the teachers' meaning-making process as they reflect on their learning.

To explore the patterns of these teachers' informal learning, I collected and analyzed data of written and oral origin authored by the eleven teacher participants (e.g., reflective journals), me as researcher (e.g., observations), and both (e.g., interviews and focus groups). To discern meanings that teachers attributed to the contexts of their informal learning from these representations, I employed ethnographic and discourse-analytic methods (Gee, 2004, 2017). The body of data collected over a 2-year period included: One-on-one, focus group, and "elite" interviews (Marshall & Rossman, 1999) with teachers and administrators (78 hours of interviews), teachers' reflective journals, artifacts and documents, a survey of all elementary teachers in each school, photographs and video images of the school and classrooms, observational field notes, and secondary sources such as educational laws and similar documents that represent national policies. In describing each layer of analysis, I summarize the means and modes of data collection and analysis.

The First Layer of Analysis

In the first (individual) layer of analysis (or the smallest nesting doll) that views each teacher as the center of inquiry, teacher learning is conceptualized as a continuous development and growth (Knight, 2002). Such professional growth involves teachers' investigation of their practice and construction of their *own* theories of teaching "rather than others getting teachers to change" (Bell & Gilbert, 1994, p. 493). This trend of research positions teachers as agents of learning who exercise freedom of what, how, and when to learn (Jurasaite-Harbison & Rex, 2005).

Such a perspective calls for a closer look at how teachers construct their own everyday learning. Thus, this level of analysis is guided by the following questions:

- What emic analytic framework forwards investigation of teachers' informal learning?
- What does it mean for teachers in different schools and cultures to be learners?
- What are elementary teachers' learning patterns in the USA and in Lithuania and how are they similar and different?

To approach the teachers' learning processes as closely as possible, I use a micro-analytic approach in discourse analysis (focusing on prosody, word choice, and the semantics of tense and syntax) while perceiving informal teacher learning as situated in the context of the teachers' everyday practice (Greeno, Collins, & Resnick, 1996; Hodkinson & Bloomer, 2000; Lave & Wenger, 1991; Quicke, 1996). My objective is to examine how in their discourse about their practice, teachers represent contexts of the inquiry that enable their professional growth. To explore the patterns of elementary teachers' informal learning emically or from the insiders' perspective, I identified and analyzed written and oral representations of teachers' learning.

This layer of analysis presents the results of an emic analytical framework for comparing the individual cultures of teachers' informal learning practices. The analysis focuses on teachers' journals in which they reflected on their learning experiences over the period of 1 year once a week. My interpretations were triangulated with seventy-nine video interviews with teachers and administrators, a survey of all the teachers in each school, and related artifacts and documents.

The Second Layer of Analysis

When discussing teacher learning in the second layer of analysis (school cultures), I employ a case study methodology to construct and comparatively analyze three separate cases of school culture across three different schools: a Lithuanian school with instruction delivered in the native language in Lithuania; a Lithuanian school with instruction delivered in Russian language; and a Midwestern school in the United States with instruction delivered in English. The population of the Midwestern US school was comparable to the other two in that it served middle-class families, was homogeneous in terms of students' ethnicity, and families had similar aspirations for their children's academic performance. Discourse analysis of interviews with teachers (Knight & Murray, 1999) in this layer is used alongside other visual and written texts again employing Bakhtinian concept of *heteroglossia*, that allowed me to identify teachers using their voice as a mother, a family person, a professional, a colleague, a friend, a leader, or a learner, thus expressing different angles of their identity. For analytic purposes, I re-construct school cultures created through interactions of multiple participants (Anderson-Levitt, 2002; Hodkinson et al., 2004) as the teachers weave their voices into the complex fabric of workplace discourses. From long-term observations of school life in cafeterias, teachers' lounges, hallways during class periods and breaks, participant interviews, teacher gatherings, and school schedules analyzed as parts of school culture, I unveil different cultural patterns and trends within each school.

To examine the teachers' perspectives and describe the meaning that the teachers assigned to the phenomenon of informal teacher learning, I analyzed semi-structured phenomenological interviews (Marshall & Rossman, 1999) with seven elementary teachers in Lithuania and four elementary teachers in the United States. The series of interviews with each teacher focused on the exploration of the teachers' past and current learning experiences, defining the individual's essential informal learning experience. In addition, I used focus group ethnographic interviews with the group of teachers to investigate culture through the participants' perspective and to elicit meanings that they ascribe to events and behaviors as a group. These interviews contained three main types of questions:

descriptive, structural, and contrast. This approach allowed generating a possible typology of cultural schemes in teachers' informal learning.

The Third Layer of Analysis

The third layer of analysis (district/national or the biggest doll) treats primary and secondary sources such as interviews with teachers and educational officials, and educational policy documents as texts to de-construct and to explore discourses of teacher learning and professional development at the district and national level. These ideas are that are reflected in these texts were ascertained for this study by performing a thematic discourse analysis (Nowell et al., 2017).

Here, I analyze district/national cultural contexts for teacher learning by using teachers' perceptions of how their educational systems position them as learners and how the district or national education systems provide or do not provide informal learning opportunities. I employ both synchronic and diachronic perspectives (Chrisomalis, 2006), providing a historical backdrop for teacher voices. The synchronic lens focuses on the meaning of the language in the moment and allows for generating categories for cross-cultural comparisons from the teachers' accounts, while the diachronic view provides a historical context for emerging cultural patterns by examining how the language has been used over time.

The comparative framework of examining synchronic and diachronic lenses provides insights into the culture of teachers' learning "through explaining the behavior of educational systems" (Grant, 2000, p. 309). On the synchronic plane, it involves analysis of specific components of national educational systems that are relevant to teachers' informal learning, such as national education goals and policies, pre-service teacher training and accreditation, systems of professional development and ways educational systems structure teachers' work. I also consider the implications these factors have for informal teacher learning. On the diachronic plane, I reflect on the countries' recent historic events and educational documents that had a strong influence on educational systems.

Thus, guided by the central objectives in each layer of analysis, the design of three layers demonstrates diverse approaches and different uses of discourse analyses. These discourse-analytic approaches could also be considered as micro-, macro-, and mega-analyses that can be used to reconstruct cultural contexts and employ carefully tailored tools that enable the examination of the essential aspects of teacher informal learning.

Relationship of the Situated Language Use to the Examination of Cultural Patterns

To analyze written (secondary sources) and spoken (primary sources) data across the three layers of analysis, I employed the method of discourse analysis that allowed me to identify patterns of social and cultural meanings that emerged from these data. I began with the assumption that language is a social construct (Bakhtin, 1981) that represents both the object and the medium of culture, which is one of the central foci in this investigation and a context for informal learning. According to Mikhail Bakhtin, there is a reciprocal relationship between a user and a context: the social context constrains the language user and, simultaneously, the language user creates and influences the context.

Also relevant to this study are Alessandro Duranti (1997), Michael Silverstein (1998), and other contemporary linguistic anthropologists' views who have studied how language use can constitute aspects of culture and identity. According to these researchers, the meaning of any utterance can be refigured in different ways by highlighting different contextual features. This view is congruent with Dell Hymes' (1972) idea that systematic aspects of speech are tuned to cultural contexts. Sometimes scholars called such manipulations "keying" (Goffman, 1986); however, Hymes and his colleagues did not explain how keying gets accomplished in practice which poses limitations for its use in this approach. A decade later, scholars introduced the concepts of "contextualization cues" (Gumperz, 1982; Gumperz & Berenz, 1993) or indexicality (Garfinkel and Sacks, 1970), which showed how contexts are constructed by pointing to a particular aspect of that context. The relationship between an utterance and its meaning is mediated by participants' construction of the context. This process of "mediation" (Wortham, 2001) or "contextualization" (Silverstein, 1992) is crucial in defining the meaning of a cultural context; therefore, the concepts of "contextualization cue" and "mediation" were helpful in my analysis of written and spoken texts as they allowed for explicating cultural meanings that participating teachers assigned in one situation or another. Through reconstruction of relevant cues (which I highlight in the analyzed texts by bolding specific parts), I developed a coherent understanding of conversations and events that I identified in the texts as recognizable types of cultural actions.

Usually, interpretation of categories involves a dialectic process where both the researcher and participants display two types of cultural knowledge that is expressed linguistically: the analysis provides interpretations of what particular cues index, and what types of specific content and enacted events engage in the context (Wortham & Rymes, 2003). Silverstein (1993, 1998) and other linguistic anthropologists refer to this dialectic process as "regimentation" of indexical cues by available cultural types of events. This means that when speakers and hearers presuppose that a particular type of event is going on, the expectable script for that type of event comes to regiment many indexical cues.

In re-constructing cultural contexts from multiple sources of data, I hold that members of any professional community explicitly and implicitly recognize complex sets of types of events that constitute culture. Gregory Urban (1996) calls such presupposed pattern or cultural feature of text a "metadiscourse". Metadiscourses are the explicit and implicit framings used in a community for understanding social events as intelligible. Thus, they are publicly circulating devices for interpreting or regimenting interactional events. The circulation of metadiscourses explains the "contextually-situated, interactional establishment, maintenance and renewal of social relations in societies" (Silverstein, 1993, p. 35). The social events, relationships, and identities characteristic of a society are made recognizable by the metadiscourses that typify them (Urban, 1996). The concepts of "metadiscourses" and "regimentation" are useful for my study for illuminating a larger social and cultural background that participants bring into their everyday interactions. By applying "contextualization cues" that metadiscourses constrain and signal indexically to a particular context, the analysis of the language-in-use reveals how participants of the interaction position themselves in a situation. For the exploratory study at the center of this book, it reflects how teachers identify themselves as learners in everyday informal situations at schools and how they represent their learning in their interactions with me as a researcher.

A Note on Trustworthiness

To strengthen the trustworthiness of the study, I adopted several processes and procedures, especially given my own cultural connections to each of these contexts. Triangulation among various participants' accounts and sources of data (e.g., documents, transcripts, fieldnotes, and teacher interviews) as well as these data analysis in different layers provided the means for clarifying and verifying my interpretations. As I participated actively within the schools' communities over an extended period (Eisenhart & Howe, 1992), thereby getting to know the teachers and the administrators well, I used journaling to reflect on possible effects of my close engagement. Being a participant-observer allowed me to notice unfamiliar in the familiarity of the everyday school life of teachers and bring these observations into the thick descriptions of the workplaces. To increase the likelihood that my cultural understandings of the communities of practice (Lave &Wenger, 1991) would fairly represent those communities in my interpretations throughout the study, I also sought out teachers' interpretations of their own school cultures, of their own professional growth, and of the opportunities for their development. Frederick Erickson (1986) suggested that such a combination of richness and interpretive perspective strengthens the validity of accounts: "Such a valid account is not simply a description: it is an analysis". Further, he wrote, "in an effective report of fieldwork, key assertions are not left undocumented by vignettes, and single vignettes are not left to stand by themselves as evidence. Rather, interpretive connections are made across vignettes, and between vignettes and other more summary forms of description" (Erickson, 1986, p. 150). This interchange of thick, interpretive, summative descriptions in the narrative provides a multidimensional, holistic view of the context of informal learning and its processes. In all the layers of analysis, I strive for both ethnographic depth and discursive detail through thick illustrative descriptions of telling cases (Mitchell, 1984). I use data to provide warrants to interpretive claims while at the same time aiming for a verisimilitude by illustrating my interpretations with excerpts from the interview transcripts (Denzin, 1994; Drisko, 2013; Tracy, 2010) that invites the reader to develop alternative interpretations.

References

Anderson-Levitt, K. M. (2002). *Teaching cultures: Knowledge for teaching first grade in France and the United States.* Cresskill, NJ: Hampton Press, Inc.

Bakhtin, M. (1981). *The dialogic imagination* (C. Emerson & M. Holquist, Trans.). Austin, TX: University of Texas Press.

Bell, B., & Gilbert, J. (1994). Teacher development as professional, personal, and social development. *Teaching and Teacher Education, 10*(5), 483–497.

Bourdieu, P., & Passerson, J.-C. (1990). *Reproduction in education, society and culture* (2nd ed.). London: SAGE.

Bourdieu, P., & Wacquant, L. J. D. (1992). *An invitation to reflexive sociology.* Chicago, IL: The University of Chicago Press.

Chrisomalis, S. (2006). Comparing cultures and comparing processes: Diachronic methods in cross-cultural anthropology. *Cross-Cultural Research, 40*(4), 377–404.

Denzin, N. K. (1994). Evaluating qualitative research in the poststructural moment: The lessons James Joyce teaches us. *Qualitative Studies in Education, 7*(4), 295–308.

Drisko, J. (2013). Standards for qualitative studies and reports. In A. Fortune, W. Reid & R. Miller, Jr (Eds.), *Qualitative research in social work.* (2nd ed., pp. 3–34).

Duranti, A. (1997). *Linguistic anthropology.* New York: Cambridge University Press.

Eisenhart, M., & Howe, K. (1992). Validity in educational research. In M. D. LeCompte, W. Millroy, & J. Preissle (Eds.), *The handbook of qualitative research in education* (pp. 643–680). San Diego, CA: Academic Press.

Erickson, F. (1986). Qualitative methods in research on teaching. In M. C. Witrock (Ed.), *Handbook of research on teaching* (3rd ed., pp. 119–161). New York: Academic Press.

Garfinkel, H. (1967). *Studies in Ethnomethodology.* Engelwood Cliffs, NJ: Prentice-Hall, Inc.

Gee, J. P. (2004). *An introduction to discourse analysis: Theory and method.* New York: Routledge.

Gee, J. P. (2017). Discourse analysis. In *The Routledge handbook of language and dialogue* (pp. 78–93). New York: Routledge.

Goffman, E. (1986). *Frame analysis: An essay on the organization of experience* (Northeastern University Press ed.). York, PA: The Maple Press.

Garfinkel, H. & Sacks, H. (1970) On formal structures of practical actions, In J. C. McKinney & E. A. Tiryakian (Eds.), *Theoretical Sociology. Perspectives and Development.* (pp. 337–366). New York: Appleton–Century–Crofts.

Grant, N. (2000). Tasks for comparative education in New Millennium. *Comparative Education, 36*(3), 309–317.

Greeno, J. G., Collins, A. M., & Resnick, L. B. (1996). Cognition and learning. In D. C. Berliner & R. C. Calfee (Eds.), *Handbook of educational psychology* (pp. 15–46). New York: Macmillan.

Gumperz, J. J. (1982). *Discourse strategies.* Cambridge: Cambridge University Press.

Gumperz, J. J., & Berenz, N. (1993). Transcribing conversational exchanges. In J. Edwards & M. Lampert (Eds.), *Talking data: Transcription and coding in discourse research*, (pp. 91–122).

Hodkinson, P., Biesta, G., & James, D. (2004). *Towards a cultural theory of college-based learning* [Paper] Manchester: The Annual Conference of the British Educational Research Association.

Hodkinson, P., & Bloomer, M. (2000). Stokingham Six Form College: Institutional culture and dispositions to learning. *British Journal of Sociology of Education, 21*(2), 187–202.

Hymes, D. H. (1972). Models of the interaction of language and social life. In J. J. Gumperz & D. H. Hymes (Eds.), *Directions in sociolinguistics: The ethnography of communication* (pp. 35–71). New York: Holt, Rinehart, and Winston.

Jurasaite-Harbison, E., & Rex, L. A. (2005). Taking on a researcher's identity: Teacher learning in and through research participation. *Linguistics and Education, 16*, 425–454.

Jurasaite-Harbison, E., & Rex, L. A. (2010). School cultures as contexts for informal teacher learning. *Teaching and Teacher Education, 26*, 267–277.

Jurasaite-Harbison, E., & Rex, L. A. (2013). Teachers as informal learners: Workplace professional learning in the United States and Lithuania. *Pedagogies, 8*(1), 1–23.

Knight, P. T. (2002). A systematic approach to professional development: Learning as practice. *Teaching and Teacher Education, 18*, 229–241.

Knight, P. T., & Murray, S. (1999). Understanding teachers' professional culture through interview: A constructivist approach. *Evaluation and Research in Education, 13*(3), 144–156.

Lave, J., & Wenger, E. (1991). *Situated learning: Legitimate peripheral participation*. Cambridge: Cambridge University Press.

Marshall, C., & Rossman, G. B. (1999). *Designing qualitative research* (3rd ed.). Thousand Oaks, CA: SAGE.

Mitchell, J. C. (1984). Typicality and the case study. In R. F. Ellen (Ed.), *Ethnographic research: A guide to general conduct* (pp. 238–241). Orlando, FL: Academic Press.

Nowell, L. S., Norris, J. M., White, D. E., & Moules, N. J. (2017). Thematic analysis: Striving to meet the trustworthiness criteria. *International Journal of Qualitative Methods*, 16(1), 1–13.

Polanyi, M. (1958/2015). *Personal knowledge: Towards a post-critical philosophy*. Chicago, IL: University of Chicago Press.

Quicke, J. (1996). Learning and context: Constructing an integrated perspective: Review essay. *British Journal of Sociology of Education, 17*(1), 103–113.

Silverstein, M. (1992). The indeterminacy of contextualization: When is enough enough? In A. DiLuzio & P. Auer (Eds.), *The contextualization of language* (pp. 55–75). Amsterdam: John Benjamins.

Silverstein, M. (1993). Metapragmatic discourse and metapragmatic function. In J. Lucy (Ed.), *Reflexive language*. New York: Cambridge University Press.

Silverstein, M. (1998). The improvisational performance of "culture" in real-time discursive practice. In K. Sawyer (Ed.), *Improvisation*. Norwood, NJ: Ablex.

Tracy, S. J. (2010). Qualitative quality: Eight "big-tent" criteria for excellent qualitative research. *Qualitative Inquiry, 16*(10), 837–851.

Urban, G. (1996). *Metaphysical community*. Austin, TX: University of Texas Press.

Wortham, S. (2001). *Narratives in action*. New York: Teachers College Press.

Wortham, S., & Rymes, B. (Eds.). (2003). *Linguistic anthropology of education*. Westport, CT: Praeger.

3 Portraits of Teachers

Overview of This Chapter

This chapter introduces the 11 teacher participants of the exploratory study and brings in their multiple voices. The teachers come from three schools in two countries—the United States and Lithuania. In Lithuania, two schools participated—one with Russian language of instruction that served a Russian-speaking community, and the other one with the Lithuanian language of instruction, serving comparable-to-the-Russian-school population of native Lithuanian speakers. The American teachers came from a school in one of the Midwestern states. Their voices are brought in through discourse analyses of their pedagogical autobiographies and reflective journals, which the teachers wrote upon the author's request. This approach provides multiple lenses on teachers' roles and experiences learning informally every day in their workplace. The portrait sketches, when possible, use the wording the teachers used to describe their paths to teaching.

Most of my professional experience is in childhood education and professional development. I have observed, prepared, talked with, and trained teachers in many countries, which is a key reason that I focused my exploration on elementary teachers. I invited teachers from three schools: an American school with an excellent reputation for serving its community, and two schools in Lithuania—one with a Russian language of instruction and the other one with a Lithuanian language of instruction, both with a brilliant status in the cities that they serve. The Lithuanian schools with different languages of instruction, which enrolled students from Russian-speaking and Lithuanian communities accordingly, made it possible to compare ethnically different schools' cultures within a single country.

When designing the study and inviting participants, I provided a written request to the three principals seeking three or four elementary teachers from different grade levels within their schools. Teachers were asked to agree to participate, and the principals introduced me to all those that did. In the end, a reading specialist and one second grade teacher, one third grade teacher, and one fourth grade teacher agreed to participate from the

Midwestern US School; two first grade teachers, one third grade teacher, and one fourth grade teacher from the Lithuanian-speaking school in Lithuania; and one first grade teacher, one second grade teacher, and one fourth grade teacher from the Russian-speaking school in Lithuania.

The teachers' portrait sketches are based on their pedagogical autobiographies and weekly journal entries in which teachers reflected on their learning; the teachers wrote both documents specifically for this study. All the texts were written in their native languages: English, Lithuanian, and Russian. I analyzed these data in the original languages and only translated excerpts that I chose to illustrate my points. Additionally, it is critical to point out that though not directly included in the sketches, individual interviews and classroom observations could have influenced my perception. Nine out of 11 teachers wrote their pedagogical autobiographies, and thusly, only nine portraits comprise this chapter. They depict each teachers' journey to and within their profession and provide a view of how they perceived themselves as teachers and learners. In the upcoming chapters in Part II, the portraits will be expanded by adding another dimension—informal learners' profiles.

Nadia[1]

(A teacher from the school with the Russian language of instruction in Lithuania)

Nadia did not decide to be a teacher until she entered university. She was always active in extracurricular activities at the school she attended as a student. During her high school years attending this very school (this is a comprehensive school, serving children from grade one to 12), a talented and creative teacher of Physics organized a youth club. In that club, they made theatrical performances, created costumes and decorations, wrote poems and songs, and performed musicals and concerts. Nadia spent all her after-school time in this club. When she cried at the graduation party, somebody told her, "Don't want to leave? Come back!" That is exactly what happened—after 10 years, she came back to this school to teach.

She chose to become an elementary teacher because teaching in elementary grades embraced all theatrical, musical, and other artistic features that she enjoyed practicing so much as a student in the youth club. At the university, she felt that she learned a lot, but not "how to really teach". At her first school, her mentor (who was an experienced teacher) and the head teacher immersed her in the process of learning by observing other teachers. After 7 years in that school, she got a job as a kindergarten teacher at the school from which she had graduated and where she was employed at the time of this study. At that time, many changes happened in her personal life (marriage and children) as well as in the life of the country (gaining Independence and joining European Union).

Teaching her kindergarten class in a separate building in the neighboring preschool was difficult for her. She was tasked with teaching a class of gifted students without knowing much about how to do it. It did not help that she was surrounded by preschool teachers and did not have any other upper level elementary teachers around. At the same time, "changes in the elementary curriculum required much more time for lesson planning" (Nadia's Pedagogical Autobiography, p. 3). It is a common practice in Lithuania for teachers to follow and teach the same group of students through all elementary school. After her second maternity leave, Nadia was assigned to teach third grade, which became a new learning experience: she took over a class that had looped with another teacher for 2 years in which students were used to a very different teaching style. She needed to adjust her teaching and she did. At the time of our interaction, she had implemented her dream of making a puppet theater with the students whom she taught from the first grade.

Nadia's journal entries were story-like narratives that described specific situations that she qualified as leaning experiences. She provided many details regarding her dilemmas and who helped her to find a solution. She also included examples and concluded her entries with reflections.

Marija

(A teacher from the school with the Russian language of instruction in Lithuania)

Marija is a head teacher in the elementary department in one of the largest and most prestigious schools in the city. At the time of her participation in the study, she had 20 years of experience. She started working as an elementary teacher and entered university simultaneously. In her pedagogical autobiography, she wrote that she "started teaching without practically any experience", "with knowledge about teaching that was only based on [her] own experience as a student at school" (Marija's Pedagogical Autobiography, p. 1). She learned the most from her experienced colleagues and young teachers as well as from her own experience while working. The school at which she was employed at the time of the study was the third workplace in her career. She started out teaching underprivileged children from low-income families, and she wrote that many of her students had behavioral and academic problems. Moving to this particular school was a tremendous learning experience for her. As she pointed out in her pedagogical autobiography, when she began working in it, she had to develop a different approach and use different methods because the majority of students were academically advanced and gifted in many different areas. When she started teaching after-school classes, she started using educational games, which she later integrated into her classroom teaching. At the time when we met, she focused her own learning on developing student assessments, integrating educational technology, and enhancing students' motivation.

Marija approached journal writing in a systematic way. She wrote entries every week since I asked the participants to record their learning experiences in their journals. Each entry was more than half a page and had a similar structure: description of a situation, identification of a problem, people involved in the situation, a moment of sharing she considered to be important for her information or experience, evaluation/implementation of the new idea and, occasionally, a commentary on its implementation.

Ramute

(A teacher from the school with the Lithuanian language of instruction in Lithuania)

Somebody asked Ramute when she was 5 years old, what she would like to be when she grew up. She responded right away—an elementary teacher. Since then, she never changed her mind. She had years of "apprenticeship of observation" (Lortie, 1975) and played "school" at home with her dolls. In high school, she was often asked to substitute for elementary school teachers when they were absent. She started working at a University school in her last year before graduating from the university with her teaching degree. She remembered that her first year as a teacher was the most difficult: most of all, she was scared to teach and worried that she would not educate her students well enough; however, a student's mother told her, "I am very happy that my daughter's class is the first in your practice. We give the most to our first ones". Ramute completely agreed with these words. She read everything she could get, listened to each new idea coming from her colleagues, and asked her professors for advice. She thought that it was significant that she started her teaching career at the University school, which was small, with a family-centered atmosphere and an outstanding leader heading it. Thus, she distinguished two periods in her teaching career: the first loop (4 years teaching the same students), and work after that. During the first period, she remembers that she almost "lived" at the school and dedicated much time and energy to her students. Later, she joined the International Child Development Project, which introduced new teaching philosophy and methods as well as brought new acquaintances and a teacher support network from all over the country into her life. She believed that, "a good teacher should learn every day and should change with the changing world" (Ramute's Pedagogical Autobiography, p. 2). At the time of the data collection, Ramute was looking forward to developing her computer skills and her knowledge of foreign languages.

Ramute's journal entries were short bullet-pointed statements, business-like, directed at naming a problem and finding ways of solving it. There was no reflection, no analysis, and no emotions in the entries; however, some entries included the exclamation "it's interesting!" Entries reflected mostly where and what she wanted to learn.

Sigute

(A teacher from the school with the Lithuanian language of instruction in Lithuania)

Sigute described her own family's atmosphere as "saturated with an image of a woman as a teacher" (Sigute's Pedagogical Autobiography, p. 1). Her grandmother, with whom she spent much time, was a teacher, and both of her parents met when studying teaching. Her elementary teacher was a person whom she could approach with any question even after Sigute moved to the middle school. She started thinking about becoming an elementary teacher in the seventh grade, when she developed a clear image of a teacher's profession. Her father would take her to the university where he taught. Often, she would take care of her cousins or help four of her neighbors' children with their homework. At that time, she discovered that when she taught others, she learned herself. In high school, she liked to stay after classes and help her teacher. Her Language Arts teacher was a role model for her—"her lessons were planned extremely well, and she always looked energizing and pretty" (Sigute's Pedagogical Autobiography, p. 4). She continued corresponding with this teacher after she graduated, sharing her accomplishments and learning more from the teacher's experiences. After school, she entered an elementary teacher education program. Though her parents warned her about hardships and low pay in this profession, she decided to learn from her own mistakes. After their student teaching experiences, a few students in her cohort realized that teaching was not for them. On the contrary, she felt happy each day spent in the classroom. She learned a lot when working on her Master's theses by visiting many schools and learning about different teaching styles. She was happy to have a small class (18 students) at the beginning of her teaching career and was glad that the associate principal was her former professor. At the time of this study, this school was the second workplace in her teaching career. She concluded that in this school, she communicated with her colleagues as with friends sharing and discussing teaching problems or having fun together. She believed that it was not enough to have a university teaching degree and claimed "it was important to learn constantly because each new day was different, and it was necessary to keep up with that" (Sigute's Pedagogical Autobiography, p. 9).

Sigute's journal entries were short (3–5 sentences). She described the situation and the problem that she would like to solve. Often, she defined how she felt discovering it (using such words as "realized", "noticed", "shocked", "frustrated"). Finally, she came up with an idea or new understanding. For example, she reported feeling shocked after meeting her new first graders and their parents on September 1 (that is when school traditionally starts in Lithuania). She realized that she would have to find different ways of working with them. It was frustrating to her that new parents were either negative or indifferent to whatever was going on. She ended the entry with a new understanding that she had developed deep attachment to her fourth graders ("as if they were my own kids") and that when they graduated, she needed to refocus on her new first graders, who would look helpless compared to the fourth graders. Sometimes, she skipped defining a problem; rather, she described multiple sources of learning as if she aimed at absorbing all possible information and experience and storing it until the right moment came.

Viktorija

(A teacher from the school with the Lithuanian language of instruction in Lithuania)

Viktorija had always dreamed of becoming a teacher; however, before becoming a teacher, she gained experience in legal business (court secretary) and later practiced education in managing entertainment events. As she wrote in her pedagogical autobiography, all these experiences shaped the kind of teacher she became. After receiving a Bachelor's degree in entertainment business, she started working in a preschool and later in an elementary afterschool program. At the time of the data collection, she was working in a prestigious school, taught at the Pedagogical University, and co-authored elementary math textbooks. She described herself as a person who took part in everything that was new. For example, she joined two projects run by a major international non-profit organization. She set up goals and constantly moved forward. She had a dream that one day when she retired, she would see her former students on the TV show "Famous people".

Viktorija had a habit of taking notes at the end of the week. When I asked her to reflect in a journal, she seemed to keep it the way she usually took notes: she did not make any distinction between keeping notes and journaling. The main goal for her was to record great ideas that she encountered in different places and in different situations. Thus, her journal looked like a bullet-pointed bank of ideas for teaching (mostly, art education).

Kristi

(A teacher from the school in the Midwestern United States)

Kristi decided that teaching is a noble profession many years ago when she spent time with her grandmother who was an elementary teacher.

Her grandmother was a role model for her, and would take her to her classroom and to teachers' conferences. She was the kind of a teacher who attended every Parent Teacher Organization (PTO) meeting, students' sporting event, and dance recital. As Kristi noted, her grandmother never seemed to be tired even though there was no end to her day. Kristi loved the way her grandmother knew what was going on in any part of her busy classroom, even though to Kristi sometimes "it looked like chaos" (Kristi's Pedagogical Autobiography, p. 1). Kristi started college as a business major, but accounting courses seemed to be tedious and boring. During the spring break, when she started doubting her choice, her grandmother asked if she ever considered teaching and spent a day telling what a great teacher she could become. Kristi tried out educational classes and liked them. After graduation, she taught first grade and was following her grandmother's suit—attending every PTO meeting, going to sporting events and dance recitals.

This school was the third workplace in her career. While working in her previous school, she started feeling that she was no longer a "new" teacher and she became more comfortable taking risks. Attending numerous professional workshops and sharing her knowledge with the staff gave her even more confidence. She noticed that the more she learned, the more her students learned. At the time of my data collection, she taught the second grade, which was new to her. In addition, she was trying something different—team teaching. She reflected that as a beginning teacher, she had relied more on her knowledge from university courses. Now, more often she relied on collaboration with other teaching professionals and her on own experience.

Kristie's journal included weekly entries in which she describes her perceived learning situations. The entries were short (5–7 sentences), often emotionally colored, and focused on unexpected events that occurred during the week.

John

(A teacher from the school in the Midwestern United States)

John did not choose the teaching profession even when he had to make a choice. At first, he followed one of his father's suggestions to go into nursing; however, during orientation, he got so nervous that he decided not to enter the nursing school. Since high school, he had been involved in a teen group promoting an alcohol- and drug-free environment. The leaders of this group advised him to go into teaching. He did so and enjoyed the program very much. His goal was "to be a good role model and help develop young minds" (John's Pedagogical Autobiography, p. 4). This school was his second workplace after graduation; he continued teaching the fourth grade in the current school. He said he was happy with where he was personally and professionally. He liked to consider himself a balanced teacher—being both strict and having a fun time whenever possible. His 'strict side' told him, "students should have high expectations and should be held accountable for their actions." while the other side argued, "School should be fun and filled with positive memories" (John's Pedagogical Autobiography, p. 5). He considered that his teaching style was a reflection of him as a person: he liked order and discipline and enjoyed a good laugh too. He believed that as a teacher, he changed over time as he learned from other teachers what worked well and what did not. He shared his ideas with his colleagues all the time. He stressed that he also learned from his students and their parents. Many times, this learning was by trial-and-error.

In his journal, John wrote about results of his learning, coming up with general conclusions of his learning experiences, though providing no details about his sources of learning. He defined what he learned that week in terms of its value for the development of his personality or for the advancement of his teaching habits (e.g., flexibility in planning; getting ready for the day). It was challenging to identify learning procedures because of the general character of his entries. Almost every entry has a conclusion such as, "We raised a lot of money" or "They passed on to me specific writing prompts as well as examples of student work...." Some conclusions such as, "I have a bigger responsibility than teaching Math and Science", or "unprepared teacher means misbehaving students", and "students appreciate when the teachers do unordinary things" sounded rather trivial in as he echoed commonly held ideas.

Bob

(A teacher from the school in the Midwestern United States)

Ever since Bob could remember, he loved working with children. At family gatherings, he used to keep track of his younger cousin. In his neighborhood, he would baby-sit and get paid for playing with kids; however, he did not know what he wanted to be and what he wanted to study in college. Thoughts about teaching never crossed his mind. He got worried about choosing the right major and could not make up his mind. One of his peers recommended that he tried Elementary Education. He enjoyed every moment of the program; the professors liked the creativity and playfulness of his lessons. People still called him "the biggest kid in the school" (Bob's Pedagogical Autobiography, p. 2). After graduation, he substituted for a year and learned many things, becoming a popular substitute teacher. Since he had been hired as a permanent teacher, he taught the fifth grade. He liked to stress to his students that people never stop learning. He was confident that he would pursue another career the day he stops learning or having fun in the classroom. Every day, he looked forward to his job and believed he had a positive impact on many children.

It looked like each entry of Bob's journal was a response to something that started a line of his thinking. In most of his entries, he seemed to continue contemplating what we had discussed in the interviews: he reflected upon his teaching philosophy, the fun of teaching, and enjoying the profession. Bob seemed to use this opportunity for rethinking his teaching philosophy, his teaching style, and the teachers' role. He defined himself as a constant learner who, in his own words, "related a lot of what [he] learned to [his] teaching every day". The structure of his entries contained problem setting, descriptions of experiences, and general thoughts about the profession; however, there was not much reflection on specific teaching problems.

Though the teachers described their different backgrounds, family histories, and paths to the profession, all of them expressed a common feature—a passion for continuous learning. In the next Part, their everyday learning is the focal point of the discussion, which will detail a variety of ways they approach it and take part in it.

Note

1 The names of all the participants are pseudonyms.

References

Lortie, D. (1975). *Schoolteacher: A sociological study*. Chicago, IL: University of Chicago Press.

Part II

Teachers as Learners

Part II
Teachers as Learners

Overview of This Chapter

The introduction to Part II discusses research related teacher learning referring to different professional development models such as mentoring and coaching, summer institutes, reflections, teacher research, lesson study, communities of practice, collaborative practice-based professional development in which teachers take initiative in expanding their professional knowledge. Further, the chapter discusses literature on teacher professional growth that includes informal learning opportunities as opposed to the traditional "delivery" models of professional development. It concludes with the review of the five chapters that comprise this part and offers a framework for studying teachers as learners using microdiscourse analysis for identifying the *individual* features of teachers' informal learning practices and processes as a core segment of the "nesting doll" design: (1) how teachers expressed their disposition to learning (opportunistic–proactive continuum), (2) how they identified sources of their learning (individual–social continuum), (3) what problems they highlighted as their focus for learning (self-oriented–teaching-oriented continuum), (4) how they described processes in which they engaged in their attempts to solve professional dilemmas (spontaneous–deliberate continuum), and (5) how they expressed their reaction to professional dilemmas (emotional–cognitive continuum).

Current social developments in the United States and the world call for new educational initiatives that require professional transformation and development to meet new expectations for teachers. Teachers become key figures and important agents of social change through their innovative and effective practices (Darling-Hammond & Bransford, 2005); however, both teachers and researchers report that in many cases, traditional professional development events that are intended to lead to professional transformation do not serve that purpose (Ball & Cohen, 1999; Borko & Putnam, 1995; Hatch et al., 2005; Lieberman & Miller, 2001; Putnam & Borko, 2000). It is also critical to note that this is the type of professional development that has largely been the most prevalent across the United States, at least in the first decade of the 21st century (Darling-Hammond et al., 2009; Wei et al., 2010). Therefore, it is highly important to find out about the alternative ways in which teachers learn, including how they learn, what they learn about, and when they learn it. The stakes for teacher learning have grown higher as links are discovered between exploding literacy demands (including recent interest in digital literacy), economic expansion, and social and political stability. As pressures for teachers to improve their students' educational achievement increase through federal, state, and district policies and accountability measures (e.g., No Child Left Behind and other government-backed reforms), formal ongoing professional development opportunities cannot keep up. The opportunities for quality teacher learning are not always there: "workshops are not tailored to teachers' needs; two-thirds of U.S. teachers state that they have no say in what or how they learn in the professional development" events (Bransford, Brown, & Cocking, 1999, pp. 180–181), and when professional development is available, it is often focused on short-term triage approaches to school- or district-based issues, not necessarily aligned to teachers' needs and desires for learning (Wei et al., 2010). Astonishingly, Ann Lieberman's (1996) summary concerning limitations of traditional approaches to professional development still seems valid today. She argued:

- Teacher development has been limited by lack of knowledge of how teachers learn.
- Teachers' definitions of the problem of practice have often been ignored.
- The agenda for reform involves teachers in practices that have not been a part of the accepted view of teachers' professional learning.
- Teaching has been described as a technical set of skills, leaving little room for invention and building craft knowledge.
- Professional development opportunities have often ignored the critical importance of the context within which teachers' work.
- Strategies for change have often not considered the importance of support mechanisms and the necessity of learning over time.
- Time and the necessity mechanisms for inventing as well as consuming new knowledge have often been absent from schools.

(p. 185)

Over the last decades, and to counter the futility of the ineffective "drive-by" workshop model so accurately characterized by Lieberman, research has introduced a new paradigm, which aims at satisfying ever-growing needs for teachers' professional growth (Morris, 2003). Darling-Hammond and Richardson (2009) describe that this new evidence-based paradigm:

- Deepens teachers' knowledge of content and how to teach it to students.
- Helps teachers understand how students learn specific content.
- Provides opportunities for active, hands-on learning.

- Enables teachers to acquire new knowledge, apply it to practice, and reflect on the results with colleagues.
- Is part of a school reform effort that links curriculum, assessment, and standards to professional learning.
- Is collaborative and collegial.
- Is intensive and sustained over time.

(para 6)

This is also supported by the findings of the National Staff Development Council's report on professional development in the United States (Wei et al., 2009), which further defined effective professional development as including the following:

- Focused on specific curriculum content and pedagogies needed to teach that content effectively.
- Offered as a coherent part of a whole school reform effort, with assessments standards, and professional development seamlessly linked.
- Designed to engage teachers in active learning that allows them to make sense of what they learn in meaningful ways.
- Presented in an intensive, sustained, and continuous manner over time.
- Linked to analysis of teaching and student learning, including the formative use of assessment data.
- Supported by coaching, modeling, observation, and feedback.
- Connected to teachers' collaborative work in school-based professional learning communities and learning teams.

(Wei et al., 2010, p. 2)

Both sets of paradigms/definitions of effective professional development call for different types of professional learning that feature collaboration, topics and activities that are aligned to students' and teachers' needs, are continuous and ongoing, and are personalized to the context of the teacher's classroom and own learning experiences. Further, the new modes of conducting PD such as modeling new strategies and creating opportunities for teachers to practice and reflect on them (Garet et al., 2001; Saxe et al., 2001; Supovitz et al., 2000) are critical because they have been shown to actively engage teachers in knowledge construction in collaborative, job-embedded professional learning activities. PD models which comprise this paradigm include: mentoring and coaching (e.g., Boreen, 2009; Fletcher & Mullen, 2012), summer institutes (e.g., Nadelson et al., 2012; Wilson et al., 1996), teacher reflection (e.g., Fishman et al., 2003), teacher research (e.g., Cochran-Smith & Lytle, 1999; Zeichner, 2003), lesson study (e.g., Fernandez, 2002; Lewis et al., 2006); communities of practice (e.g., Lave & Wenger, 1991; Lieberman & Miller, 2008; Talbert & McLaughlin, 2001; Wenger,

2010), and collaborative practice-based professional development (e.g., Ball & Cohen, 1999; Lieberman & Pointer-Mace, 2010). The teacher-researcher movement (Cochran-Smith, & Lytle, 2009a, 2009b) has grown over the years and has resulted in the inclusion of classroom and action research into these types of professional learning (e.g., Alexakos, 2015; Esposito, & Smith, 2006; Hopkins, 2008). Within this paradigm, teachers take initiative as they see fit to expand their knowledge and do so in ways that are in context of their daily classroom practice.

Informal learning (Greeno et al., 1996; Quicke, 1996) seems to be part of many of these models that build on teachers' practice and permeate teachers' everyday activity. Becher (1999) argues that it plays "a significant part in the enhancement of professional capacity [so that] to fail to acknowledge [its] significance is to considerably underrate the extent to which practitioners maintain the quality of their work" (p. 205). Davis and Krajcik (2005) notice that "teachers' learning is situated in their daily practice" (p. 4); however, most research of teacher learning has not paid enough attention to studying teacher informal learning. Paradoxically, in the field of professional learning only a few studies (e.g., Jurasaite-Harbison, 2012; Jurasaite-Harbison, & Rex, 2013; Kyndt, & Baert, 2013; Kyndt et al., 2016; Marsick, & Watkins, 2016) investigate how teachers learn in informal settings, e.g., through their interactions with school administrators, colleagues, parents, co-planning sessions, communications during lunch and coffee breaks and similar situations, leaving room for and requiring further formal examination of the topic.

Teacher Learning as Professional Growth

In this section, conceptualization of teacher professional growth differs from a widely held view that emphasizes participation in PD as the main source for teacher learning. Contrary to the traditional language of "delivery" (Timperley et al., 2007), the language I use underscores a complex, situative, and continuous nature of learning that leads to professional growth. Earlier, we discussed the Clarke and Hollingsworth model, confirming the incremental, iterative nature of teacher professional growth and highlighting variation between individuals and across contexts (e.g., Jurasaite-Harbison & Rex, 2010; Jurasaite-Harbison & Rex, 2013). The change in language reflects professional learning as a more inclusive concept, and represents a deeper shift from a professional development to a professional learning paradigm seen in Clarke and Hollingsworth's (2002) Interconnected Model of Professional Growth. By including a broad variety of learning opportunities and stressing the role of an individual's knowledge and beliefs within the larger socio-cultural context, this model acknowledges multiple possibilities for teacher learning, while accounting for variation in teacher professional growth. Recently, other researchers (e.g., Adams, 2017; Goldsmith, Doerr, & Lewis, 2014; Opfer & Pedder, 2011; Pedder, & Opfer, 2013) also discussed the intricate and dynamic nature of such learning using the lens of Complex systems theory according to which events and actors interact within nested systems (in our case—individual, school, and broader learning cultures) in a variety of ways with various possible learning outcomes. Such learning is a part of teachers' everyday practice and occurs in a range of contexts where traditional or alternative PD is just one of the contexts for learning. Thus, it involves teachers' investigation of their practice and construction of their *own* ways of growing professionally "rather than others getting teachers to change" (Bell & Gilbert, 1994, p. 493). This approach positions teachers as agents of learning who exercise freedom of what, how, and when to learn (Jurasaite-Harbison, & Rex, 2005).

By focusing on the concepts of agency and choice, the chapters in this Section provide a better understanding of how teachers can be agents of their own professional learning. In this context, professional learning is viewed as "an orchestration" of different kinds of knowledge that develop in and through interaction with others, texts, and environments (Leont'ev, 1981/1974). Peter Knight's (2002) conceptualization of learning—that it develops from multiple sources and in multiple contexts—points out the importance of both formal and informal learning and the close relationship between the two. Seeing the need to find out how these two types of learning interrelate, and filling in the void of theoretical perspectives on informal learning, Knight pays special attention to the relationship between a person's tacit and explicit knowing that develops within an individual (intuitive, conscious) and in a group (collective, cultural, objectified). Knight echoes Aleksey Leont'ev's, view by stating, "the ways in which learning occurs vary with the level of interaction involved" (p. 231).

This approach to learning—one that develops from multiple sources and in multiple contexts, makes it possible to consider the multiple ways in which teachers learn in and from practice (Bransford, Brown, & Cocking, 1999; Hoekstra, Beijaard, Brekelmans, & Korthagen, 2007). It also enables us to observe the spontaneity of teacher learning in informal contexts. This stance highlights the importance of informal learning in general (Becher, 1999; Eraut, 2000, 2004) and teacher learning in particular (Day, 1993; Helsby & Knight, 1997, Lortie, 2002), and further accounts for a special dimension of professional growth that occurs in workplace settings that are not specifically designed for professional learning.

Although teachers' informal learning is not generally considered a part of professional development, researchers have taken seriously teachers as knowers and learners (see, e.g., Clandinin, & Huber, 2005; Connelly & Clandinin, 1999; Conway, 2001; Fenstermacher, 1994; Florio-Ruane, 2000; Korthagen, 2001; Lampert, 1985, 2001; Malcom et al., 2003; Richardson & Fallona, 2001; Shulman, 1987; Zeichner, 1998). Their studies disperse along a continuum between investigation of mainstream professional development by 'delivery models' and viewing teachers as lifelong learners with recent research moving distinctively toward conceptualizing teacher learning as growth (e.g., Clarke & Hollingsworth, 2002; Knight,

2002). Current policy efforts follow this tendency. Policies aimed at transforming teaching are rooted in understanding that "regulations cannot transform school; only teachers, in collaboration with parents and administrators, can do that" (Darling-Hammond & McLaughlin, 1996, p. 6).

About This Part

Given the importance of a detailed teacher informal learning investigation, this Part includes five chapters and discusses the core of the multilayered nesting doll design described in Chapter 2. It offers a framework for studying teachers as learners using an emic analytical framework for identifying the ***individual*** features of teachers' informal learning practices and processes as a core segment of the design. It also discusses how the teachers approach their learning as continuous development and professional growth. Using microdiscourse analysis (prosody in speech, frequency of word occurrence, and grammatical and lexical patterns in written text) and a grounded theory procedure (Strauss & Corbin, 1998) when analyzing the teachers' journals, I generated five major themes based on which each teacher's portrait was enriched with a unique combination of specific features on the continuum of these themes: (1) how teachers expressed their disposition to learning (opportunistic–proactive continuum), (2) how they identified sources of their learning (individual–social continuum), (3) what problems they highlighted as their focus for learning (self-oriented–teaching-oriented continuum), (4) how they described processes in which they engaged in their attempts to solve professional dilemmas (spontaneous–deliberate continuum), and (5) how they expressed their reaction to professional dilemmas (emotional–cognitive continuum). Each of the following chapters (Chapters 4–8) discusses one theme in detail by demonstrating how it was constructed.

The analysis in Chapters 4–8 involves teachers' journals in which teachers reflected on their learning experiences on a weekly basis over a period of 1 year. The question guiding the analysis was, *how do teachers construct their professional informal learning?* Interpretations were triangulated with seventy-nine hours of video interviews with teachers and administrators, ethnographic observations in each school, and related artifacts and documents.

I analyzed patterns of teachers' language of their journal entries as representations of their informal learning. For this purpose, I applied Bakhtin's (1981) perspective on the language as a social construct, and Hymes' (1972) perspective that systematic aspects of speech are tuned or "keyed" (Goffman, 1986) to specific contexts. This approach enabled me to identify what teachers as learners ***do*** when they find themselves in a learning situation (it also provided me with information about what each considered a learning situation). The process of developing these categories included finding patterns in empirical data, categorizing these patterns, going back to data to look for confirming and disconfirming evidence for these categories and refining descriptions of the categories based on understandings that emerged from the recurrent data analysis. Specifically, I first coded the teachers' reflective journals to surface the ways they position themselves as learners, paying specific attention to the entries' structural, grammatical, and lexical patterns. Second, using a grounded theory approach (Strauss & Corbin, 1998), I generated five descriptive themes with two sub-themes in each, which I used as a heuristic for defining individual teachers' learning. Third, I synthesized characteristic features that described each theme and defined them as analytic categories, which led me to hypothesize a possible typology of informal professional learning. To test this hypothesis and using information gathered from their journals, interviews, and observations, I wrote narratives that defined each teacher as a learner in terms of the five categories based on the frequency of the teachers' identification with each of them.

Different Types of Informal Learners

Though all teachers received the same instructions for how to keep their journals, their entries were not uniform. The structure of the entries as well as their language differed in terms of (1) how teachers expressed their disposition to learning, (2) how they identified sources of learning, (3) what problems they highlighted as their focus for learning, (4) how they described processes when they attempted to solve professional dilemmas, and (5) how they expressed their reaction to professional dilemmas. These differences comprised the basis for defining the five categories (see Table 2.1) that

Table 2.1 Types of learners by categories

	Group 1	*Group 2*	*Group 3*
Dispositions	**Opportunistic** Bob, Kristi, John, Daina	**Balanced** Ramute, Viktorija, Debbie, Sigute	**Proactive** Nadia, Marija
Focus	**Self-oriented** John, Kristi, Ramute	**Balanced** Bob, Sigute, Debbie, Daina	**Teaching-oriented** Nadia, Marija, Viktorija
Reaction	**Emotional** Kristi, Daina, Bob, John	**Balanced** Nadia, Viktorija, Debbie, Ramute	**Cognitive** Sigute, Marija
Sources	**Individual** John, Kristi	**Balanced** Nadia, Ramute, Debbie, Sigute	**Social** Bob, Daina, Marija, Viktorija
Process	**Spontaneous** Bob, Kristi, John, Daina	**Balanced** Nadia, Viktorija, Debbie, Ramute	**Deliberate** Sigute, Marija

served as a lens for examining ways in which the teachers engaged in learning and positioned themselves as informal learners.

I treated each category as a continuum bounded by two sub-categories or modes that represent opposite and extreme positions. To identify each teacher's specific position on the continuum, I calculated frequencies of codes depending on how they described their involvement in the process of informal learning. Within the categories, in multiple instances of informal learning that they described, almost all the teachers displayed both modes (sub-categories); however, one or another mode prevailed in some teachers' learning. Table 2.1 illustrates the distribution of teachers' characteristics as informal learners by the categories. Though each combination of the modes is unique, there are observable patterns that suggested a possibility of placing the participants into three groups within each category, which represents three types of learning. The following chapters offer a detailed analysis of the five categories.

The structure of the teachers' journal entries as well as their language differed in terms of (1) how teachers expressed their disposition to learning (opportunistic--proactive, (2) how they identified sources of learning (individual–social), (3) how they expressed their reaction to professional dilemmas (emotional–cognitive), (4) what problems they highlighted as their focus for learning (self-oriented–teaching-oriented), and (5) how they described processes when they attempted to solve professional dilemmas (spontaneous–deliberate). These differences expressed in the frequencies of codes comprised the basis for defining the five categories.

References

Adams, G. (2017). Using a narrative approach to illuminate teacher professional learning in an era of accountability. *Teaching and Teacher Education*, *67*, 161–170.

Alexakos, K. (2015). *Being a teacher| researcher: A primer on doing authentic inquiry research on teaching and learning*. New York, NY: Springer.

Bakhtin, M. (1981). *The dialogic imagination* (C. Emerson & M. Holquist, Trans.). Austin, TX: University of Texas Press.

Ball, D., & Cohen, D. (1999). Developing practice, developing practitioners: Toward a practice-based theory of professional education. In L. Darling-Hammond & G. Sykes (Eds.), *Teaching as the learning profession: Handbook of policy and practice* (pp. 3–32). San Francisco, CA: Jossey-Bass.

Becher, N. (1999). *Professional practices: Commitment and capability in a changing environment*. New Brunswick, NJ: Transaction Publishers.

Bell, B., & Gilbert, J. (1994). Teacher development as professional, personal, and social development. *Teaching and Teacher Education*, *10*(2), 483–494.

Boreen, J. (2009). *Mentoring beginning teachers: Guiding, reflecting, coaching*. Portland, ME: Stenhouse Publishers.

Borko, H., & Putnam, R. (1995). Expanding a teacher's knowledge base: A cognitive psychological perspective on professional development. In T. Guskey &

M. Huberman (Eds.), *Professional development in education: New paradigms and practices.* New York: Teachers College Press.

Bransford, J. D., Brown, A. L., & Cocking, R. R. (1999). *How people learn.* Washington, DC: National Academy Press.

Clandinin, D. J., & Huber, M. (2005). Shifting stories to live by. In *Teacher professional development in changing conditions* (pp. 43–59). Dordrecht: Springer.

Clarke, D., & Hollingsworth, H. (2002). Elaborating a model of teacher professional growth. *Teaching and Teacher Education, 18*(8), 947–967.

Cochran-Smith, M., & Lytle, S. (2009a). *Inquiry as stance: Practitioner research for the next generation.* New York: Teachers College Press.

Cochran-Smith, M., & Lytle, S. (2009b). Teacher research as stance. In S. Noffke and B. Somekh (Ed.), *The SAGE handbook of educational action research* (pp. 39–49). Thousand Oaks, CA: Sage.

Cochran-Smith, M., & Lytle, S. L. (1999). The teacher research movement: A decade later. *Educational Researcher, 28*(7), 15–29.

Connelly, F. M., & Clandinin, D. J. (Eds.). (1999). *Shaping a professional identity: Stories of educational practice.* New York: Teachers College Press.

Conway, P. F. (2001). Anticipatory reflection while learning to teach: From a temporally truncated to a temporally distributed model of reflection in teacher education. *Teaching and Teacher Education, 17,* 89–106.

Darling-Hammond, L., & Bransford, J. (2005). *Preparing teachers for a changing world: What teachers should learn and be able to do.* San Francisco, CA: Jossey-Bass.

Darling-Hammond, L., & McLaughlin, M. (1996). Policies that support professional development. In M. McLaughlin & I. Oberman (Eds.), *Teacher learning: New policies, new practices.* New York: Teachers College Press.

Darling-Hammond, L., & Richardson, N. (2009). Research review/teacher learning: What matters. *Educational leadership, 66*(5), 46–53.

Darling-Hammond, L., Wei, R. C., Andree, A., Richardson, N., & Orphanos, S. (2009). *Professional learning in the learning profession* (p. 12) Washington, DC: National Staff Development Council.

Davis, E. A., & Krajcik, J. (2005). Designing educastive curriculum materials to promote teacher learning. *Edussscational Researcher, 34*(3), 3–14.

Day, C. (1993). Reflection: A necessary but not sufficient condition for professional development. *British Educational Research Journal, 19*(1), 83–93.

Eraut, M. (2000). Non-formal learning and tacit knowledge in professional work. *British Journal of Educational Psychology, 70,* 113–136.

Eraut, M. (2004). Informal learning in the workplace. *Studies in Continuing Education, 26,* 247–273.

Esposito, J., & Smith, S. (2006). From reluctant teacher to empowered teacher-researcher: One educator's journey toward action research. *Teacher Education Quarterly, 33*(3), 45–60.

Fenstermacher, G. D. (1994). The knower and the known: The nature of knowledge in research on teaching. In L. Darling Hammond (Ed.), *Review of research in education* (Vol. 20). Washington, DC: American Educational Research Association.

Fernandez, C. (2002). Learning from Japanese approaches to professional development: The case of lesson study. *Journal of Teacher Education, 53*(5), 393–405.

Fishman, B. J., Marx, R. W., Best, S., & Tal, R. T. (2003). Linking teacher and student learning to improve professional development in systemic reform. *Teaching and Teacher Education, 19*(6), 643–658.

Fletcher, S., & Mullen, C. A. (Eds.). (2012). *SAGE handbook of mentoring and coaching in education.* Thousand Oaks, CA: SAGE.

Florio-Ruane, S. (2000). *Teacher education and the cultural imagination: Autobiography, conversation, and narrative.* Mahwah, NJ: Lawrence Erlbaum Associates.

Garet, M., Porter, A., Desimone, L., Birman, B., Yoon, K. (2001). What makes professional development effective? Results from a national sample of teachers. *American Educational Research Journal, 38*(4), 915–945.

Goffman, E. (1986). *Frame analysis: An essay on the organization of experience* (Northeastern University Press ed.). York, PA: The Maple Press.

Goldsmith, L. T., Doerr, H. M., & Lewis, C. C. (2014). Mathematics teachers' learning: A conceptual framework and synthesis of research. *Journal of mathematics teacher education, 17*(1), 5–36.

Greeno, J. G., Collins, A. M., & Resnick, L. B. (1996). Cognition and learning. In D. C. Berliner & R. C. Calfee (Eds.), *Handbook of educational psychology* (pp. 15–46). New York: Macmillan.

Hatch, T., Ahmed, D., Lieberman, A., Faigenbaum, D., White, M. E., & Pointer-Mace, D. H. (Eds.). (2005). *Going public with our teaching: An anthology of practice.* New York: Teachers College Press.

Helsby, G., & Knight, P. (1997). Continuing professional development and the National Curriculum. In G. Helsby & G. McCulloch (Eds.), *Teachers and the National Curriculum* (pp. 127–141). London: Cassell.

Hoekstra, A., Beijaard, D., Brekelmans, M., & Korthagen, F. (2007). Experienced teachers' informal learning from classroom teaching. *Teachers and Teaching, 13*(2), 189–206.

Hopkins, D. (2008). *A teacher's guide to classroom research.* London: McGraw-Hill.

Hymes, D. H. (1972). Models of the interaction of language and social life. In J. J. Gumperz & D. H. Hymes (Eds.), *Directions in sociolinguistics: The ethnography of communication* (pp. 35–71). New York: Holt, Rinehart, and Winston.

Jurasaite-Harbison, E. (2012). Workplace learning in informal contexts: Transnational comparison of teacher professional growth in Lithuania and the United States. In M. Ginsburg (Ed.), *Preparation, practice, and politics of educators: Problems and prospects in comparative perspective* (pp. 79–100). Rotterdam, Netherlands: Sense Publishers.

Jurasaite-Harbison, E., & Rex, L. A. (2005). Taking on a researcher's identity: Teacher learning in and through research participation. *Linguistics and Education, 16,* 425–454.

Jurasaite-Harbison, E., & Rex, L. A. (2010). School cultures as contexts for informal teacher learning. *Teaching and Teacher Education, 26,* 267–277.

Jurasaite-Harbison, E., & Rex, L. A. (2013). Teachers as informal learners: Workplace professional learning in the United States and Lithuania. *Pedagogies, 8*(1), 1–23.

Knight, P. T. (2002). A systematic approach to professional development: Learning as practice. *Teaching and Teacher Education, 18*(3), 229–241.

Korthagen, F. (2001). Learning from practice. In *Linking practice and theory: The pedagogy of realistic teacher education* (pp. 20–50). Mahway, NJ: Lawrence Erlbaum Associates.

Kyndt, E., & Baert, H. (2013). Antecedents of employees' involvement in work-related learning: A systematic review. *Review of Educational Research, 83*(2), 273–313.

Kyndt, E., Gijbels, D., Grosemans, I., & Donche, V. (2016). Teachers' everyday professional development: Mapping informal learning activities, antecedents, and learning outcomes. *Review of Educational Research, 86*(4), 1111–1150.

Lampert, M. (1985). How do teachers manage to teach? Perspectives on problems in practice. *Harvard Educational Review, 55*(2), 18–35.

Lampert, M. (2001). *Teaching problems and the problems of teaching*. New Haven, CT: Yale University Press.

Lave, J., & Wenger, E. (1991). *Situated learning: Legitimate peripheral participation*. Cambridge: Cambridge University Press.

Leont'ev, A. N. (1981/1974). The problem of activity in psychology. In J. V. Wertsch (Ed.), *The concept of activity in Soviet psychology*. Armonk, NY: M. E. Sharpe.

Lewis, C., Perry, R., & Murata, A. (2006). How should research contribute to instructional improvement? The case of lesson study. *Educational Researcher, 35*(3), 3–14.

Lieberman, A. (1996). Practices that support teacher development: Transforming conceptions of professional learning. In M. W. McLaughlin & I. Oberman (Eds.), *Teacher learning: New policies, new practices* (pp. 185–201). New York: Teacher College Press.

Lieberman, A., & Miller, L. (2008). *Teachers in professional communities: Improving teaching and learning*. New York: Teachers College Press.

Lieberman, A., & Miller, L. (Eds.). (2001). *Teachers caught in the action: Professional development that matters*. New York: Teachers College Press.

Lieberman, A., & Pointer-Mace, D. (2010). Making practice public: Teacher learning in the 21st century. *Journal of Teacher Education, 61*(1–2), 77–88.

Lortie, D. C. (2002). *Schoolteacher: A sociological study* (2nd ed.). Chicago, IL: The University of Chicago Press.

Marsick, V. J., & Watkins, K. (2016). *Informal and incidental learning in the workplace*. London: Routledge.

Malcolm, J., Hodkinson, P., & Colley, H. (2003). The interrelationships between informal and formal learning. *Journal of Workplace Learning*, 15(7/8), 313–318.

Morris, K. (2003). *Elementary teachers' opportunities for learning: An ethnographic study of professional development*. Unpublished doctoral dissertation, University of Michigan, Ann Arbor, MI.

Nadelson, L. S., Seifert, A., Moll, A. J., & Coats, B. (2012). i-STEM summer institute: An integrated approach to teacher professional development in STEM. *Journal of STEM Education: Innovation and Outreach 13*(2), 69–83.

Opfer, V. D., & Pedder, D. (2011). Conceptualizing teacher professional learning. *Review of Educational Research, 81*(3), 376–407.

Pedder, D., & Opfer, V. D. (2013). Professional learning orientations: Patterns of dissonance and alignment between teachers' values and practices. *Research Papers in Education, 28*(5), 539–570.

Putnam, R. T., & Borko, H. (2000). What do new views of knowledge and thinking have to say about research on teacher learning? *Educational Researcher, 29*(1), 4–15.

Quicke, J. (1996). Learning and context: Constructing an integrated perspective: Review essay. *British Journal of Sociology of Education, 17*(1), 103–113.

Richardson, V., & Fallona, C. (2001). Classroom management as method and manner. *Journal of Curriculum Studies, 33*(6), 705–728.

Saxe, G., Gearhart, M., & Nasir, N. S. (2001). Enhancing students' understanding of mathematics: A study of three contrasting approaches to professional support. *Journal of Mathematics Teacher Education*, *4*, 55–79.

Shulman, L. (1987). Knowledge and teaching: Foundations of the new reform. *Harvard Educational Review*, *57*(1), 1–22.

Strauss, A., & Corbin, J. (1998). *Basics of qualitative research: Techniques and processes for developing grounded theory* (2nd ed.). Thousand, Oaks, CA: SAGE.

Supovitz, J. A., Mayer, D. P., & Kahle, J. B. (2000). Promoting inquiry-based instructional practice: The longitudinal impact of professional development in the context of systemic reform. *Educational Policy*, *14*(3), 331–356.

Talbert, J. E., & McLaughlin, M. (2001). *Professional communities and the work of high school teachers*. Chicago, IL: University of Chicago Press.

Timperley, H., Wilson, A., Barrar, H., & Fung, I. (2007). *Teacher professional learning and development: Best evidence synthesis iteration*. Wellington, New Zealand: Ministry of Education.

Wei, R. C., Darling-Hammond, L., Andree, A., Richardson, N., Orphanos, S. (2009). *Professional learning in the learning profession: A status report on teacher development in the United States and abroad*. Dallas, TX: National Staff Development Council.

Wei, R. C., Darling-Hammond, L., & Adamson, F. (2010). *Professional development in the United States: Trends and challenges* (Vol. 28). Dallas, TX: National Staff Development Council.

Wenger, E. (2010). Communities of practice and social learning systems: The career of a concept. In *Social learning systems and communities of practice* (pp. 179–198).London: Springer.

Wilson, S. M., Lubienski, S. T., & Mattson, S. (1996, April). *What happened to the mathematics: A case study of the challenges facing reform-oriented professional development*. Paper presented at the *American Educational Research Association*, New York.

Zeichner, K. M. (1998, June 2–4). *The role of practitioner research in personal, educational, and social reconstruction*. Paper presented at the *Conference on Action Research (Aksjonforskining)*, University of Tromso, Norway.

Zeichner, K. M. (2003). Teacher research as professional development for P–12 educators in the USA [1]. *Educational Action Research*, *11*(2), 301–326.

4 Dispositions

Opportunistic—Proactive Learners' Continuum

Overview of This Chapter

This chapter focuses on how teachers expressed their disposition to learning. Based on the discourse analysis of the participants' journal accounts of when they enter the learning process (word choice, choice of tense) and frequency count of the words used to describe their dispositions in their reflective journals, this chapter determines that the teachers demonstrate a certain stance on the continuum between highly opportunistic (taking on a learning opportunity whenever one comes along) and highly proactive (actively seeking answers to a professional question) learners. It appears that the teachers' stances in their disposition toward learning serve as a driving force in their engagement in informal learning situations. Opportunistic openness to learning allows them to submerge in a learning process spontaneously and turn many informal situations into learning experiences. Proactive rationality in approaching learning situations brings an analytic component into teachers' disposition toward learning that is represented in the sequence of steps they undertake when entering their learning experiences.

Introduction

Participating teachers each differed in their disposition toward learning. In some situations, the teachers chose to go along with the routine and rhythm of their everyday professional lives and learn something that could be useful for their teaching without conscious anticipation. In other cases, the teachers were inclined to improve their own teaching in general, without focusing on any specific objective or theme, by looking for learning opportunities whenever they appeared. Though both cases presented differently, in both, teachers did not take any preplanned actions in order to learn anything specific; rather, they were open to any kind of learning, which conveyed an *opportunistic disposition* to learning. When the teachers chose to be *proactive*, they set specific goals for learning sources and took certain steps to reach those goals: they talked with their colleagues

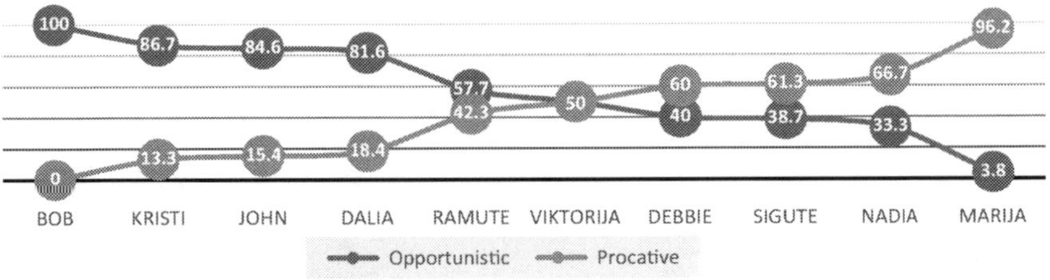

Figure 4.1 Teachers' disposition to informal learning

seeking advice for their teaching challenges; shared their teaching quandaries with other teachers; looked for books; searched the Internet; signed up for relevant seminars. The teachers would display both opportunistic and proactive dispositions depending on the situation; however, some of the teachers clearly leaned toward one disposition—either opportunistic or proactive—while others exhibited features of both.

Figure 4.1 demonstrates the distribution of teachers' dispositions on an Opportunistic—Proactive continuum by the percentage of opportunistic and proactive features that they displayed in their weekly journal entries when describing ways of approaching their teaching dilemmas (Lampert, 2001). On average, the participating teachers tended to approach informal learning situations slightly more opportunistically than proactively. When coding data for opportunistic or proactive dispositions, I considered three aspects: a structural composition of an analyzed unit (a journal entry, an utterance in interviews), grammatical features (choice of tense) and lexical features (word choice). The proportionality of these features determined the position each teacher occupied on the continuum. The following analysis illustrates how accounts of the participating teachers reveal similarities and differences of these aspects.

Opportunistic Learners

Bob, Kristi, John, and Daina belonged to the far opportunistic end of the continuum. The **structural pattern** of their journal entries was similar. As compared to other teachers, they tended to provide a simple structure: they described a learning situation, expressed their emotional attitude, and concluded with a general closure. For example, Kristi did not define her learning goals but rather reacted to problematic situations by describing them and coming up with general conclusions. In one of her journal entries she wrote:[1]

> (1) This week I have learned (again!) how important it is to be flexible! (2) My plans have changed many times. (3) My second grade team plans together. I love that. We are able to collaborate by sharing ideas, as well as responsibilities.

> We started the week with a snow day. I was happy to get my 4:30 am phone call, but that meant my plans had to change. Monday was to be our Valentine's Day party. It went to Tuesday's agenda. We *had visitors scheduled* throughout the week that had *to be rescheduled*. My team partner will not be here on Friday. Her sub plans had *to be redone*.
>
> Flexibility is key in this profession!

Similar to Kristi, John did not seem to predict, anticipate, or plan things that he would like to learn. Rather, the structure of his entries reflected what had already happened and how he felt about it. For example, one of his most typical entries read:

> This week I have learned again what it's like *to be doing* too much at one time. Because I have so much *going on* (graduate school, multiple student projects to grade, meetings...) I *am feeling* overwhelmed and stressed out this week. I *am finding* it difficult to do my regular teaching when I have these other things *needing* to get done. I also find I take it out on others around me by being short with them, sometimes rude, and impatient. But next week is a new week, and hopefully back to normal.[2]

Bob also did not define what he wanted to learn or what kinds of problems he wanted to solve; however, differently from Kristi and John, he embraced any opportunity to learn something about himself and the profession. For example, he pondered his learning as well as his role and place in the classroom, referring to the movie *Dead Poets Society* where the teacher had students' attention as well as respect. He described his attitude to learning, contrasted it with a common view of teachers, and paralleled his stance with the movie's character:

> I got to thinking after my first interview about why I teach and what teaching means to me.
>
> For starters, I love kids and that's why I teach in an elementary school. I believe that I teach (and enjoy it) because *I have a love of learning*. I *love to learn* new things and *I'm always watching* the Discovery Channel, the History Channel, The Learning Channel and Animal Planet (not to mention news shows). I relate a lot of what I learn to my teaching every day. I am a firm believer that you learn something new every day and *I'm always telling* my students that.
>
> When most people think of teaching, they think of the teacher that stands in front of the room and instructs. That approach might work for some, but not for me. I like to move around and get the kids' attention. I find that if you get their attention right away, the lesson goes a lot easier than if you are trying to get their attention in the middle of the lesson. *I always think* of the movie "The Dead Poets' Society" [sic]. The teacher in that movie had their attention as well as their respect.

Similar to Kristi and John, Daina reported an event or described a situation, justifying her choice of a story for the journal entry by describing a strong emotional impact that she had experienced in the situation (the school's birthday celebration with her students, Teachers' Day celebration, a trip to the railway museum, guest musicians at the school) and finding proof for her thoughts and attitudes (the value of ethno-cultural education). Even on those rare occasions when she did write about her teaching experiences, she chose to report that she had spent a great deal of time preparing for the lesson and instead described the procedures of reflecting on her learning from that experience. Like Kristi and John, her learning outcomes were saturated with emotions. Usually, her learning outcomes took the shape of unexpected ideas that emerged randomly from a situation in which she took part. Like Bob, she seemed to take an active stance, looking for learning experiences in different situations. Like the other members of this group, the structure of her passages consisted of a situation description, a paragraph that expressed an educative value of the experience for her students, and a closure that featured a new idea that emerged from this situation. For example, in one of her entries, Daina wrote:

> Ambassadors' wives made Christmas toys and souvenirs for donation, and our elementary students were asked to decorate paper bags for them. I gave this job to those who wanted to do it without putting any pressure because a donation is a DONATION for it is done voluntarily, without any pressure. I was very pleased with my students' effort in doing it. There appeared beautiful drawings on simple bags that became wonderful masterpieces. I think that everyone who received it was pleased.
>
> I wanted to share the joy of participating in this good mission in which our elementary students, my class, took part in a much-needed activity! That is a very meaningful, genuine, and necessary support, which is most necessary for those who miss attention especially now, with big holidays approaching.
>
> That idea inspired a thought to decorate plain envelopes, where I put students' artwork for birthdays.

A similar pattern (description, emotional reaction, a new idea/understanding) emerged in other entries by Daina, Bob, John, and Kristi.

Grammatical and linguistic patterns were also similar among this group of teachers; they tended to use the passive voice, transferring agency to another person or event. They also used the present continuous tense, communicating instability and signifying their emergent learning rather than their focus on a specific theme or result. For example, in the quoted passage, Kristi used the passive voice when she described the work that she should re-do because of the snow day. Even when she used the active voice (sentence 2: *My plans have changed many times*), she was not an agent in the sentence—her plans were acting rather than she. In sentence three (*My second-grade team plans together*), she removed herself from being an active agent and placed herself within the team of actors (the second-grade teachers). It the passage presented above, John used the present continuous tense (*like to be doing*, *going on*, *I am feeling*, *I am finding*, *things needing to get done*), which signaled that he positioned himself as being in the process rather than taking active steps to learn certain things.

By repeating the structure "*I'm always [doing something]*" three times in the quoted above journal entry, Bob placed himself as an agent in the continual process of learning. He reinforced this picture of himself as an incessant learner by underlining his strong emotional relation to learning; however, his openness to learning did not have any specific focus. He did not seem to be planning to learn anything specific about his teaching.

The word choice was indicative of the stance the teachers took as learners. The teachers in this group used many verbs that expressed emotions (*love*, *like*, *feeling*). Daina extensively used adjectives that conveyed her appreciation (*wonderful*, *beautiful*) and her positive attitude (*much needed*, *meaningful*, *genuine*). These teachers' vocabulary and syntactic features (verb choice, the passive voice, the present continuous tense and repetitive use of this structure) confirmed that they tended to approach their learning opportunistically.

In sum, the structure of the journal entries and their grammatical and lexical patterns showed that opportunistic learners welcomed any learning opportunities that came along. Bob and Daina often took an active stance and looked for learning opportunities. Kristi and John displayed a passive stance: they did not define their learning goals but rather emotionally reacted to problematic situations by describing them. They concluded their entries with general statements, and unexpected ideas emerged randomly from learning situations in which they took part. Interestingly, this group of teachers includes three American and one Lithuanian teacher (see Table 2.1 in the introduction to this part).

Opportunistic/Proactive Learners

Viktorija, Sigute, Ramute, and Debbie comprised the second group of teachers, who displayed both opportunistic and proactive dispositions to learning with almost equal emphasis. In its form, Debbie's journal was similar to other American teachers—a narrative in which she described events and/or feelings about those events. In contrast, the three Lithuanian teachers (Viktorija, Sigute, Ramute) constructed their journal entries as short bullet-pointed statements. All the teachers, except for these three, kept these journals specifically for this study. Viktorija, Sigute and Ramute mentioned that they have practiced journaling before and continued recording ideas and experiences by keeping concise notes as lists of things to remember do. Though the structure of their entries was similar, the content slightly differed in terms of each teacher's disposition to learning. For example, under the heading "March", Viktorija had four entries (one for each week) and each entry conveyed a few different ideas. In one of the entries, she wrote:

- We have visited Czech schools and learned about their curriculum. I liked their students' art works. There were different collages, made with using produce waste (plastic bottles). I liked that wonderful work is being created out of simple things. That is not hard for the kids to do.
- Together with my class, I took part in an environmental protection action "I would like to live", which was dedicated to protecting plants and animals in spring. Children drew pictures, created poems. We discussed the works with my colleagues. There were interesting suggestions. Margarita became a winner.

Both entries illustrate an opportunistic disposition in that Viktorija did not define her learning goals, yet she still actively took part in different practices. She sought and reported on her learning outcomes like Bob and Daina. In her other entries, Viktorija demonstrated her proactive disposition; she did not explicitly define her learning goal but rather made her learning focus evident in her reflections. For example,

> I taught an open[3] lesson "I am growing up healthy" using multimedia. Teachers L. and D. observed it. New technologies are interesting but there are not enough skills to use them professionally.
>
> Later, I observed Birute's lesson "The Battle of Zhalgiris [Grunewald]." We discussed the lesson. Children are interested in the use of technology during lessons, but that activity requires a very big preparation.

Ramute's disposition to learning had more in common with the opportunistic stance than the others' in this group. Her journal entries usually followed a simple structure: she described a situation or experience and then concluded with an explanation of what was important for her as a teacher. For example, she wrote about visiting Gambia, where people lived without electricity and running water and where children rushed to cars for candy. Upon returning from her trip, she talked with her students about the values that they usually take for granted in our everyday lives. In another entry, she commented on reading Anderson's fairy tales with her students. She discovered "on the spot" that the students did not know many of them. Like Bob, Daina, and Viktorija, Ramute's opportunistic learning was active. She did not wait for opportunities to come, but vigorously took part in different events, visited various places and brought ideas to her teaching from her rich experiences. On the other hand, she was clearly proactive when she looked for ways of developing her own skills (i.e., enhancing computer skills, joining international projects, or doing her new part-time trainer job). For example, in one of the entries she wrote:

- (…) Interview for eTwinning consultants. Needs to be attended.
- A preparatory visit for Comenius Project will be in November. The documents need to be prepared.
- I want to go to an international seminar for elementary education in Belgium, Holland and France.
- I passed the competition for eTwinning consultants. Hurray. I will be a consultant.
- I am going to teach a seminar for Telshiai region teachers on June 16.
- Teacher L. shared an idea from a seminar. Choose a fairy tale and all the week, give assignments related to it. I should try.
- I need to find a place for the seminar in Telshiai. It is great to have Internet.

In addition to characteristics of opportunistic learners and like Ramute, Sigute also displayed characteristics of a proactive learner. She wrote about students with problems, defining her efforts in helping them. She talked about selecting a fiction book for reading at home that related to teaching. With her colleagues, she discussed strategies of keeping parents focused on bringing students to classes on time. She wrote about preparation for a field trip, planned for her former students to come and help her, utilized her colleague's ideas about teaching fun classes on the last day before the break, and thought through ways of talking with her students about the tragic day of January 13, 1991.[4] She anticipated what factors could be at work when she taught an "open lesson", went to an exhibition to check whether it would be interesting for her students, incorporated her prior negative experiences with a parents' meeting to design the next one, selected ideas from communication with her colleagues and her grandmother to use in her teaching. Her opportunistic stance came forward in her description of initial meetings with students' parents, in ways in which she found connections of her everyday experiences with her teaching, in her comments on participation in all-school events and fieldtrips.

Sigute's entries' structure was closer to the one displayed by the teachers that belong to the proactive group of learners. Sigute described her problem, provided evidence that supported her understanding of the situation, planned actions to solve the problem, and sometimes reported on the results of her actions. For example,

> I worry immensely about my student R. The Music teacher, social counselor, my other colleague and I noticed that R. perceives environment not adequately to his age as well as is not able to do many things that children of his age are able to do easily. We have a problem: what

> to do? I have a feeling that it is necessary to talk with the school's psychologist.

A few days later, she continued with the story:

> The psychologist tested R. on two tests: the child's development and perception. She told me that the child is about two years behind in his level of perception. She recommended using colors and numbers while teaching him the curriculum and just experiment [what works for him].

In contrast to the other three members of this group, Debbie wrote a narrative of her learning experiences rather than recording them in a bullet-point format; however, Debbie's disposition to learning also incorporated both proactive and opportunistic stances, with a slightly stronger inclination toward proactive. She demonstrated an analytic approach by creating a learning situation for herself with a specific goal in mind. She did not define the goal explicitly, but her purposeful actions, which lead toward new understandings, demonstrated what she had in mind. For example, she wrote:

> I learned a lot today just by listening to my students read. The behaviors they have are quite outstanding. However, one area seems to be a pitfall among all my students receiving special reading instruction: the ability to be flexible with vowels at a point of difficulty in the story. Each one of my students will try only one vowel sound and neglect to think about the meaning of a nonsense word. Instead of reading and trying another sound for the tricky part to make the story more meaningful, they continue to plunge through the story, leaving the nonsense words unfixed.
>
> So: I have learned just through observation of my students a teaching strategy I have neglected to instruct. By sitting back and becoming a careful observer, one can learn a lot about oneself.

Debbie's structure of entries, though similar to Sigute's, was more complex. She started with making a claim (*I learned a lot today just by listening to my students read*). Next, she defined a problem (*However, one area seems to be a pitfall among all my students receiving special reading instruction; the ability to be flexible with vowels at a point of difficulty in the story. Each one of my students will try only one vowel sound and neglect to think about the meaning of a nonsense word. Instead of reading and trying another sound for the tricky part to make the story more meaningful, they continue to plunge through the story, leaving the nonsense words unfixed*). Then she reported on her learning (*So: I have learned just through observation of my students a teaching strategy I have neglected to instruct*); and wrapped up with a conclusion (*By sitting back and becoming a careful observer, one can learn a lot about oneself*). This complex structure represents the logically organized thinking process that is characteristic of proactive learners.

Grammatical and lexical patterns demonstrated that teachers in this group took an active part in events even when they did not plan to learn anything specific. Their sentences were short. Usually, the authors were the subjects (Ramute: *I want*, *I passed*; Viktorija: *I took part*, *I visited*, *I liked*; Sigute: *I worry*, *I have a feeling*; Debbie: *I have learned*, *I have neglected*). They used simple or perfect tense. Usually, these teachers employed active verbs (*visited*, *discussed*, *learned*, *took part*, *observed and recommended*). They seemed to avoid using adjectives or adverbs as if they wanted to move on faster to doing something. In their experiences, they presented themselves as active and purposeful agents who made choices in which learning situation to participate. They anticipated what they might learn and actively sought settings that enriched their experiences, which they planned to apply in their teaching.

In sum, the opportunistic/proactive group combined features that were characteristic of both stances, taking opportunistic stances in some situations and proactive in others, yet they still actively took part in different learning practices. As opportunistic learners, these teachers did not define their learning goals, yet they made their learning focus evident in their reflections. Similar to proactive learners, the structure of their entries was more complex than that of opportunistic learners'. They pursued learning opportunities and reported on their learning outcomes, as did proactive learners.

Proactive Learners

The final group of teachers included Nadia and Marija (both from a Russian school in Lithuania). These teachers demonstrated a highly proactive mode of disposition to informal learning. From the previous group, I noticed that the structure of Debbie's and Sigute's entries was the closest to those in the proactive group; however, in this group, the structure was even more complex. Marija and Nadia usually defined a situation and a problem, described steps they took to research and solve it, reflected upon and evaluated new understandings, and tried (or planned) to apply them in their practice. For example, Nadia wrote:

> [1] Since I started working in this school (in 1991), I taught Music only one year at the very beginning. [2] The rest of the time, specialists taught it, though my education + Music school [diploma] allowed me to teach these lessons, though, may be, of course not on such a high professional level. [3] But this year, I was put in the position (received only 11 weekly hours) of taking over Music lessons. [4] For 12 years, I have not touched these lesson plans (except of preparing for concerts), no help from the specialist was

> expected—she was upset; counting on myself was the only option. [5] Teacher A.K. helped me with literature, explained the Music Standards; I read the curriculum, some things should have been recollected, and I composed the thematic plan. [6] Of course, I would like to observe an open lesson.

Though in this journal entry, Nadia did not define her specific learning goals, she seemed to know what she needed to learn by assessing her prior knowledge of Music (sentences 1–2). Then, she defined a problem (sentences 3–4) and described the steps that she took for solving it and then, she reported on the results of her actions (sentence 5). She concluded with a wish to learn more and identified a specific way of doing it (sentence 6). Her entries, usually, did not involve all the structural elements that were characteristic of the proactive learning mode.

Marija, who also displayed a proactive stance in her entries, presented a complex structure of identifying, defining, resolving her professional dilemmas, and applying new ideas. She did not wait for a learning opportunity to emerge. Rather, she actively looked for and created learning situations by approaching her colleagues, asking them questions and appreciatively listening to their experiences, sharing her own experiences with them, and joining conversations. For example, in one of the journal entries, Marija wrote:

> The first graders like to play most of all. Because of that, I constantly look for new didactic games and think up different playful situations. On November 10, I was checking my students' workbooks in the teachers' lounge. The second grade teacher T.I. sat down right next to me. She pulled out some kind of cards and started writing something on them. Of course, I got interested in her work right away. T.I. told me that a few days ago she looked through some old "Elementary School" ("Nachalnaja shkola" in Russian) magazines and came across a description of Math games. I asked her to tell me more about those games. She not only told me about them but also brought these magazines the next day. That is how more educational games were added to my games' "piggy bank."

The structure of Marija's entries reflected that she was a strategic learner. Whenever she formulated a problem, she seemed to have a plan for solving it.

Chronologically, her entry structure reflected the following steps:

1. She described a situation, identified a problem and the participants.
2. She shared specific information or her experience.
3. She collected information and researched the problem.
4. She defined her new understanding.

5. She evaluated or implemented a new idea.
6. She, occasionally, commented on its value for development of her teaching or on results of its implementation.

Grammatical and lexical patterns revealed that teachers in this group constructed their learning through reflecting on their professional experiences and identifying things that they needed to find out. Nadia's and Marija's entries told stories about their informal learning. They used complex grammatical structures that defined how they positioned themselves in a situation. In the example above, Nadia used impersonal constructs (*some things should have been recollected*) or the passive voice (*I was put in the position*) to show that there was another layer in the story and an additional agent—the problematic situation was created by the district and the school administration. She switched to the simple past or the past perfect when she wrote about her own actions in solving the problem. Marija used the simple or the perfect tense. Her sentences had an active subject (herself, a student, or a colleague). Both teachers in this group used active verbs (*took over*, *read*, *composed*, *look for*, *pulled out*, *came across*, *brought*), which helped them maintain the flow of the story; they seldom used adjectives or adverbs. These teachers positioned themselves as active and determined agents who decided what they wanted or needed to learn, how they would do that and how they would apply their new understandings. On rare occasions when they decided to enter a learning situation without a specific goal, they identified a reason for doing that, reported on specific things that they learned, and reflected on how it was applicable to what they tried to resolve.

To conclude, among those teachers who chose an **opportunistic disposition** more frequently, I distinguished two kinds of stances: (1) Go along with daily routines or any situations that they encounter (John, Kristi); (2) be open to learning and seek any experiences that could contribute to enriching their teaching practices (Bob, Daina). Teachers who commonly displayed an opportunistic disposition to learning tended to be less reflective and more emotional. They reacted rather than acted.

The second group of teachers tended to use an opportunistic mode in some situations and a proactive mode in others (Ramute, Sigute, Viktorija, and Debbie). Usually when they chose to take on an opportunistic stance, they were active and open to learning. When they exercised a proactive mode, they either focused on a wider area of learning or chose a specific teaching dilemma.

Two kinds of **proactive dispositions** to informal learning emerged in the teachers' entries. They either (1) identified a larger focal area and looked for various possibilities for developing in this precise area (Nadia); or (2) defined a specific professional dilemma and took a sequence of steps to resolve it (Marija). Teachers, who took a proactive stance more often, constructed their learning strategically. They seemed to exercise certain habits of mind (Costa & Kallick, 2008) in using teaching dilemmas to continually develop and grow professionally.

Teachers' stances in their disposition toward learning served as a driving force in their engagement in informal learning situations. Opportunistic openness to learning allowed them to submerge in a learning process spontaneously and turn many informal situations into learning experiences. Proactive rationality in approaching learning situations brought an analytic component into teachers' disposition toward learning that was represented in the sequence of steps they undertook when reflecting upon their learning experiences. The following chapters present the analyses of the four remaining features that characterize teachers' individual learning stances in workplace: source of learning, orientation to learning problems, engagement in learning process, and reactions to learning problems/instances.

Notes

1 In following excerpts, *Italics* signify key grammatical and lexical patterns.
2 This excerpt will be analyzed in Chapter 8, in which it will serve to illustrate a different point.
3 A lesson taught in front of other colleagues to be discussed with them later, similar to the Japanese lesson study.
4 The Lithuanian Republic was the first of the former Soviet Republics to declare independence from the Soviet Union on March 11, 1990, and thereafter underwent a difficult period of emergence. Tensions rose sharply during the first days of 1991. On January 10, the president of the Soviet Union, Mikhail Gorbachev, addressed the Supreme Council, demanding restoration of the constitution of the USSR in Lithuania and the revocation of all anti-constitutional laws. He mentioned that a military intervention could be possible within days. On the morning of January 11, Speaker of the Supreme Council Vytautas Landsbergis and Prime Minister Albertas Šimėnas were presented with another ultimatum from "Democratic Congress of Lithuania" (a Lithuanian pro-communist organization) demanding that they comply with Gorbachev's request by 15:00 on January 11. In Vilnius, the capital of Lithuania, independence supporters gathered around the main governmental and infrastructural buildings to protect them. At 1:50 a.m. on January 13, Soviet tanks and soldiers encircled the TV tower. Soldiers fired overhead and into civilian crowds gathered around the building. Tanks drove straight through lines of people. Fourteen people were killed in the attack, most of them shot and several crushed by tanks. One Soviet paratrooper was killed by friendly fire. For more information, see http://news.bbc.co.uk/onthisday/hi/dates/stories/january/13/newsid_4059000/4059959.stm.

References

Costa, A. L., & Kallick, B. (Eds.). (2008). *Learning and leading with habits of mind: 16 essential characteristics for success.* Alexandria, VA: ASCD.

Lampert, M. (2001). *Teaching problems and the problems of teaching.* New Haven, CT: Yale University Press.

5 Sources of Learning

Individual–Social Learners' Continuum

Overview of This Chapter

In this chapter, discourse analysis of the teachers' written accounts results in placing them on the continuum between individual and social learners depending on how they identify sources of their learning: some take preference in finding a book or an article on their own while others find solutions to their professional dilemmas by talking to their colleagues. When engaging in the process of informal learning, teachers pursue learning resources either on their own or in interaction with colleagues, students, parents, and administrators. The chapter demonstrates the teachers' distribution along the continuum between individual and social learning. Two of the groups include teachers whose learning characteristics lean toward one of the opposite sides of the continua, and one group (in the middle) includes teachers who almost equally employ learning features from both sides. Teachers' individual profiles demonstrate that most of the teachers utilize social learning sources, even when they draw more often than others upon individual resources.

Introduction

After having applied the same pattern of analysis that I used in chapter 4, I expected to find that teachers differed in the ways they looked for resources for learning informally. The analysis of their reflective journals showed that some teachers most frequently worked on their own (individual learners), others turned to their colleagues and other people (social learners), and some used a combination of both modes with almost equal frequency. As individual learners, the teachers analyzed their own teaching, mainly focusing on its effectiveness; they also turned to books, journals, or the Internet for information to help resolve their dilemmas. They reflected on their teaching through "the generation of rich, impressionistic narrative accounts of the writer's own experiences regarding a particular phenomenon of interest" (Holbrook, 2005 as cited in Rod, 2011, p. 6). This subjective personal introspection is the characteristic feature of

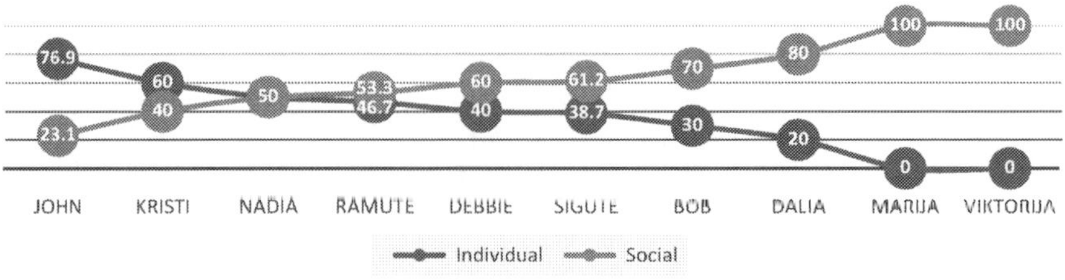

Figure 5.1 Teachers' sources of informal learning

individual learners. As social learners, they discussed their practice with their colleagues, administrators, and other people, and experimented with ideas that they found valuable. On the Individual—Social continuum, the teachers comprised three groups: individual, social/individual, and social learners. Figure 5.1 demonstrates the participating teachers' distribution on the continuum. Interestingly, it also shows that most of the teachers tend to look for and use resources as social learners, with only two teachers leaning toward an individual learning mode. This category helps to understand what resources teachers use in their informal learning and how they utilize them.

Individual Learners

John and Kristi seemed to rely on their individual experience and prior knowledge most of the time. Usually, their entries contained evidence of reflection. They looked at their practice in order to understand what they could do better. For example, journal entries indicate that John's main source of learning was his personal experience (marked in bold). In one of the entries, John wrote:

> This week **I** learned the effect of working with other teachers new to a grade level. This year **I've** worked with two teachers who were new to 4th grade and new to regular education (previously special ed.). Really **I've** learned all year the effects of being the "senior" teacher at a grade level. **I've** learned that it can be very taxing to be the person constantly sharing and "teaching" others about the in's and out's of a grade level. Don't get me wrong, **I** have greatly enjoyed working with my 4th grade counterparts, but **I** can reflect on the year and see the effects of me giving up time throughout the year in order to help others. **I'm** glad **I** could be helpful to them, but it did take a toll on my effectiveness as a teacher towards my students. This has shown me that teachers really do learn from each other. **I** can also see how tough it can be on a teacher who is consistently helping others to learn.

In this entry, John claimed that there was a value in learning from others; however, it was not he who learned from his colleagues, but rather that they were positioned to learn from him. He saw himself exclusively as a learning provider who did not benefit from such interactions. Nevertheless, he submitted this entry as his learning experience, which he described as his learning to offer less time to others because the experience he described took a toll on his effectiveness as a teacher in his own classroom.

Individual learners tended to reflect on their personal or professional problems and dealt with their dilemmas on their own (John: learning to be flexible, learning the value of good planning, realizing the effects of being more experienced in the grade level; Kristi: being more flexible, managing her time, problems caused by snow days). Interactions with colleagues and students as sources of learning did not appear in their journal frequently. For example, only on a few occasions did John mentioned doing things together with his colleagues (working with his grade level colleagues on addressing educational needs better, talking with fifth grade teachers about ideas for teaching persuasive writing, staff performing together).

Kristi's learning procedures included an extensive communication with her colleagues both at her grade level at the school and outside the building (at a dinner, on the bus trip, golfing); however, even in these potentially social instances of learning, she seemed to place herself as both subject and object of narration. For example, in one of the entries she wrote:

> This week has been crazy as well. **I** have been sick, and **I** have sick kids at home. **I** was out Wednesday. My husband stayed home with my daughters yesterday. Even though **I** was here, **my** mind was there.
>
> It seems like even on a day that on paper looks like not much is going on, lots come up. **I** feel glad that **my** grade level is so organized. As organized as we are, there is always something to be done. Next month is reading month. **I'm** on the committee. Not enough prizes came in, so we are having to order more, and hope they will be in soon. Who knows? Things that make sense to **me**, don't always to others. Why is that?

Sources of learning for individual learners originate both from observation, reflection, as well as from interactions—with colleagues, parents, and students. It seems to be very important for Kristi to have friends at work. In an interview, she admitted that she missed such a network of friends in this new building (comparing it to her old workplace), so she attempted creating one. She seemed to have a need to verify her understandings with her colleagues; however, learning for her and John seemed to come from and be about themselves. They positioned themselves outside the described situations, signifying that their new realizations stemmed from their (often negative) perceptions of the context.

Grammatical and lexical patterns. The teachers who belong to the group of individual learners used pronoun "I" and its possessive form "my" extensively. For example, similarly to the previously quoted John's passage, in a different entry, he wrote about his individual understandings, again constructing his narrative around self:

> **I** learned this week that as a teacher you must take time for some of the "little" problems students come up against. As Spring continues, students get more active and excitable. Because of this they may hurt another in the class emotionally. This week **I** had two occasions with this. It shows me that **I** have a bigger responsibility than teaching math or science. Sometimes **I** have to take time to address the emotional needs of 9 and 10 year old kids.

The structure of the sentences that contain pronoun "I" was simple. The ideas discussed in sentences with such a structure revolved around self, without making deep connections with a broader context.

Individual/Social Learners

Nadia, Ramute, Debbie, and Sigute comprise the group of teachers who utilized both individual and social sources of learning. The teachers in this group used reflection to solve their professional dilemmas from which they learned. Nadia, for example, developed new understandings through on-the-spot and retrospective reflection, by working on curriculum design or modification, by looking for connections between ideas learned in seminars and her own work, by observing other teachers or performers, and by preparing for "open" lessons. Ramute reflected on her experiences teaching with multimedia, she looked for information on the Internet, she defined focus areas for herself (i.e., prepared papers for the Comenius visit, signed up for computer courses, prepared slides with PowerPoint for computer courses). Sigute reflected on something that went wrong in her teaching (emotionally involved with her former graduates, an unsuccessful patents' meeting, a successful parents' meeting), utilized other experiences to improve her teaching (used the movie's "Shrek" example in teaching her students about teeth hygiene, from observing the 12th graders' theater performance and their influence on younger students, decided to involve her former students—fifth graders, used her grandmother's embroidery patterns for egg-dying, found attractive a system of students' evaluation, used by her friend in another school). Debbie reflected on her classroom observations, and on her readings. For example, in one of her entries, she wrote:

> I am reading a book about a boy in a terrible situation. This makes me wonder how some children can come expected to learn and carry

> out classroom activities. When children are abused, not loved, and neglected how they can be held accountable for the same benchmarks and federal legislations as NCLB. I have learned from this boy's experience that even though life has handed some children a can of rotten worms, most of them carry on with the courage to move forward. Teachers are faced with these type of children every year. It is only our love for them that these children need to keep going, as they do not get it from their home environment.

Even though she derived her new understandings from her personal readings, she built a connection with her professional standpoint and extended her thinking to her students.

Teachers in this group also learn from communications with their colleagues. They collaborated with their colleagues, interacted with them during formal meetings and informal encounters, learned from their stories about interesting seminars, discussed their teaching dilemmas, and socialized with them.

In addition, these teachers learned from their participation in various events. For example, Ramute wrote about her learning experiences when visiting the Art Education Center (using plural "we" rather that singular "I") or when she reflected on her participation in art shows. Like Ramute, other teachers in this group communicated with participants at seminars and learned from going on field trips. On occasion, they reported that they learned from their students and other people.

Grammatical and lexical patterns. The structure of the sentences in these teachers' narratives was more complex compared to that of the individual learners'. Variations of clauses in a paragraph illustrate the authors' departure from one-dimensional ("I") interaction with the world that is characteristic of individual learners to a multifaceted perception of a learning situation. The subjects of the sentences vary from the first person singular to the third person singular and plural, illustrating how the authors developed their understandings by constructing multiple connections with their previous experiences. Such sentence structure provides a multilayered picture of learning sources.

Social Learners

Social learners (Bob, Daina, Marija, and Viktorija) engaged in different types of communication with a variety of people, who provided them with feedback. In most of their journal entries, they depicted their learning experiences as interactions with others, and in different situations, they employed a variety of social learning techniques. Overall, their sources of learning were more diverse than the other two groups. They held conversations with a wide range of colleagues: elementary, middle, and high school teachers, administrators and other specialists in their buildings, their former colleagues, and teachers in other buildings. For example, on one occasion Marija wrote:

> In my class, there is a boy, who seems not to know how to communicate with other children. Children complain that he often pushes and hits them. For a few days, the school psychologist visited my classroom. **I asked her** to observe this boy. On the 23 of September, she told me about her observations in the teachers' lounge**. According to her opinion**, this boy really wants to communicate with other children but does not know how to attract their attention. That is why he often takes others' things, pushes and hits them. In addition, **she drew my attention** to the fact, that during lessons, this boy wants to be different by doing everything at a different time than other students. For example, all the children would start doing a One-Minute Gym, while he would continue writing, but when children would get back to writing, he would stand up and do a One-Minute Gym. **The psychologist suggested me** to involve this boy in everything they do (assign him to lead a One-Minute Gym, call on him first to come to the blackboard and so on) and praise him more often. Of course, I knew that all myself, but it seems that I have not used it often enough. Well, **I will try to follow the psychologist's advice**.

Usually, they initiated communicative process by asking questions, sharing their experiences, and asking for feedback (see Marija's entry above). When they joined conversations, they were active participants—they showed interest by asking for advice and readily discussed with others what they did in their classrooms. They seemed to be positive and open about their practice and others' advice.

They learned:

- From and with their students (Bob and Viktorija);
- Communicating with colleagues in hallways, cafeterias, teachers' lounges (Bob and Viktorija);
- Observing and discussing colleagues' experiences, ideas and lessons (Viktorija);
- Discussing with colleagues interesting ideas that they encounter (Viktorija);
- Discussing their own teaching experiences (Viktorija);
- Interacting with educators from other schools, cities, countries (Viktorija and Marija);
- Participating in exhibitions and shows with their students (Viktorija);
- Working with colleagues on common projects (Marija).

Often, these teachers wrote about implementing ideas that they have discussed in their journals (Viktorija: Teaching a new lesson with multimedia; creative transformation of ideas). They seemed to be open to learning from everything they did or got involved with (Bob: relating TV programs' information to his teaching; thinking about his profession and how the society relates to it; working with different students' personalities; thinking through the school year).

Complex sentences distinguish these teachers' **grammatical and lexical patterns** from the previous groups. Their sentence structure contained multiple clauses, through which the teachers depicted profound connections that they built with the world. They identified multiple sources for learning and drew on their rich experiences. They positioned themselves within an interactive environment in which the main activity was communication with others. For this reason, frequently, other colleagues, students, and their parents were the subjects in the sentences. Their narratives often incorporated dialogues that the author of the story reproduced in an indirect speech (Marija: "I asked her", "according to her opinion", "she drew my attention to", "the psychologist suggested me"). Sometimes, a narrator refers to me, their most likely audience, directly (Bob: I will have to keep you updated on any new news) or indirectly (Daina told stories about how much fun she had with her students as if trying to illustrate what she perceived my idea of "good teaching" was).

In sum, **individual learners** usually learned by reflecting on their practice and analyzing it on their own, keeping an implicit dialogue with themselves or turning to printed resources and media for solutions. They placed themselves in the center of narration, constructing their account of learning around the self. Individual introspection was the characteristic feature of this group, and the main sources of learning for individual learners originated mainly from observation and reflection.

Social learners tended to share their dilemmas with someone and expected feedback, or they explicitly asked for advice on a specific issue. They described their learning experiences as interaction with others, and their sources and means of learning were diverse. They were both good listeners and engaged talkers who were active participants in each of their interactions with others. On many occasions, they were the initiators of the communicative process by expressing their interest in and positive attitude to their collocutors' practices.

Social/individual learners utilized both individual and social sources of learning. The teachers in this group used reflection to solve their professional dilemmas and learn from them. Even though they derived their new understandings from personal experiences, they built connections with their professional stance. These teachers learned from their participation in various events, and on multiple occasions, they communicated and collaborated with their colleagues.

When engaging in the process of informal learning, teachers pursued learning resources either on their own or in interaction with colleagues, students, parents, and administrators. Table 2.1 illustrates the teachers' distribution among three groups (individual, social and balanced social/

individual). Two of the groups include teachers whose learning characteristics lean toward one of the opposite sides of the continua, and one group (in the middle) includes teachers who almost equally employ learning features from both sides. Teachers' individual profiles demonstrate that most of the teachers utilized social learning sources, even when they drew more often upon individual resources as, for example, Kristi and John did.

References

Holbrook, M. (2005). Customer value and autoethnography: Subjective personal introspection and the meanings of a photographic collection. *Journal of Business Research, 18*(1), 45–61.

Rod, M. (2011). Subjective personal introspection in action-oriented research. *Qualitative Research in Organizations and Management: An International Journal, 6*(1), 6–25.

6 Reactions to Dilemmas

Emotional–Cognitive Learners' Continuum

Overview of This Chapter

This chapter uses discourse analysis to provide evidence of how teachers express their reaction to professional dilemmas. Some of the teachers express their emotions (either positive or negative) more often, while others start analyzing the dilemma at hand and design a road map to its resolution. Most of the participants display a combination of emotional and cognitive reactions according to which they occupy a close-to-middle position on the continuum between the two opposites. Cognitive reactions would help teachers analyze a dilemma and find resources for resolving it, while emotional reactions would inspire and motivate them to pursue change. By identifying the different reactions that teachers display in response to their professional problems, this chapter paves the way for further investigation of how, for example, teachers react to specific situations and problems, and how these reactions relate to their engagement in learning.

Introduction

Teachers differed in how they reacted to a teaching dilemma that they identified, which usually followed by a learning experience. When describing such situations in their reflective journals, some of the teachers primarily displayed a range of emotional reactions. They comprised the group of *emotional* learners. Other teachers belonged to the group of *cognitive* learners who approached their dilemmas using *cognitive* processes that resembled the Deweyan phases of reflective thinking: (1) suggestion, (2) intellectualization, (3) the guiding idea, hypothesis, (4) reasoning, and (5) testing hypothesis by action (Dewey, 1933/1989). The teachers who used both modes for reacting to their professional dilemmas comprised the *emotional/cognitive* learners' group.

Emotional Learners

Kristi, Bob, and John often finalized their entries with platitudes and generalized trivial conclusions (e.g., Kristi: "it's all about confidence", "flexibility is key in this profession", "everything has a good side and a bad side", "great having an organized team"). Daina, usually, concluded her entries with a phrase expressing emotions. For example, on one occasion she wrote:

> It is the schoolteachers' team carnival, a party with the Middle Eastern theme. We tried to look very Eastern. We tried to pull information out of whoever bought any interesting clothing. I also shared my shopping findings! It was not in vain! And that was pleasant! Because it is so important just to play! We had a good time! We all the elementary teachers wanted to be united!
>
> It is great to be on this team, not only exchanging (Christmas) presents, but just be there!
>
> Why did I choose to write about this episode? Because I want to share about this enjoyable party, isn't it the best to be among your own teammates, and "see" them not only in the rut, but also have fun together. That is our strength!

The teachers in this group seemed to be aware of their professional "ups" and "downs". Occasionally, to reflect on their emotional states, these four teachers displayed cognitive reactions. Bob, for example, described his previous good experiences with team-teaching and felt that many things went wrong this time. He was both cognitive and emotional in addressing this problem. To reflect on this dilemma, he returned to this experience in another entry; however, he was not analyzing but rather reporting on what was going on and how he was feeling about the decision ("feeling bad, like [he] is giving up"). To reinforce his reactions, Bob graphically expressed his emotional states: he added a smiley or a sad face at the end of each entry. He also communicated an emotional attachment, when he referred to his students' parents' notes and cards, which he saved from all the years of his teaching to remind him about happy moments. Often, he went back and read them "to make the right choices in the future".

Grammatical and lexical patterns. The teachers who belong to this group extensively used exclamations to express their emotionally colored accounts (e.g., Kristi: "We have lives too!", "I am very ready for spring break this year!", "Only a little over a week! (…) and we still couldn't find the way!" "How exciting!"). Kristi and Daina usually put an exclamatory mark at the end of the entry, as if drawing a conclusion in an excited manner. In addition, Daina used exclamatory expressions to highlight appealing ideas ("just an idea about how to use a paper maché technique using balloons!"), to describe the atmosphere in the classroom ("I was very glad that we had a great time that day missing each other after vacations, so nobody really cared for learning that day!"), and to express her feelings ("It feels like playing!"). In some entries, Daina used more exclamation marks than any other punctuation signs (e.g., six exclamation marks when describing the teachers' Christmas party).

These teachers tended to use vocabulary that reflected their emotions (Daina: "It was very nice!", "I made it!", "I am happy about…", "it was so much fun!", "I liked…"). In addition, Daina frequently used intensifying adjectives ***wonderful***, ***great***, ***amazing***, and adjunct intensifying adverbs ***very much***, ***highly***, ***a lot***.

Often, these teachers weaved a slogan or an abstract statement into the texture of their narrative (Daina: Creativity is freedom! Bob: "It is a great experience for the kids though!" "There will always be 'ups' and 'downs' in life. Hopefully you will have more ups!", "I teach!" Kristi: "Flexibility is key to this profession!", "Everything has a good side and a bad side!", "We have lives too!").

Emotional/Cognitive Learners

Sigute and Nadia reacted to learning situations using both cognitive and emotional modes with almost equal frequency. In some entries, they analyzed problematic situations and came up with a plan to solve their dilemmas. In other entries, like the emotional learners, they expressed negative emotions, which seemed to ignite desire for changing something and figuring out how to do it (Sigute: "a 'tragic' parents' meeting;" "I could not imagine that my first graders would try so hard;" "I doubt that I would take my kids to meet with this guest musician again;" "I will have to show an 'open lesson'" to British critical thinking teachers. That will be Monday, the first lesson, first graders. It's stupid…"). Nadia also frequently expressed negative emotions: disappointment for not being able to implement great ideas in her school, skepticism about using small group activities because of the chaotic nature of such activities, and administrators' intolerance of any disorganized activities.

Sigute and Nadia used a reporting rather than a reflective style of journaling; however, differently from the emotional learners, they often described their reactions to teaching dilemmas using some reflection. Nadia, for example, wrote:

> A lesson for the future first graders.
>
> Russian Language.
>
> My students helped—they presented a play "The Red Sun." My children took care of the little ones with great enthusiasm. I thought that there would not be enough time, but there even remained some time.
>
> I found out that those children who are entering the first grade are "readers." It is time to get rid of letters' cases.

In this entry, Nadia described a context, shared her new understanding of her future first graders' reading skills, and defined how she would adjust her teaching strategies. Nevertheless, about one third of her entries explicitly referred to her emotional state. For example, she declared a pedagogical victory when she had created a comfortable situation for a shy and sensitive student in her class to stand up and contribute to her team's success:

> A nontraditional lesson—show "Come on, girls!" The goal of this lesson is to develop students' appreciation of their mothers' work at home and build the team spirit in the class. Since November, there is a new girl in our class. The girl is capable, works hard, but she is very sensitive (starts crying if anything).
>
> She attends gymnastics.
>
> During this lesson, there was a situation, when each team had to present something. We managed to persuade M. that she should do it. That was a victory![1]

Both Sigute and Nadia did not mention ways of assessing their learning. Only once did Sigute refer to her previous entry and wrote that she used the idea of inviting her former students to help her work with her current (younger) students who needed more help. In other instances, Sigute mentioned that she would do something differently next time, but she did not report if she ever had tried it out.

Grammatical and lexical patterns. Like the emotional learners, these teachers used exclamations, rhetorical questions, and metaphors to emphasize the intensity of their feelings and to highlight interesting ideas. Sigute employed interrogative sentences to stress her disagreement with a situation ("What's to be done?"; "What would you expect from children?"; "And who ever decided to save [money] on the walls of the auditorium and buy such unpractical boards?"; "What is the custodian doing?").

Like the cognitive learners, these teachers identified steps in their learning process. For example, Nadia described a context and a problem in one of her entries. While working on thematic plans, she realized that the textbook that she had used was no longer accepted as a main textbook and she had to teach from a book that had served as their additional reading source. Since there were no thematic plans or any systematic approaches to teaching Language Arts offered in the new book, she defined what she had done to solve the problem. She grounded her thematic units in the book that she had taught before and linked themes with the texts in the new textbook. Finally, she expressed satisfaction with the results ("it turned out to be an interesting plan").

In their cognitive accounts, Sigute and Nadia used verbs that expressed ways they processed information (Sigute: "I learned", "I noticed", "I thought", "I contemplated", "I decided"; Nadia: "I wanted to abandon this method", "I noticed"), but they described rather than reflected on the learning situations.

Cognitive Learners

Ramute, Viktorija, Debbie, and Marija reacted to problems that they encountered in a cognitive way. In most entries, they were specific in listing ideas and ways in which they could be useful in the future. Viktorija, for example, provided precise descriptions of ideas that she liked (the idea about student-made books; the idea about making puppets from pieces of fabric; the ideas [listed ten of them] from the seminar on "Teaching by Stories"; the idea of using produce waste for art projects). She seemed to look for ways for using the ideas that caught her attention. In some entries, she wrote about how she has implemented them (e.g., enacted the Russian fairy tale "The Golden Fish" with her students; implemented ideas from an exhibition in the hallway). In other cases, she planned on using ideas later (next year do some story teaching; more practice in using technologies). Marija often used her journal to record her colleagues' suggestions and graphical representations of their ideas as in Figures 6.1 and 6.2:

> It seems that there is nothing simpler than the topic of addition and subtraction within 10 in the first grade. However, I have students in my class, who have difficulties with this topic, though they have a number line right in front of them on the board. I say to my children, "If we add 1 to a number, we will get the next number. If we subtract—we'll get the previous one." Some students look at me but cannot respond.
>
> On the 18th of January, during the "window" [special lessons when students go with a specialist and the teacher has a prep time], I shared this problem with my colleague R.T. in the teachers' lounge. She suggested animating the number line by letting them "talk with arrows and math signs." The following number line appeared:

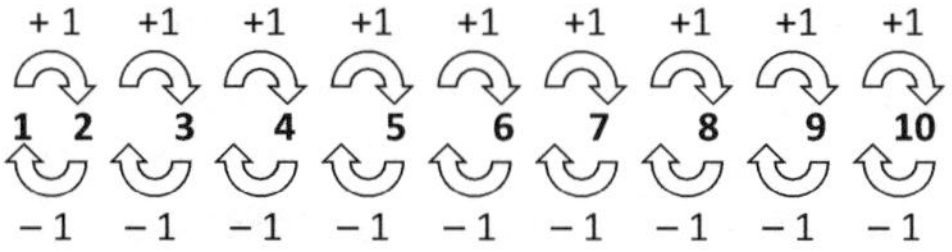

Figure 6.1 The Animated Number Line for +/- 1

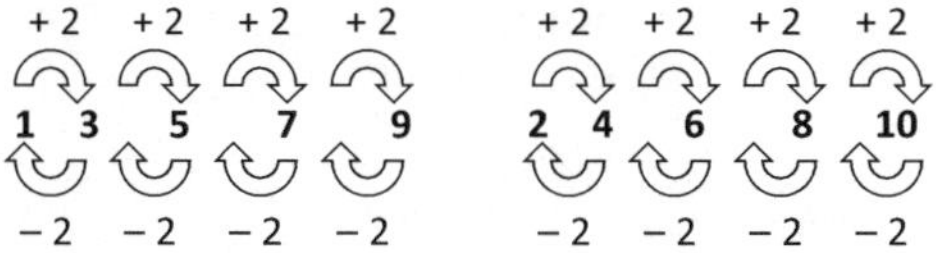

Figure 6.2 The Animated Number Line for +/- 2

> For working on problems (+ –) 2, 3, 4 and so on, one can make several number lines. For example,
>
> R.T. [her colleague] said that students like working with such number lines, and you can memorize such tables faster. The main thing, she emphasized, is that students should take an active part in making these images.

Cognitive learners laid out their expectations for learning (e.g., technology courses for Ramute) and tailored their learning to their professional needs; therefore, they did not seem to have any unexpected instances. They approached obstacles that they encountered in the process of looking for solutions to their dilemmas as a natural part of their learning process. These teachers expressed desire for implementing ideas they discovered in their own or others' practice (e.g., Ramute: "we'll try to catch up on Andersen", "I will try implementing the idea", "I need to arrange a meeting with the author", "I would like to try out teaching with stories").

Ramute, Viktorija, Debbie, and Marija stayed focused and determined until they reached their anticipated results. For example, even though similar to the emotional learners, Ramute's entries contained almost no reference to specific dilemmas of teaching. When Ramute realized that it was difficult to find partners for the project, she continued thinking about the problem ("the idea has to wait till the next year") and kept working on it until she found partners. The results of her efforts in making her ideas happen seemed to be the main assessment tool of her learning experiences (signed up for eTwinning, found partners for the International project). As reflective thinkers, these teachers first described "a state of doubt, hesitation, perplexity, mental difficulty, in which thinking originates", and then they provided a rich description of "an act of searching, hunting, inquiring, to find material that will resolve the doubt, settle and dispose of the perplexity" (Dewey, 1933/1989, p. 121).

Grammatical and lexical patterns. The verbs that the teachers used defined rational and consistent processes that they described (Marija: "I talked with colleagues", "drew my attention", "I once again analyzed"; Viktorija: "discuss ideas", "discuss students' works", "got acquainted with the Check curriculum", "I implement this idea"; Debbie: "I learned…"; Ramute: "one could use" [this for the lessons]). The teachers also described reflective processes that they underwent (Debbie: "I learned by listening", "I have learned through observation", "I am thinking and wondering", "this makes me wonder"; Marija: "I contemplated", "I analyzed"; Ramute: "I realized"; Viktorija: "I observed", "I think that…"). In additon, their language demonstrated that they employed logical thinking processes (Marija: "the evidence of", "as a result", "solving a problem"; Viktorija: "found interesting solutions").

In the last sentence of their entries, the teachers usually summarized their main points. For example, Debbie wrote, "Working w/a team allowing people to share ideas in a non-threatening environment where peoples' beliefs are mutually respected and [tied] closely to their values in education". Viktorija noted, "It is important for a child to understand the idea; I liked this idea because in practice it is desirable to have a more interesting view of common things; I think that the story-teaching idea is interesting for elementary kids and the next year a project could be done choosing a fairy tale once a week". Marija concluded, "This way, parents practically saw the necessity to personally attend parents' meetings; Therefore, I started including geometrical concepts in my lessons more often".

In sum, the teachers expressed two different reactions to the problems that they described in their journals: emotional and cognitive. The first group of teachers that I call **emotional learners** reacted to their professional problem emotionally. Often, they conveyed contrasting emotions. They concluded their entries with generalized inferences or exclamations. Sometimes they reflected on their emotional states and displayed cognitive reactions; however, they did not analyze but rather reported on what was going on and how they felt about it.

Like the "emotional" ones, in some entries, **emotional/cognitive** learners expressed negative emotions, which seemed to enhance their desire for changing something and figuring out how to do it. In other entries, like the cognitive learners, they analyzed problematic situations and came up with a plan to solve their dilemmas. They used a reporting rather than a reflective style of journaling and depicted events without mentioning ways of assessing their learning.

Finally, **cognitive learners** were specific in listing ideas and ways in which these ideas could be useful in the future. The language of their entries defined rational and consistent processes that they described. They provided rich descriptions of ideas that appealed to them and looked for ways of using them in their teaching. They laid out their expectations for learning and stayed focused and determined until they reached their anticipated results.

The analyses of teachers' reactions (cognitive or emotional) highlight ways in which teachers respond to a potential learning situation (see Figure 6.3). Cognitive reactions would help teachers analyze a dilemma

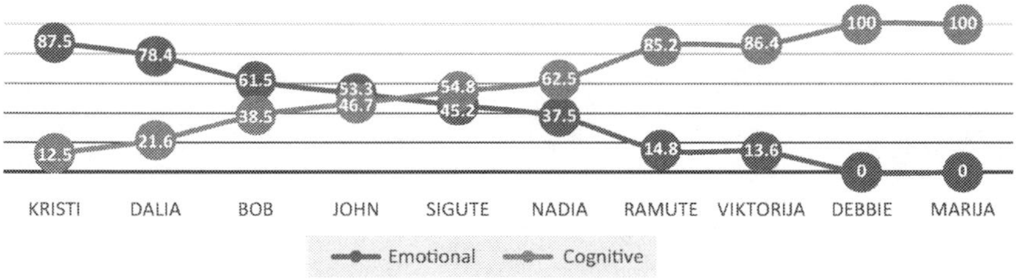

Figure 6.3 Teachers' reactions to teaching dilemmas

and find resources for resolving it, while emotional reactions would inspire and motivate them to pursue change. By identifying the different reactions that teachers displayed in response to their professional problems, this chapter paves the way for further investigation of how, for example, teachers react to specific situations and problems, and how these reactions relate to their engagement in learning.

Note

1 This excerpt will be also analyzed in the next chapter to demonstrate that the same excerpt could be informative and useful in making several points.

References

Dewey, J. (1933/1989). How we think. In J. A. Boydston (Ed.), *John Dewey: The middle works* (Vol. 8, pp. 105–352). Carbondale: Southern Illinois University Press. (Original work published in 1933).

7 Orientation to Problems for Learning

Self–Teaching-Oriented Problems

Overview of This Chapter

This chapter highlights what problems the teachers choose to focus on as they learn informally. Depending on how they describe the essence of their dilemmas, the participating teachers disperse on a continuum between viewing professional dilemmas either as self-oriented and/or teaching-oriented. For example, some teachers reflect on a problematic schedule that cause them inconvenience in teaching—being concerned with improving their working conditions (self-oriented), while others are trying to find out how to help their students increase their reading fluency skills, focusing on the improvement of their professional performance (teaching-oriented), yet others display both sides of the continuum. Such a distinction in orientation might reflect further differences in the teachers' perceptions of their profession and the role they as professionals play in society. This chapter aims at postulating these possible relationships and sets the ground for future investigation.

Introduction

Teachers differed in their orientations to kinds of problems upon which they focused in their informal learning instances. The teachers in all three schools considered two kinds of problems: (1) They were concerned about accommodating their professional commitment with other roles that they took on in their lives (*self-oriented*), or (2) they focused on their professional growth so that they could find answers to their teaching dilemmas and become better teachers (*teaching-oriented*) (see Figure 7.1). Depending on what kinds of problems they focused on in their learning, the teachers comprised three groups: self-oriented, teaching-oriented, and self/teaching-oriented. This category is important in understanding how teachers position themselves as learners, how they perceive themselves as professionals, and how they perceive teaching as a profession.

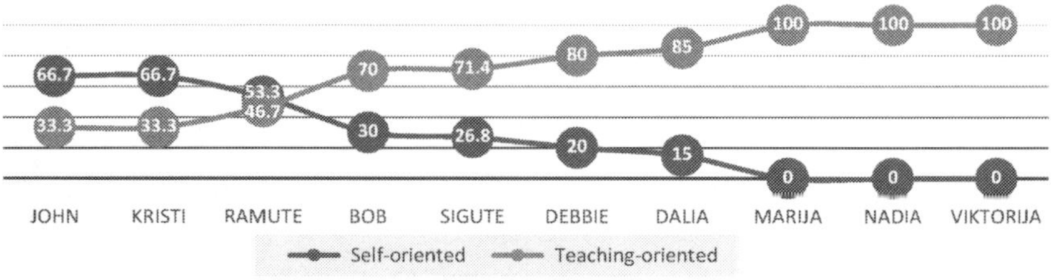

Figure 7.1 Teachers' focus on problems for learning

Self-Oriented Learners

The teachers in this group (John, Kristi, and Ramute) were concerned about personal rather than professional problems. For example, Kristi expressed frustration about many things that were going on at the same time, working but having her thoughts focused at home with her sick daughter and having to change lesson plans because of the snow days. On one occasion, she wrote:

> We have just come back to school after having two new snow days! As much as I love staying home on those days, really don't want any more! We'll be going later into the summer if this continues.
>
> On the snowdays [sic] we were supposed to have an assembly to kick off reading month. Now a few days have been lost of that too. Everything has a good side and a bad side.

Kristi seemed to focus on problems that pulled her out of her established routine and rhythm and required a special effort from her to perform her job. These problems did not directly relate to the teaching process, rather, they arose from inconvenience that her profession brought to her life. John also did not focus on specific teaching problems. He contemplated ways of becoming a better person and developing general skills (writing things down, being flexible—"can't count on everything you plan", take time to plan, working well with others).

John and Kristi assigned high value to having friendly relationships with their colleagues; however, rather than considering these good relationships as a source for their learning, these teachers expressed the need for a friendly atmosphere because it provided them with a comfortable feeling in their work environment. For example, John wrote about the value of enjoyable colleagues and working with other grades' teams. Kristi seemed to enjoy planning together with her other three same grade level colleagues. To establish closer relationships of trust and understanding with them, she set a goal of creating personal relationships with her colleagues.

These teachers also focused on things that they would like to accomplish outside of their teaching process, which were not directly related to becoming better professionals. For example, Kristi wrote in her reflective journal about making students' placements for the next year, "turning things upside down to teach" for the test, debating a Parent Teacher Association (PTA) meeting message that parents wanted teachers to attend more after-school events, and discussing the district level language assessment.

Even when these teachers wrote about their own professional growth, they seemed to do it for personal reasons: the teaching problems they addressed were rather general. For example, on multiple occasions, Ramute seemed to be occupied with ideas of developing her computer skills, trying out new job experiences, and building international partnerships. Only a few of John's entries addressed specific teaching problems (e.g., how to teach students to "hear" each other's emotions and how to do a persuasive writing with students). Some problems reflected John's critical attitude toward what he did (doing too much, not seeing other things that his students do at school, allocating too much time to help new teachers, not being prepared to teach enough). When Kristi addressed teaching problems, she discussed issues such as her concerns about academically low achieving students, not giving enough credit to her students, and building up her students' confidence. Teachers in this group often referred to their negative professional experiences and in many cases, it seemed that teaching was either a roadblock for their personal goals or a vehicle for reaching them.

Grammatical and lexical patterns. In their descriptions of informal learning, rather than pondering teaching dilemmas, self-oriented teachers usually described what had happened to them. Expressing their dissatisfaction with their current situation, these teachers tended to juxtapose their previous experiences (usually, positive) with their current (usually, negative) ones or with their different states of mind. In order to feel comfortable, they seemed to look for ways of recreating their past. For example, in one of her entries Kristi wrote:

> Mary and Claudia [pseudonyms] are going to join my summer golf league. I am excited to spend more "personal" time with them. Although professionally we have been getting along great, I miss having personal relationships with colleagues. I have [sic] been in my old building such a long time that I had created many friendships outside of work. It makes it feel so much more than just a job when some of my friends work with me. I really miss that.

Or,

> [...] We are really getting into the busy time for school now. This Friday is our Fine Arts Festival, lots of field trips coming up, etc...
>
> It also means pressure to finish things (math units, science curriculum...). I love this time of year for the weather, fun culminating activities, etc... but hate it for the busy work it brings.

Self-oriented learners were particular about their time spent on work. Their journal entries had frequent temporal references (John: "this week—2 times", "every day", "the next day", "in a week"; Kristi: "getting into the busy time", "this Friday", "coming up", "this time of the year", "now"). They kept their sentence structure simple and traditional: subject+verb+object, what Berk (1999) called "unmarked" (pp. 51–52) that suggested a generic perception of the described events, which did not involve deep reflection. They usually included transitive (with direct objects) and intransitive verbs that present a situation in terms of a simple, single-layered event. Though the teachers in this group did not use existential "there", which also signals generic "aboutness" (Williams, 2006), the non-referential character of their sentences gave an impression that they chose to communicate their experiences on the surface, without deeply analyzing them.

In addition, these teachers seemed to be terser—their entries were shorter than those of the other teachers, suggesting that they might have given their responses less thought. This style of writing also gives the impression that the teachers took less time to write their entries. For example, John's entry on average contained 91 words, Kristi's—105 words, compared to Bob's—177 words, Daina's—130 words, and Marija's—114 words. The language of their narratives was not as varied and rich as the other teachers': they tended to repeat the same words several times in one entry (John repeats "I learned"—2 times, "were[n't] completed"—2 times, "to do, done, doing"—3 times, "this week"—2 times in the 60-word entry).

Self/Teaching-Oriented Learners

Bob, Sigute, Debbie, and Daina comprise a group of teachers who focused on problems that both referred to them as individuals as well as to their teaching process with more frequent mention of teaching-oriented dilemmas. A few instances when the teachers demonstrated an individual orientation dealt with the teachers' better understanding of their professional commitment. For example, Bob focused on reflecting upon his professional affiliation. He defined himself as a learner; he circumscribed his ways of being a teacher; he reflected on what it meant to him to go to the camp with his students, what it meant to have the wall between the classrooms put up, what it meant to be a teacher in American society, and what it meant for him to make a difference to his students. Daina included a few episodes about her personal growth as an original and creative person. For example, on one of the occasions she wrote:

> I found studio-gallery "Delmona" very accidentally. Beautiful works in paper techniques, shawls and scarves hand-decorated looked very attractive. I asked if I could buy anything, and received a question to my question, if I would like to learn to do it myself. I was very happy.

> And I joined this game. I started attending this studio. The first task was very big—to prepare some silk for work, put some color on it, some tone and some collage.
>
> I made friends with a colleague, a teacher of home technologies from Lazdynai district. My instructor seemed to be very interesting, active, challenging, critical and helpful.
>
> Why did I choose to write about this episode? Because it was very important to see if I could learn to paint on silk, make silk-and-paper cards. Just to try and then teach my kids (students). Also make something that I could present to the loved ones, because what is authentic, individual is also warm and nice. And it is better to give something warm rather than something bought.
>
> I believe that this one lesson will not end with only technical interest; I believe that interaction is also very necessary, not only what I have mentioned already.
>
> Getting to know this artist is my great discovery! It is for me, for my learning, for self-realization.

Though the content was rather broad-spectrum and the choice of problem was still closely connected with the teachers' personal comfort on the job and development of specific other-than-teaching skills, most of the problems that these teachers discussed in their journals are teaching-oriented. Bob mainly addressed larger educational problems, such as when kids learned best, how having the wall between his and the adjacent classroom closed affected his teaching and his relationship with colleagues, what attending the camp meant for his students, working with parents, teaching students of different types of personalities, and keeping contacts with his students after they graduate. There were only two specific teaching problems that he referred to—a teacher–parent conference and his further interactions with that family and relationships with one of his colleagues after closing the wall. Similar to Bob, Debbie reflected on larger issues. She wrote:

> I am thinking and wondering about temperaments of people. Why are some people so difficult to get along with? This is a huge factor that effects group dynamics and learning in informal situations. I know research has classified people into 3 different categories: easy, cautious, and difficult. These 3 temperaments make a community of teachers in one building very critical to others' learning. As some people have intimidation and influence over others, as some people cannot make decisions for themselves and choose to follow in others' footsteps.

Sigute was more specific in defining her professional dilemmas. She pondered how to teach students who had academic difficulties in the classroom, how to work productively with her students' parents, where to go on field trips, how to make interesting art projects, how to teach her first graders about important dates in Lithuanian history, and how to teach with multimedia.

Grammatical and lexical patterns. Similar to those who are self-oriented learners, the teachers in this group tended to describe what has happened to them; however, their descriptions were more detailed and expressive and their sentence structure was more complex and more diverse. To highlight certain points in their narratives they used "marked" sentences (Berk, 1999, pp. 51–52). They differed from a traditional subject+verb+object structure and signified the authors' special points of interest (Daina: "Why did I choose to write about this episode?" and "Getting to know this artist is my great discovery!"; Debbie: "Why are some people so difficult to get along with?"; Sigute: "What would you expect from children?", "One more thing…").

Teaching-Oriented Learners

Marija, Nadia, and Viktorija comprise a group of teachers who exclusively discussed teaching dilemmas in their journal entries. Some of their topics originated from their immediate teaching experiences: they pointed out something that they would like to improve in their teaching right away. Nadia, for example, reflected on the outcomes of her lessons, classroom activities, and when she tried new methods; analyzed her preparation for "open lessons"; solved problems in motivating students. Most of the themes represented some special events in her practice rather than everyday teaching dilemmas. Marija also pondered specific teaching problems such as how to help a particular student interact with others, how to assess first graders' learning, how to motivate her first graders, how to teach her students to read fluently, how to motivate advanced students to work hard, and how to have most of the parents come to the meetings. Her problems were described in detail and tied to her everyday practice. Similar to Marija, Viktorija's learning themes reflected her day-to-day teaching experiences. For example, on multiple occasions she focused on creative approaches to teaching art (not ways of teaching but rather final products).

Other ideas focused on possible changes in the teachers' future practices. For example, in a few entries, Viktorija discussed important teaching issues such as reading comprehension or teaching a new Math curriculum, which she authored herself. Marija contemplated what she should pay attention to in order to get her students ready for middle school, how to help students get ready for writing dictations, how to teach addition and subtraction, how to teach students to write faster, what Thematic Weeks were and how she could use them in her practice, and how to use books and toys in her instruction.

Highlighting interesting ideas they acquired from seminars was also a prominent feature of the entries of the teaching-oriented learners. For example, Viktorija listed appealing ideas from a seminar about thematic teaching and the seminar about reading tests, while Nadia also described what she learned attending seminars. For example, she depicted her experiences learning about a puppet theater:

> (I) took part in a thematic practical seminar for the leaders of school puppet theatres. The seminar more resembled an exchange of experiences between creative people, who are involved in an amateur puppet theater "Cheese." It was very interesting, I was very satisfied and saw many interesting puppets. But where is it possible to find time and resources for making them? At the school, they pay us only for 1 hour per week to do extracurricular activities.
>
> There was an interesting experience in controlling large group of children while they watch a performance (for our school it would not be really appropriate—it is required to be completely silent, but it is so hard for little kids). During "Cheese" performances children are allowed even to lay down on the floor and that did not disturb actors (as seen on the videotape).

These teachers seemed to be looking for more than success in teaching. They wanted their teaching to be fun for both their students and them. Viktorija emphasized having fun teaching, and she focused on finding the best place for classroom rules and figuring out ways of teaching Economics in an interesting way. Marija looked for ways of teaching more playfully, and Nadia reflected on what she could use in her teaching from watching theater performances.

Grammatical and lexical patterns. Students were in the center of these teachers' narratives. Describing and reflecting upon their teaching dilemmas, the teachers in this group provided multidimensional accounts of their learning by employing foregrounding to highlight a learning situation and backgrounding to describe its context. They utilized transitive and intransitive verbs, which, according to Berk (1999, p. 161), "serve to push the action to the forefront." Additional tools (stative verbs, copulas, and agentless passives) helped them depict the background of their events, and the use of multiple syntactic tools allowed the teachers in this group to present a complex picture of teaching and learning to teach. For example, Nadia wrote:

> A nontraditional lesson–show "Come on, girls!" The goal of this lesson is to develop students' appreciation of their mothers' work at home and build the team spirit in the class. Since November, there is a new girl in our class. The girl is capable, hard working, but she is very sensitive (starts crying if anything).
>
> She attends gymnastics.
>
> During this lesson, there was a situation, when a team had to present something. An attempt to persuade M. to present was successful. Was [it] a victory!

In this entry, alongside usual or "unmarked" (Berk, pp. 51–52) sentence structures (i.e., transitive structures with verbs *to develop*, *to build*, *attends*, *to present* something *and to persuade* that transfer an action to a direct object; intransitive structures such as *to present*; and copulas: *the goal of the lesson is*, *the girl is capable*, *hard working*, *but she is very sensitive*, that refer to the same individual as the subject of the sentence), Nadia also exploited a special construction called existential *there*, as in *there was a situation*, that served as a "pointing out" syntactic construction (Berk, 1999, pp. 158–160), which draws readers' attention to a specific place in the story. To highlight the significance of the situation, she used "marked" sentences (those that stand in contrast to our normal expectations of a subject+verb+object sentence structure): for example, *A non-traditional lesson-show "Come on, girls!," Was [it] a victory!* These sentences marked the beginning and the end of the entry, which signify the importance of the enclosed narrative. In the way these teachers wrote their entries, they signaled a rich interest in the problems of teaching. They provided thick descriptions of particular learning situations, including contextual detail, and their style of writing demonstrated a multidimensional perception of the nature of a teaching problem.

To conclude, teachers' orientations toward learning problems demonstrate that some teachers were concerned with improving their working conditions while others focused upon improvement of their professional performance while others displayed both sides of the continuum. Such a distinction in orientation might reflect further differences in the teachers' perceptions of their profession and the role they as professionals play in society. This chapter aims at postulating these possible relationships and sets the ground for future investigation.

References

Berk, L. M. (1999). *English syntax: From word to discourse*. New York: Oxford University Press.

Williams, E. (2006). The subject-predicate theory of there. *Linguistic Inquiry*, *37*(4), 648–651.

8 Engagement in Learning Process

Spontaneous–Deliberate

Overview of This Chapter

In this chapter, discourse analysis reveals how the teachers describe processes in which they engage as they attempt to solve professional dilemmas. The teachers' engagement in learning processes demonstrates that in some learning instances, they would switch from being a teacher to being a learner spontaneously; in other situations, they would deliberately plan, engage, and implement what they learned. Yet as the analysis above reveals, some teachers tend to engage in learning situations more spontaneously and others take on challenges more deliberately. This chapter also includes a discussion of emerging patters across all five categories and general conclusions for Part II. It is possible to conclude that the analysis of the five categories illuminates patterns of teachers' informal learning pointing out to probable sets of features that characterize certain types of informal learners.

Introduction

Teachers differed in the ways they involved themselves in the process of informal learning (see Figure 8.1). In some cases, they accidentally or unintentionally learned something that they could use in their practice (*spontaneous involvement*). In other cases, they seemed to have a detailed plan (usually, in their heads) of what they wanted to learn, how they would learn it, and how they were going to implement their new understandings (*deliberate involvement*).

This category might seem similar to the first category, disposition to learning; however, disposition explains the teachers' perception and anticipation of a possible learning situation, while this category illuminates patterns of the actions teachers took to solve the problems they identified. This category is useful for defining how the teachers act when they find themselves (intentionally or not) in a learning situation in the workplace.

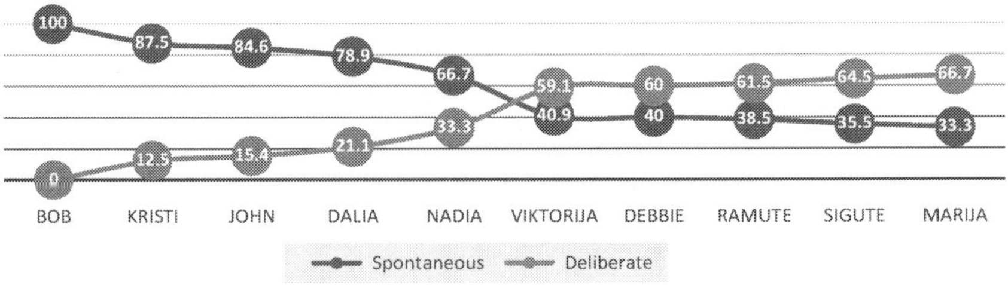

Figure 8.1 Teachers' participation in the learning process

Spontaneous Learners

Bob, Kristi, John, and Daina comprise a group of *spontaneous learners*. The teachers in this group did not seem to design their learning process but instead, they tended to utilize any experience for their learning without looking for specific learning situations or being aware of them—learning from whatever comes along. They seemed to be teaching (and learning) "in the moment" all the time: they were responsive to their students and the environment, weaving curriculum into it. Learning for Bob, for example, involved thinking about and choosing his actions that he would consider be the most adequate for the moment. He learned from everything every day and he shaped those experiences so that they became sources for his teaching. He seemed to be an impulsive teacher who taught from a blend of experiences, emotions, and personality. Bob thought of his teaching role as existing beyond only teaching in the classroom. In the following excerpt, Bob wrote about what was important for his students and what their needs were:

> After I thought for a while,—I thought about some things I said at an interview I had. I'd like to elaborate on what I said when I spoke relating to kids.
>
> I think that being a teacher is more than just instructing in the classroom. I enjoy eating with the kids in the cafeteria and playing with them on recess when I get a chance. I think this is great for many reasons. For one, I get to talk with the kids about different things and not "teach" them. We've had some pretty interesting conversations down in the lunchroom! Second, I think that it's important for the kids to see their teachers in a different way, especially having fun and enjoying life. During recess, I get to run around with the kids and get exercise at the same time. It's a win-win situation! The kids love it when I go outside and eat with them and I think it helps me gain respect because I treat them kindly and do some of the same things they do. Most importantly, it's fun!

Kristi also learned mostly spontaneously; however, her spontaneity of learning was different from Bob's. She engaged in learning by unexpectedly finding herself in problematic situations (e.g., having to reschedule the whole week; having an unpredicted outcome in a meeting with a student's mother; getting tired from the workload; being concerned about low-achieving students and students that did not qualify for special education) or having a positive but unexpected experience (student-led conferences, an interesting field trip; planning for the end of the year). She did not seem to be looking for any learning experiences, rather, according to her comments, she tended to avoid them because they caused her inconvenience by turning her world upside-down.

Similar to Kristi, for John, unexpected circumstances (e.g., absence of a substitute; change in the schedule), uncomfortable situations outside the classroom (e.g., giving up time to help others; administration's support having received low scores on the State writing test) or personal discomfort (e.g., doing too much, putting extra effort into getting ready) stimulated his informal learning. Constructive experiences also inspired it: he seemed to realize that he had learned something while writing a journal entry; however, it is not easy to identify his learning procedures because of the generic character of his descriptions. For example, he wrote:

> This week I have learned again what it's like to be doing too much at one time. Because I have so much going on (graduate school, multiple student projects to grade, meetings…) I am feeling overwhelmed and stressed out this week. I am finding it difficult to do my regular teaching when I have these other things needing to get done. I also find I take it out on others around me by being short with them, sometimes rude, and impatient.
>
> But next week is a new week, and hopefully back to normal.

Daina's mode of engagement in informal learning was similar to Bob's. She learned from the situations in which she found herself and seemed to be comfortable with surprises that such situations presented. Though Daina usually displayed characteristics of a spontaneous learner, she tended to describe her learning process in terms of deliberate procedures more often than other teachers in this group did.

Grammatical and lexical patterns. In these teachers' entries, the word choice indicated spontaneity and concern with time (e.g., John: "by chance"; Daina: "accidentally"). Daina chose generic words to describe her experiences (i.e., "rather interesting", "big impression", it was interesting", "I was preparing for this lesson very much"), which suggests that she did not have a specific focus for learning and did not reflect on particular dilemmas.

The teachers in this category used temporal adverbs and clauses of duration (John: "all year", "consistently"; Kristi: "busy time", "this time of year") that described a longer period during which events occurred spontaneously rather than depicting a specific episode. The simple present or the simple past tenses guided the narration through a basic and straightforward storyline. Their presentation of what had happened to them within a longer period (a week) did not involve any follow up or finite conclusions about the outcomes of their learning.

Spontaneous/Deliberate Learners

Nadia, Viktorija, Debbie, and Ramute embody both features of spontaneous and deliberate learners. For example, Nadia wrote about her learning experiences *post factum* as if they have happened by accident (Nadia thought that her students would be independent in the this grade and did not expect their parents coming to the class on the first day of the new school year, but they did). When she took a deliberate stance, she defined a problem and ways she had solved it (e.g., a specific situation when she had to develop units for teaching Music, which she had not taught for 14 years); however, all the entries reported on what had already taken place rather that pondering an existing problem and planning a way of resolving it.

Teachers in this group engaged spontaneously in events, which did not require their full commitment and thorough preparation. In such events, they were usually regular participants; yet, when they were in charge of a lesson, event, or a presentation, they demonstrated qualities of deliberate learners and leaders. Viktorija, for example, engaged in both modes of informal learning with a slightly stronger deliberate tendency. Spontaneous learning occurred when her students and colleagues reacted differently to her display of classroom rules, when she reflected on the positive outcomes of her students' art projects, when she participated in a conference about reading as a social skill, when she took her students to the Art Education Center, and, when she noticed interesting ideas participating in whole school events. Deliberate learning took place when she planned and reflected on the outcomes of activities, when she approached new tasks of teaching Economics and used multimedia, when she made a presentation at a conference and observed how a teacher taught a lesson from the teacher's book, which she authored; when she prepared her students' art works for a show, when she looked for interesting ideas for a Mother's Day project, when she made a list of main ideas from a seminar on thematic teaching and planned to use them the coming year, and, finally, when she enjoyed her students' greetings for her birthday and picked up interesting ideas to use for their graduation that was coming up in 2 years.

Debbie and Ramute engaged in both deliberate and spontaneous learning, but more often displaying features of deliberate learners. Spontaneous learning for both teachers happened when they went through routine daily experiences and found out something new about students, about teaching resources, about self, and about helpful ideas for teaching.

Often, these teachers deliberately defined their learning steps and chose learning situations. Ramute did that when she wrote about her goals and efforts to find international partners, to develop computer skills, or to go through the selection process for a trainers' job. For example, she wrote in different journal entries:

- The deadline for Socrates Comenius project's proposal submission is February. It is necessary to hurry up looking for partners.
- Found partners for Comenius project in Spain. (We) can start working.
- The preparatory visit for Comenius project is in November. Need to prepare documents.

Debbie described a sequence of steps in her learning process and reflected on specific situations, or she presented a generalized summary with a reference to an implicit situation that had triggered her thoughts. For example, she engaged in deliberate learning when discussing how to move her students through the reading program, observing her students, seeking advice from colleagues about how to guide instructional practices at the end of the school year, and wondering how to work with different colleagues.

Grammatical and lexical patterns. These teachers' word choices reflected spontaneity of learning in unexpected situations (Nadia: "I counted upon ..., but was mistaken"; Viktorija: "it was interesting to see what students think of us"; Ramute: "When visiting Gambia, I realized..."; Debbie: "I am reading a book ... This makes me wonder") and deliberateness (Nadia: "help from the specialist would not be expected"; Viktorija: "I observed a lesson ... It has been well thought through"; Ramute: "I have signed up for computer courses"; Debbie: "we sat down together and developed a plan").

These teachers expressed temporality differently from the previous group. They defined specific dates or discussed time-bound learning experiences (Debbie: "talking with a teacher today"; Viktorija: "planning for the Teachers' Day", "during the Art and Technology lesson"; Ramute: "on the 4th of March", "I signed up").

They employed a variety of ways to highlight their planning and determination to act. Ramute used the simple future tense ("I will lead") and modal verbs ("I would like", "I have to prepare"); Debbie wrote a paragraph to summarize her experiences ("So: I have learned just through observation of my students a teaching strategy I have neglected to instruct. Sitting back and becoming a careful observer, one can learn a lot about oneself"); Viktorija reported about implementation of new ideas ("Having returned, I shared ideas with my colleagues, and made a performance 'The Golden Fish' with my students"), and Nadia summarized her learning experiences in a sentence or two ("What have I learned?—To be ready with several alternatives and keep in mind that parents want to see a celebration on the 1st of September"). In sum, teachers in this group were more specific in defining their learning time and planning their future actions. They were able to do that because they summarized their learning experiences. Yet, in some cases, they seemed to learn from spontaneous situations and reflect on their experiences afterward.

Deliberate Learners

In most of the journal entries, Sigute and Marija represented features of *deliberate learners.* As such, they took part in learning processes striving to find out something specific in order to solve a dilemma that they faced at the moment. Their determination was explicitly expressed or implied in ways they dealt a problem. For example, Sigute first described either a problem or a challenging moment that she experienced in her work, or an interesting idea that she noticed when listening to or observing her colleagues teach. Then, she made a plan to deal with it or suggested ways of using these ideas in her work. Marija also actively looked for and created learning situations by approaching her colleagues, joining conversations, asking them questions and appreciatively listening to their experiences, and sharing her own experiences with them.

In the majority of the situations described in their journals, Sigute and Marija initiated communication with their colleagues. They seemed to be curious about what other teachers did. Marija, for example, held conversations with a wide range of her colleagues: elementary, middle and high school teachers, administrators and other specialists in her building, her former colleagues, and teachers in other buildings. On one occasion, she wrote:

> The first half [of the year] is coming to an end. My […]-graders already know many letters; when dictated, they can write letters and syllables; they can copy words. I decided to check their knowledge and skills, that is, to write a small dictation with them. On December 15, I overheard two teachers of Russian language, who work in high school, talking in the teachers' lounge. One teacher told that kids make a lot of mistakes in dictations and essays. The other teacher explained that students don't read enough and do not understand meaning of some words. Then she said that every dictation is stressful for students, for that reason she often practices dictations with additional preparation at home or in class. Having heard this conversation, after the lessons, I came up to the second grade teacher and asked her about ways she prepared her students last year for dictations. She told me that preparation for dictations would take about two lessons. At first, children would read sentences, and then they would identify orthographs, after that they would copy sentences from the board. The next lesson, children would read sentences again, repeat orthographs, and only after that the teacher would erase the text and dictate it [for them to write it down].

In this and many other narratives, Marija was an active participant. In one instance, the high school language teachers pointed out a problem that attracted her attention: their students were making many mistakes in their writing. Marija decided to find ways of teaching better spelling skills in elementary grades and turned to her colleagues for help. In her interactions, she asked questions, invited her colleagues to come to her classroom, and shared with them what she did. She also seemed to be positive about her practice and open to others' advice. She received immense support: her colleagues did not hesitate to share their experiences or materials with her. They brought her games, tasks, diagrams, scenarios, and other materials, shared their success stories and ideas.

Sigute and Marija seemed to be strategic learners. Whenever they identified a dilemma, they would frame a problem and develop a plan for solving it. Their journal entries' structure reflected this process: first, they described a situation, identified a problem and relevant participants; then, they shared specific information or experience; further, they evaluated or implemented a new idea, and, finally, they occasionally, commented on its value for development of their teaching skills or reflected on the results of its implementation.

Grammatical and lexical patterns. This consistent structure of Marija's and Sigute's entries represented steps that seemed to have become their habit of mind; they thought through the steps and followed them to resolve each teaching problem that they identified. Their determination to learn and to resolve their professional dilemmas is formulated in the sentences that often were found in the middle of their narratives, where they presented themselves as agents and subjects of action (Berk, 1999, pp. 15–16). For example, Sigute: "I met my students and parents yesterday", "I was ready to order"; Marija: "I approached my colleagues", "I asked her to observe". They also positioned themselves as experiencer subjects (Schlesinger, 1992), those who exercised agency was evident in their verbs' use that describe experience (Sigute: I learned, I recollected, I was nervous; Marija: I know that, I saw an interesting task). They chose active verbs to depict their own or their colleagues' actions. Their agentive power was focused immediately on the receivers of this power, on their direct objects (colleagues, students, parents). For example, Marija: "I asked her", "I shared this problem"; Sigute: "I met my students and their parents".

These teachers reported their new understandings and findings explicitly (Sigute: "I should try that out in my class") or implicitly reflected on them. Their implicit realizations became visible in the use of the indirect object in the noun phrase. For example, Marija wrote, "(…) dictation is stressful for students, I came up to the second grade teacher [because] she prepared her students [for it]". These deliberate learners constructed their sentences in such a way that an indirect object followed the verb directly, which made "the sense (…) stronger than when the indirect object appears later in the sentence" (Berk, 1999, p. 41). Sigute's entry illustrates how the indirect object (in bold) emphasized her points of learning:

> The events of January 13 **are important for every Lithuanian**. However, at school there are some difficulties with this date, because students who were born in independent Lithuania have trouble understanding that there was no war that day. This year, I **started talking with the students** about that early on. **The assistant principal (a historian) advised me** to. Children had time to think calmly about everything, and discuss that with parents and grandparents.

Marija and Sigute were specific in determining the timeframe of the described episodes (Marija: "On December 7, I took part..."; Sigute: "on February 7, [I] will have to teach an open lesson using Critical Thinking"), as well as location (Marija: "Today, before the classes, in my classroom"; Sigute: "In our classroom, there is a girl..."). To pinpoint the time of her learning experience, Marija often started her entries with a double set of temporal adverbs (Today, before the classes; Yesterday, before the meeting).

Summary

In this category, teachers comprised three groups depending on the ways they involved themselves in an informal learning process: spontaneous, spontaneous/deliberate, and deliberate. **Spontaneous** learners did not design their learning process but learned from whatever opportunities or persons that came along. Their language reflected spontaneity and concern with time spent on a task. They learned either under unexpected circumstances when they felt discomfort and frustration, or from teaching in the moment, opening themselves for any learning experiences.

Spontaneous/deliberate learners wrote about what had already taken place rather than pondering an existing problem and planning a way of resolving it. They described their learning experiences as if they had happened by accident. They tended to engage in events that did not require their full commitment and thorough preparation, and in which they were ordinary participants rather than initiators; however, when they were in charge of a lesson, an event or a presentation, they demonstrated qualities of deliberate learners and they selected their learning situations and defined their steps toward achieving a resolution of the challenge.

Deliberate learners were motivated to find out something specific in order to solve a dilemma that they faced at the moment. They expressed their determination to solve the problem explicitly or implied it in the way they approached a problem. They came up with a plan or suggested ways of using innovative ideas that they found when they talked with or observed their colleagues. They expressed curiosity in what other teachers did by initiating conversations and being appreciative listeners. These teachers were strategic learners: (1) they described a situation, (2) they identified a problem and participants, (3) they shared specific information or experiences, (4) they evaluated or implemented a new idea, and (5) they, occasionally, commented on its value for improvement of their teaching or analyzed results of its implementation.

The teachers' engagement in learning processes demonstrated that in some learning instances, they would switch from being a teacher to being a learner spontaneously; in other situations, they would deliberately plan, engage, and implement what they learned, yet as the analysis above reveals, some teachers tend to engage in learning situations more spontaneously (e.g., Kristi—87.5% spontaneous) and others take on challenges more deliberately (Marija—66.6% deliberate), which is also true for the other four categories. Thus, it is possible to conclude that the analysis of the five categories illuminates patterns of teachers' informal learning pointing out to probable sets of features that characterize certain types of informal learners. In the following segment, I examine emerging patterns by comparing the teachers' stances and looking for possible similarities and differences within and between the categories.

Emerging Patterns

Individual teacher learning profiles emerged as a composite of plotting of their most frequently recurring features on the continua of the five categories. The teachers are unevenly distributed on the continuum within each category, which was determined by the frequency of their displayed stances. Surprisingly, there are more teachers in the comparatively balanced middle group than in any of the extreme groups on the continua. This center position reflects the teachers' tendency to combine both sides almost equally, resulting in a balanced fusion that equips them with a broader assortment of learning apparatuses.

This tendency to alternate different tools in the process of informal learning depending on a learning context would be expected, especially from more experienced professionals. Almost all the teachers demonstrated qualities that are characteristic of both ends of each of the five continua within all five categories, yet each teacher's learning profile, reflected by her/his position on all five continua is unique. For example, John, an American teacher, more frequently displayed features of an opportunistic, self-focused, emotional, individual, and spontaneous learner; Marija, a teacher from a Russian school in Lithuania, more often was proactive, teaching-focused, cognitive, social, and deliberate in her learning in the workplace. This finding requires further attention because I did not expect to find consistency in teachers' affiliation with the specific ends of the continua meaning that certain characteristics tend to appear together. And yet, I found just that. For example, Kristi and John's learning profiles are similar and appear to occupy a spot on the far end of one side of the composite continua, while Marija's is on the other side, making them almost extreme opposites.

Furthermore, when all the five categories are viewed together, relationships across the categories could be observed that suggest a certain stability of patterns that allow making predictions in defining types of informal learners. For example, the teachers who were opportunistic in their disposition to learning also tended to be emotional in their reactions and spontaneous in their learning process. Similarly, those teachers who were cognitive in their reactions were also deliberate in their learning process. In addition, obvious patterns emerged when looking at them through the cultural lens. In the majority of cases, American and Russian teachers tended to occupy the opposite sides of the continua, while Lithuanian teachers were more likely to be in the middle.

Conclusions

This Part (Chapters 4–8) discusses how the teachers in two schools in Lithuania and in one in the United States construct their learning in informal settings at their workplaces. Discourse analysis of the teachers' journal entries and interviews, focusing on how they position themselves as learners in their everyday practice, revealed specific patterns that I organized into five categories: Dispositions, Focus, Sources, Processes, and Reactions. These five categories emerged from the ways teachers communicated their informal learning through writing and in speech. While developing these categories, I also noted different dimensions of the stances of teachers' learning within each category. Plots of the qualities of the stances within each category emerged as continua between the opposite stances (e.g., emotional–cognitive).

I did not aim at assigning a value judgment to the learning stances that the teachers displayed. In some learning situations, one stance seemed to enhance teacher learning; in other contexts, a different stance seemed to produce observable learning outcomes; however, the situated nature of informal professional learning calls for a learning stance to be in accord with the context. Hence, in some situations, when a teacher's learning stance appeared to be in dissonance with a learning context (e.g., when Kristi complained about the necessity of changing her plans), professional learning did not seem to occur. Though it is not the focus of this study, in the future it would be worthwhile researching the kinds of learning that emerge from relationships between certain contexts and learning stances that teachers take.

The five-category model and its dimensions proved trustworthy when I triangulated my interpretations across different interview data of the same 11 teachers. It could robustly represent the diversity of teachers' informal learning as a complex of multiple dimensions that assume different, yet family related patterns, which further in the book are examined as embedded in culturally specific contexts of learning. Thus, the model also serves as a framework for hypothesizing cultural patterns of teacher learning within schools' and broader educational settings. It calls for an in-depth exploration of cultural similarities and differences in teacher learning within an international comparative perspective.

The further utility of the suggested framework lies in the now-possible investigations into the following: how teachers learn through casual interactions with students, colleagues, and administrators; how school culture relates to informal learning; how personal culture influences professional teacher identity; and how teachers make choices to identify themselves one way or another in a learning situation. Pursuing these questions could provide teacher educators and administrators with additional knowledge to assist teachers in becoming life-long learners and achieving higher quality in their professional performance.

References

Berk, L. M. (1999). *English syntax: From word to discourse.* New York: Oxford University Press.

Schlesinger, I. M. (1992). The experiencer as an agent. *Journal of Memory and Language*, *31*(3), 315–332.

Part III

School Cultures as Contexts for Informal Workplace Learning

Part III

School Cultures as Contexts for Informal Workplace Learning

Overview of This Chapter

The introduction to Part III provides a literature review of research on school culture, specifically focusing on schools as learning organizations that offer or fail to offer opportunities for informal learning for teachers. An anthropological approach is used to create a framework for researching the three schools, according to which culture is viewed as an interactive web of meanings whose parts continuously interact in relation to each other and which includes tacit and explicit knowledge, values and attitudes, propositions and theories, and knowledge-in-practice and embodied knowledge. This part explores how teachers construct and act upon their professional identities of teachers-as-learners that are shaped in the workplace. Discourse analysis is applied to examine how teachers in different schools perceive themselves as learners and how school cultures create opportunities for their everyday informal professional development. Each ensuing chapter includes: first, the discussion of the school in the context of the community, moving to the examination of the school's mission, then discussing the architectural design of the school building, further taking a look at the teachers' classrooms to see how they represent teachers' identities, then discussing the administrative arrangements to see how they allow for teacher informal learning, then looking into the school traditions and the teachers' role in implementing them, and finally discussing the professional relationships—all of which uniquely represents school culture.

Current educational policies put significant pressure on elementary school teachers to modify their practices in many areas like, content, pedagogy, and social emotional approaches simultaneously. These changes require professional development to focus on a wide variety of subject areas with their unique epistemologies, instructional practices, and teaching resources (Elmore, 2000). To mediate government and districts' initiatives, elementary teachers must employ their knowledge and skills more effectively and develop approaches necessary for teaching in ever-changing contexts. If the reforms are to succeed, teachers need various opportunities for learning and continuous professional growth. As I argued in the previous chapters, within the context of school, such professional growth largely occurs through workplace learning, and more often through informal approaches rather than formalized structures.

Researchers suggest that the most productive educational change develops from within schools (e.g., Fullan, 1991) and that "[school] teachers' professional development is critical to systematic educational reform and school improvement focused on enhancing learning outcomes for all children in public education" (Brendeson, 2000, p. 64). This approach confirms that professional knowledge develops within the mind of the individual and, is contextually situated and intrinsic to the contexts within which and with which the individual interacts. As such, teachers' workplace learning and professional development play a strategic role in the success of any educational change, and understanding the cultural, physical, social, historical, and personal aspects of professional knowledge within these contexts calls for investigations from an anthropological perspective (Schoen & Teddlie, 2008; Yinger and Hendricks-Lee, 1993).

Approaching this examination from an anthropological perspective, which studies school culture (Alexander, 2000; Prosser, 1999a) as a content and a context for teacher learning, is crucial in understanding and supporting any educational change, for it has a profound impact upon the meaning teachers ascribe to any innovation (Fullan, 1993). The sense teachers make of prescribed innovations and ways of implementing them is mediated by the sense-making norms that are unique to their school cultures. Prescribed educational innovations are usually introduced to teachers through systems of professional development, thus, professional development serves as an immediate context for teachers' sense-making. However, research found that different school cultures allow for different learning opportunities and experiences beyond structured professional development. For example, isolationist school cultures limit learning environments and opportunities, while collaborative school cultures, on the other hand, support active learning and collaborative inquiry, strengthen professional learning communities, and enhance teacher self-efficacy (Schipper, de Vries, Goei, & van Veen, 2020). A school culture that encourages and supports teacher learning through creating opportunities and providing a stimulating context for teachers' professional change is critical in implementing educational reform (Acker, 1990; Schoen & Teddlie, 2008). While it is a critical factor, school culture cannot account for all teacher learning. Although school culture has been shown to influence how teachers make sense of new professional knowledge, researchers have indicated that in their professional performance, teachers also draw on a variety of personal and professional experiences, on other explicit knowledge, and on their own ideas (Buchmann, 1989). Research also points out that teachers co-construct their understandings of innovations by sharing, collaborating and learning from each other and through reflection on their experience; however, such research on how best to stimulate collaborative workplace learning in schools is still evolving (Evans et al., 2007; Knight, 2002; Moen et al., 2012, Poekert, 2012; Thomas & Akdere, 2013), leaving room for further exploration and examination. To find out how such learning occurs within a school culture, I examine how teachers interact with others at schools in the process of their professional learning.

Research on teachers' formal in-service experiences that are commonly held outside schools has shown that their impact on teachers' practice is limited (e.g., Goldenberg & Gallimore, 1991; Lieberman, 1996; Van Veen et al., 2012). At the same time, researchers argue that environments within schools can have significant influence upon teacher development: "the most powerful forms of teacher development are fostered most directly and powerfully by conditions unlikely to be found outside the school" (Leithwood et al., 1999, p. 150). These findings call for a major re-appraisal of professional learning systems because they imply that "the quality of teachers' learning comes from the quality of their departments and/or schools as learning organizations" (Knight, 2002, p. 293). Therefore, the quality of teacher learning is deeply embedded in the school context in which it occurs (Opfer, 2016). To determine elements of school culture that enable quality professional learning, in this part of the book, I examine "conditions in schools that enable teachers to learn throughout their careers" (Eisner, 2000, p. 349). Thus, with the goal of contributing to better understanding of the opportunities of informal teachers' workplace learning afforded within school contexts, this part of the book investigates a scarcely explored link between organizational (school) culture and professional informal workplace learning of the organization's members (teachers).

Perspectives

Acknowledging that teachers learn in many informal settings, I posit that school environment, which is often defined through the concept of school culture, is crucial for teacher professional learning. It is the place where teachers perform their professional roles over 6 hours per day, where they interact with students, colleagues, and parents, and where they shape and express their professional identity. Therefore, I argue here and in the following chapters, that school culture creates (and is created) and embodies contexts and opportunities for workplace informal teacher learning. Hence, school culture alongside teacher informal learning is the central concept discussed in the pages that follow.

To determine what is meant by school culture, let us first examine a few definitions of culture, and then of organizational culture. Hundreds of definitions highlight aspects of culture that are relevant for different fields and facets of inquiry. For example, culture in its broadest sense is a way of constructing and understanding reality, whereas different cultures represent alternative constructions of reality. According to Williams (1995), most of the definitions of culture fall into one of three broad categories: culture as (a) "a general process of intellectual, spiritual and aesthetic development", (b) culture as "a particular way of life, whether of a people, a period or a group", and (c) culture as "the works and practices of intellectual and especially artistic activity" (p. 90), the last of which would most closely relate to viewing teacher learning as embedded in school culture if viewing teaching as art.

It has been noticed that each school has an identity of its own, with complex rituals of personal relationships, a set of folkways, irrational sanctions, and moral codes represented in multiple dimensions (Maslowski, 2006). Definitions of school culture are closely related to the concept of organizational culture where school culture is perceived as a factor of organizational performance and is associated with taken-for-granted values, underlying assumptions, expectations, and collective memories (Cameron & Quinn, 2011). It is important to note that school culture is always in flux "being constructed—that is, produced and reproduced—by human activity, often but not exclusively, collective activity" (Hodkinson et al., 2004, p. 5). To expand on this view, I suggest that school culture, involving practices of all the community members (teachers, students, administrators, parents), entails an idea of agency—the participants actively construct, relate, and retain culture through interaction and communication (Biesta, 2004, 2011). Following Biesta and Tedder's (2007) ecological understanding of agency, I emphasize that "the achievement of agency will always result from the interplay of individual efforts, available resources and contextual and structural factors as they come together in particular and, in a sense, always unique situations" (p. 137). In other words, agency "is not to be understood as something that people can have; it is something that people do. It denotes a 'quality' of the engagement of actors with temporal–relational contexts-for-action, not a quality of the actors themselves" (Priestley et al., 2013, p. 187). In addition, the study I discuss in this book utilizes Kathryn Anderson-Levitt's (2002) perspective, which is similar to Clifford Geertz's (1983) representation of culture as an interactive web of meaning whose parts continuously interact in relation to each other. According to Anderson-Levitt (2002) an anthropological understanding of culture includes tacit and explicit knowledge, values and attitudes, propositions and theories, and knowledge-in-practice and embodied knowledge. Building on each other, these definitions represent the concept of culture as a social phenomenon constructed through interactions between the members and the operational contexts of an organization. Culture is reflected in the common knowledge of the members who develop, share, and use it to interpret the world within and outside their workplace and generate social behaviors manifested through values, attitudes, and different kinds of knowledge. In addition, the "culture-as-webs-of-meaning"

(Anderson-Levitt, 2002) perspective points to the fluid and agentive character of culture, in which members of an organization construct, interpret, and reinterpret the meanings of events and phenomena. In the next section, I discuss research on school culture as a unique organization.

School Culture through the Lens of Research

Educational research on school culture evolved from theories of organizational culture. In the 1960s and 1970s, studies attempted to measure school culture by applying instruments to evaluate organizational climate (Halpin and Crofts, 1963; Stern, 1970; Finlayson, 1973). A decade later, researchers attempted to both define a holistic meaning of school culture, and also analyze school sub-cultures in the context of their relationship to school change and improvement. More specifically, educational researchers identified generic and unique features of school cultures (Fink et al., 2012; Schein, 2010), arguing that each school had a different reality or mindset for school life and that each had its own set of attitudes and approaches toward what occurred in its environment. Thus, school cultures, as they claimed, were "situationally unique" (Beare et al., 1989/2018). Culture, as studied in this scholarship, was inferred from "the values, norms, expectations and traditions that described human interaction within the school system" (Hallinger & Leithwood, 1996, p. 104).

A decade later, Jon Prosser (1999b) identified four different meanings of the term "culture" as it relates to schools: (a) The broader culture within which schools function; (b) the culture of a school as an educational organization; (c) the unique culture of a specific school; and (d) the "perceived culture" of a school or an image of a school that others (e.g., parents) hold. Most research on school culture was developed under the umbrella of organizational studies, within which cultural studies of schools focused on themes of leadership and school improvement and on schools as learning organizations (e.g., Bidwell, 2001; Detert, Seashore Louis, & Schroeder, 2001; Firestone, & Louis, 1999). The focus on learning organizations and learning cultures frames the narrative of Part III of this book. The complexity of learning discussed previously here is viewed as deeply embedded within schools that "are complex organizations" (Miller & Lieberman, 1988, p. 7).

The complex nature of the phenomenon caused problems in providing adequate accounts of school culture and led many researchers to concentrate on one specific aspect of organizational culture: the role of leadership and management in organization and exploration of organizational cultures as contexts for school leadership (e.g., Ainscow, & Sandill, 2010; Deal, & Kennedy, 1982; Fullan, & Hargreaves, 1992; Schein, 1992; Sparks, 2009). An adequate representation of culture remains difficult to achieve, for what counts as "adequate" differs depending on circumstances, perceptions, timeframes, etc. The examination of school culture in this book takes into account its dynamic nature, which means that if "culture is created by its participants, it inevitably changes as participants change" (Stoll and Fink, 1996, p. 83).

In the deeper analysis of school culture, it is necessary to discuss its typology and structure (Handy & Aitken, 1986; Hargreaves, 1994, 1999). The structure of school culture is represented as a system with sub-systems (Prosser, 1999a) in terms of "observed behavioral regularities" (Stoll, 1999, p. 33) and in terms of organizational membership (Ogbonna, 1993; Ogbonna & Harris, 2000). In addition, researchers have distinguished institutional dimensions of school culture (MacGilchrist et al., 1995) and identified multiple characteristics of effective school cultures (school-effectiveness and school-improvement movements, e.g., Creemers, 2002; Creemers, & Reezigt, 2005; Hargreaves, 1995, Hopkins, 1996; Prosser, 1999b; Reynolds & Packer, 1992; Sammons, 2007); however, the usefulness of the practical applications of these representations has yet to be confirmed. Peter Knight (2002) pointed out that it is "far from obvious how to use those descriptions to improve schools" (p. 287).

More useful representations have focused on schools' cultures as learning contexts (Fuller et al., 2005; Hodkinson et al., 2008). Acknowledging Brown's and his colleagues' contribution to the study of situated cognition (Brown et al., 1989), Hodkinson and Bloomer (2000) argued from a socio-cultural perspective for the importance of social conditions or the situatedness of learning. Along the same lines, Putnam and Borko (2000) claimed that "the physical and social contexts in which an activity takes place are an integral part of the activity, and … the activity is an integral part of the learning that takes place within it. How a person learns a particular set of knowledge and skills, and the situation in which a person learns, become a fundamental part of what is learned" (p. 4), also discussed by Lave and Wenger (1991).

However, many researchers within this tradition focused on relationships between institutional culture and students' learning (Murphy & Hallinger, 1989; Hallinger & Leithwood, 1996), and few researchers addressed teachers' professional development and learning; if they did, they explored it within the context of school improvement. For example, David Hargreaves (1995) argued that school culture defined reality for those within the social organization by describing how things were and by acting as a lens through which members of the organization viewed the world. Andy Hargreaves (1994) looked at school culture through a more specific lens: he defined school culture as a context for professional learning and development. Importantly, he concluded that culture gave participants support and identity and "form[ed] a framework for occupational learning" (p. 165). Barbara MacGilchrist and her colleagues (1995) also investigated relationships between school culture and teachers' professional development, which they defined through three interrelated dimensions (i.e., professional relationships, organizational arrangements, and opportunities for learning). These three authors provide a useful lens for investigation of school culture from the socio-cultural perspective from which I constructed a theoretical framework for the anthropological approach to informal workplace teacher learning that builds upon their frameworks and ideas and around which the following chapters were organized. In addition, this theoretical framework is shaped by the study of the impact of ten organizational features on teacher efficacy, community, and expectations (Newmann, Rutter, & Smith, 1989) and the study of school leadership as a catalyzing element for teacher growth in the privatized and marketized professional development environment (Law, 1999). The latter two studies, differently from my anthropological approach, provided insights into teachers' professional development in their workplace by using organizational theories as a lens for analysis. They did not assume the socio-cultural perspective that I am taking on that highlights the interactional nature between teacher learning and cultural features of the three focal schools.

Thus, as I analyze my data, I keep in mind the categories of cultural features that are derived from the organizational theory: Administrators' responsiveness, teachers' influence on decision making, encouragement of innovation, teachers' knowledge of other teachers' work, teachers helping each other to improve instruction, teacher leadership, in-service programs specific to staff needs, collaboration time, and staff development time (Newmann et al., 1989). I also trace Law's (1999) organizational elements of supportive professional development culture: (a) The effective management of information/communication flows; (b) the development of shared and open planning processes; (c) the operation of clear resource allocation procedures with focused aims and targets; (d) the establishment of clear evaluation strategy used as a basis for ongoing review and development; and (e) the development of open networking opportunities to facilitate mutual support and reflection. Differently from Law's goal of evaluating school cultures, my framework builds upon her emphasis on communication and networking opportunities that characterize a school culture as a learning environment.

School Cultures and Knowledge Creation

Viewing schools as knowledge creation communities (Hargreaves, 1999) opens the way for examining teachers' informal learning. Scholars argue that all professionals depend on working knowledge, or "the organized body of knowledge that [...] [people] use spontaneously and routinely in the context of their work, [...] a special domain of knowledge that is relevant to one's job" (Kennedy, 1983, pp. 193–194). Yet, teachers do not often recognize the opportunities for improving their practice in their workplace and consequentially, do not contribute to and draw upon the collective knowledge that they possess. At the same time, they do not know what collective knowledge they are lacking and are not able to identify where new knowledge needs to be created. David Hargreaves (1999) claimed that "we lack sophisticated theories and models of knowledge creation in education simply because such activity has not been seen as a key to educational improvement" (p. 127). He proposed exploring Nonaka & Takeuchi's (1995) model of professional knowledge creation,[1] and advocated that it could serve as "a suggestive bridge to the exploration and conceptualization of professional knowledge creation and its management in schools" (p. 127).

The Nonaka and Takeuchi (1995) model postulates that knowledge creation arises from the interactions between two basic elements—explicit knowledge and tacit knowledge. They assert that socialization creates shared experience through apprenticeship and on-the-job training, which generates tacit knowledge. Further, along with other researchers (e.g., Baxter, 2011, Rogoff, 2003), they argue that communication and collective reflection among members of the professional community elicit externalization through which tacit knowledge is transformed into explicit knowledge. At the same time, learning-by-doing encourages internalization, by which explicit knowledge is converted into tacit knowledge—as in skill acquisition; what is initially explicit becomes tacit through individual experience. Finally, they claim that people "with different knowledge coming together through networking results in 'combination', a process of systemization and elaboration of explicit knowledge by combining different bodies of knowledge" (Hargreaves, 1999, p. 127).

Applied to school learning cultures, this model suggests that by explicating tacit knowledge teachers learn and, moreover, they also expand a cognitive map of their professional community and create learning opportunities for their colleagues through knowledge management (Hargreaves, 1999; Schön, 1984). According to Hargreaves, the object of knowledge management is to help an organization act intelligently to achieve success and realize its "intellectual capital" (p. 124). Further, he argued that this learning process is characteristic of "knowledge-creating schools", which possess four elements of knowledge management: "1. Audit their professional working knowledge; 2. Manage the process of creating new professional knowledge; 3. Validate the professional knowledge created; and 4. Disseminate the created professional knowledge" (p. 124).

Furthermore, Hargreaves (1999) suggested that four factors or "seeds" of professional knowledge creation already exist within schools. The first one, "tinkering", is widely spread among professions and crafts. Hargreaves called it "an individualized embryo of institutional knowledge creation" (p. 131). Explicit knowledge transforms the embryo into enacted processes of knowledge creation. The second factor, according to Hargreaves, is the school involvement in college teacher training programs (collaboration between cooperating teachers and student-teachers). The third factor acknowledges that creation also occurs when teachers engage in research that, consequently, involves internal and external networking. Finally, as the fourth factor, Hargreaves stressed the importance of the effective use of middle managers in the knowledge creation process. In brief, Hargreaves' study shows relationships between tacit and implicit knowledge in the process of collective knowledge creation within a school culture. This framework of four knowledge creation factors is useful for analyzing how professional relationships create opportunities for teacher informal learning. Peter Knight (2002) and other authors (Brown & Duguid, 2000; Hodkinson et al., 2004; Nonaka & Takeuchi, 1995; Wenger, 1999) took this idea further to assert that "learning happens with the interplay of knowledge and practice" (Knight, 2002, p. 283); it is created by doing and distributed throughout the community through interaction; it is "an emergent property of the community of practice that is partly explicit and partly outside consciousness" (Knight, 2002a, p. 232).

About Part III

This part focuses on the next layer in "the nesting doll" design—the relationship of school cultures to teacher learning. The previous part hypothesized about cultural mediation of relationships between the nature of informal learning and its content in different educational cultures by looking at how individual teachers learn in the workplace. This part continues building upon the similarities and differences in individual learning patterns and explores how teachers construct and act upon an important part of their professional identities that are shaped in the workplace—teachers as learners. I apply an emic perspective (Hymes, 1972) and examine how teachers in different schools perceive themselves as learners and how school cultures create opportunities for their everyday informal professional development.

Earlier, I examined culture within the broad array of definitions and meanings ascribed to the general concept of culture as well as organizational culture in particular, and defined the role that a cultural lens could play in conceptualizing informal workplace teacher learning. In the following chapters, I offer detailed accounts of culture in the three focal schools and examine how teachers define their institutional cultures and opportunities for professional development within them. Finally, I present the implications and raise questions for future research that emerges from the analysis of teacher learning at schools through a cultural lens.

This part continues the anthropological inquiry of informal teacher learning by focusing on schools as units of analysis. I describe informal learning by discursively examining written and verbal accounts of eleven individual teachers as they reflect upon their informal professional learning. Here, I examine how teachers view school cultures as contexts that provide opportunities for their informal learning and how they engage in professional growth within these contexts.

The Cultural Lens

Part III focuses on the examination of relationships between school cultures and teacher professional development by investigating how school cultures create opportunities for informal learning for teachers and how teachers identify themselves as learners within their school cultures. Hodkinson et al.'s idea of culture as a social phenomenon (2004) and his colleagues' Anderson-Levitt's (2002) concept of culture as an interactive web of meaning provide key constructs for the conceptual framework for the study. Together, these constructs focus the investigation on the relationships between informal learning contexts that exist in schools and highlight the ways teachers position themselves as learners while using existing opportunities as well as creating new occasions for their professional growth.

In addition, I use elements of interactional ethnography (e.g., Castanheira et al., 2000; Castanheira et al., 2007; Green & Dixon, 1993; Rex, 2006) to investigate how teachers' informal learning relates to school cultures. Created in and for educational research, "by viewing teaching and learning as inseparable and by studying them as interactional events" (Rex, 2006, p. 2), this approach enables a re-construction of cultural contexts as they emerge from participants' interactions with and within them. Together with interactional ethnographers, I perceive these cultures as constantly co-constructing themselves through interactions between members of the community and its contexts.

Therefore, in Part III, I focus on interactions that manifest teacher learning in the immediate situations occurring in the workplace. In doing so, I first characterize schools' contexts by focusing on traditional elements of anthropological accounts such as descriptions of community, buildings and classrooms, schools' philosophies, traditions, and the general school population. I do this by presenting ethnographic accounts, or cases, of three schools, weaving together the researcher's participant-observer perspective and teachers' voices as they shared their views on informal professional learning in 78 hours of interviews (Dyson & Genishi, 2005).

Within each case, in addition to the above-mentioned traditional elements of school culture, I apply MacGilchrist's et al. (1995) framework that highlights three interrelated dimensions of school culture: *Opportunities for learning*, which are created through *professional relationships* and *organizational arrangements*. While the traditional anthropological categories describe the context, these three dimensions highlight interactional processes within which teacher learning occurs in each school.

To deepen the analysis within each of the MacGilchrist et al. (1995) three categories, I elaborate upon them by employing complementary constructs. Professional relationships are understood through the concept of "knowledge-creating schools" (Hargreaves, 1999). From the teachers' perspective, I explore how the process of knowledge creation is reflected in their professional relationships and look for ways in which tinkering, transfer, research of practice, and facilitation by middle managers (Hargreaves, 1999) provide useful pathways for understanding teachers' learning processes within their schools' organizational arrangements.

To examine organizational arrangements, I observe ways in which school principals set the overall "tone", "pattern", and attitude" for teacher learning (Law, 1999), as well as how they organize and stimulate (if at all) collaborative learning. By examining how school cultures construct opportunities for professional learning and how teachers use these opportunities, I imply that opportunities are "socially signaled and recognized phenomen[a] that [are] context-, content-, time-, and participant-dependent" (Rex, 2006, p. 15). I analyze knowledge creation by observing the range of interactional spaces, the cultural norms, and "the roles and relationships ... [among] actions, talk, and texts" (Rex, 2006, p. 17). In these ways, I make teachers' informal learning opportunities in school settings visible for systematic examination.

Data Collection and Analysis

This layer of the "nesting doll" design includes participant observations (Delamont & Atkinson, 2001) at the three schools featured earlier in this book, teacher reflective journals, semi-structured interviews, and focus groups. The individual teachers' profiles that were discussed in Part II also inform this analysis. These data serve as a context for analysis of the teacher interviews that I focus on in this part. In their interviews, teachers responded to questions that related to the school ecology such as: *What does the school mean to you? How, when and where do you learn in your workplace? What does the school provide you for your learning?* The analysis of the interviews that are contextualized within the above-mentioned other sources serve as building blocks for the three school cases that define learning cultures on the institutional level. In each case, school culture is defined both from the teachers' point of view by emphasizing participants' interpretations of cultural elements, and from the researcher's perspective by synthesizing ethnographic data. This combination of ethnographic richness and interpretive perspective increase the likelihood that my own cultural understandings of the learning communities would fairly represent those communities throughout the analysis, and thus strengthen the validity of the study.

I systematically explore the data using methods from case study analysis, discourse analysis, and ethnographic analyses to understand how teachers learn in their workplace; how school cultures relate to informal learning and create opportunities for teachers to learn informally in their workplace; and how teachers construct their professional identities as learners in their workplace. The examination of the data guided by these questions aims at informing teacher educators and administrators about ways of helping teachers to become critical and reflective professionals who continuously improve their practice through formal and informal learning.

In the following three chapters, school cultures become visible through the webs of meanings that are explicit in utterances or implicit in conversational moves. These meanings interweave in different ways and to different degrees in different schools. To nuance the emerging understandings of different school cultures, I use the metaphor of polyphony (Fløttum, 2005) in portraying my (as a participant-observer's) and the teachers' representations of these cultures. To capture and define how the cultures of the three schools create, reinforce, and reflect teachers' professional learning, I describe schools within their social contexts.

The construction of each school case involves examination of multiple layers in which culture existed and was manifested in the schools. These layers/manifestations were often described as a tripartite of artifacts, (espoused) values, and basic assumptions. At one layer, cultural artifacts are revealed by the tangibles that one sees, hears and feels when entering an organization. Artifacts include the unique symbols, heroes, rites and rituals, myths, ceremonies and sagas of an organization (Hofstede, 1991; Masland, 1985). These manifestations of culture are "easiest to observe but arguably the most difficult to interpret" (Schein, 1992, in Detert et al., 2001, p. 187). At another layer, which represents relations between school leaders' and teachers' individual cultures, I observe particular dynamics that are expressed in the style of interactions with colleagues and leaders and with the world inside and outside the school. At one more layer, verbal and behavioral expressions of common values and assumptions produce a sense of an atmosphere at a specific school, which is challenging to piece together but easier to interpret by taking into account interpretations of members of this community.

In the narrative that follows, I triangulate the analysis of teacher interviews with interviews with school administrators, teacher focus groups, and with ethnographic artifacts such as the schools' mission statements. With teachers, I co-constructed meanings that they ascribed to informal learning via dialogic interviews with each of them (Knight & Saunders, 1999). To do so, I chose excerpts from the semi-structured interviews with the eleven teachers featured in the study. By highlighting key words and phrases, I explicated meanings that utterances carry. By weaving these meanings into a story about a school's culture, I re-construct each school's culture making it visible. I chose illustrative examples from the interviews for each analytic category of teacher informal learning, some of which repeat the ideas that the teachers have already shared in their journals. Reiterative analysis of all the data enables a greater refinement in the identification of cultural aspects of teacher learning (Green, Dixon & Zaharlick, 2003).

The Schools

The descriptions of the school cultures that follow are organized in an order in which a visitor to the school might experience them. This approach offers a fluid perspective and brings specific artifacts and teachers' voices to represent each school by providing multiple stances (Fløttum, 2005). Each case details the context in which teachers informally learn and introduces teachers' voices as they interact with that context. While these contexts are specific to each country and each institution, they reflect circumstances that are common to teachers in schools nationwide and internationally.

Six facets of school culture (Hallinger, & Leithwood, 1996) that provide opportunities for informal teacher learning are discussed in each case:

- school mission that reflects philosophy and collective values of the school community;
- architectural features of a school building that provide or fail to provide spaces for teacher informal learning;
- classrooms that represent both the administration's and individual teachers' approaches to professional learning;
- organizational arrangement that features different opportunities for teacher learning;
- traditions that extend contexts for informal learning; and
- professional relationships that provide or fail to provide opportunities to learn from each other.

The order of introducing schools (first, the Midwestern school in the United States, followed by the Russian School in Lithuania and concluding with the Lithuanian School) is dictated by the logic based on the findings discussed in Part II, which demonstrated that teachers as learners in the Midwestern school in the United States share very few characteristics with teachers in the Russian School in Lithuania; however, teachers in both of these schools share common features with teachers in the Lithuanian school. For this reason, I first present cases of the schools in which teachers seemed to be very different and conclude with the case of the school that is "in the middle" and incorporates characteristics of both "opposites". In bold, I highlight phrases and words that are key to understanding how the texts (interviews, websites, etc.) represent meanings. In the first case, when discussing professional relationships, I detail professional knowledge creation as tinkering, transfer of knowledge, research of practice, and facilitation by middle managers (Hargreaves, 1999) to explain how these four categories provide lenses for analyzing informal learning processes as socio-cultural phenomena. To avoid unnecessary repetition, in the other cases, I maintain the same structure and interpretive frame but construe meanings without explicit reference to Hargreaves.

Note

1 Nonaka and Takeuchi (1995) created their model based on industrial settings.

References

Acker, S. (1990). Teachers' culture in an English primary school. Continuity and change. *British Journal of Sociology of Education, 11*(3), 257–273.

Alexander, R. (2000). *Culture and pedagogy.* Oxford: Blackwell.

Ainscow, M., & Sandill, A. (2010). Developing inclusive education systems: The role of organisational cultures and leadership. *International Journal of Inclusive Education, 14*(4), 401–416.

Anderson-Levitt, K. M. (2002). *Teaching cultures: Knowledge for teaching first grade in France and the United States.* Cresskill, NJ: Hampton Press, Inc.

Baxter, L. A. (2011). *Voicing relationships: A dialogic perspective.* Thousand Oaks, CA: SAGE.

Beare, H., Caldwell, B. J., & Millikan, R. H. (1989/2018). *Creating an excellent school: Some new management techniques.* London: Routledge. (Originally work published in 1989).

Bidwell, C. E. (2001). Analyzing schools as organizations: Long-term permanence and short-term change. *Sociology of Education, 74*, 100–114.

Biesta, G. J. (2011). From learning cultures to educational cultures: Values and judgements in educational research and educational improvement. *International Journal of Early Childhood, 43*(3), 199–210.

Biesta, G. J. (2004). Education, accountability, and the ethical demand: Can the democratic potential of accountability be regained? *Educational theory, 54*(3), 233–250.

Biesta, G., & Tedder, M. (2007). Agency and learning in the lifecourse: Towards an ecological perspective. *Studies in the Education of Adults, 39*(2), 132–149.

Brendeson, P. V. (2000). Teacher learning as work and at work. *Journal of Inservice Education, 26*(1), 63–72.

Brown, J. S., Collins, A., & Duguid, P. (1989). Situated cognition and the culture of learning. *Educational Researcher, 18*(1), 32–42.

Brown, J. S., & Duguid, P. (2000). Balancing act: How to capture knowledge without killing it. *Harvard business review, 78*(3), 73–80.

Buchmann, M. (1989). The careful vision: How practical is contemplation in teaching? *American Journal of Education, 98*(1), 35–61.

Cameron, K. S., & Quinn, R. E. (2011). *Diagnosing and changing organizational culture: Based on the competing values framework.* Hoboken, NJ: John Wiley & Sons.

Castanheira, M. L., Crawford, T., Dixon, C. N., & Green, J. L. (2000). Interactional ethnography: An approach to studying the social construction of literate practices. *Linguistics and Education, 11*(4), 353–400.

Castanheira, M. L., Green, J., Dixon, C., & Yeagerb, B. (2007). (Re) Formulating identities in the face of fluid modernity: An interactional ethnographic approach. *International Journal of Educational Research, 46*(3–4), 172–189.

Creemers, B. P. (2002). From school effectiveness and school improvement to effective school improvement: Background, theoretical analysis, and outline of the empirical study. *Educational Research and Evaluation, 8*(4), 343–362.

Creemers, B. P., & Reezigt, G. J. (2005). Linking school effectiveness and school improvement: The background and outline of the project. *School Effectiveness and School Improvement*, *16*(4), 359–371.

Deal, T., & Kennedy, A. (1982). *Corporate cultures: The rites and rituals of corporate life*. Reading, MA: Addison Wesley.

Delamont, S., & Atkinson, P. (2001). Doctoring uncertainty: Mastering craft knowledge. *Social Studies of Science*, *31*(1), 87–107.

Detert, J. R., Seashore Louis, K., & Schroeder, R. G. (2001). A culture framework for education: Defining quality values and their impact in US high schools. *School Effectiveness and School Improvement*, *12*(2), 183–212.

Dyson, A. H., & Genishi, C. (2005). *On the case* (Vol. 76). New York: Teachers College Press.

Eisner, E. (2000). Those who ignore the past... *Journal of Curriculum Studies*, *32*(2), 343–357.

Elmore, R. F. (2000). *Leadership of large-scale improvement in American education*. Washington, DC: A. Shanker Institute.

Evans, K., Hodkinson, P., Rainbird, H., & Unwin, L. (2007). *Improving workplace learning*. Routledge.

Fink, G., Dauber, D., & Yolles, M. (2012). Understanding organisational culture as a trait theory. *European Journal of International Management*, *6*(2), 199–220.

Finlayson, D. S. (1973). The school perceptions of teachers of differential status. *Research in Education*, *9*(1), 83–92.

Firestone, W. A., & Louis, K. S. (1999). Schools as cultures. In J. Murphy & K. S. Louis (Eds.), *Handbook of research on educational administration* (2nd ed., pp. 297–322). San Francisco, CA: Jossey-Bass.

Fløttum, K. (2005). The self and the others: Polyphonic visibility in research articles. *International Journal of Applied Linguistics*, *15*(1), 29–44.

Fullan, M. (1991). *The new meaning of educational change* (2nd ed.). New York: Teacher College Press.

Fullan, M. (1993). *Change forces: Probing the depth of educational reform*. London: Falmer Press.

Fuller, A., Hodkinson, H., Hodkinson, P., & Unwin, L. (2005). Learning as peripheral participation in communities of practice: A reassessment of key concepts in workplace learning. *British Educational Research Journal*, *31*(1), 49–68.

Geertz, C. (1983). Common sense as a cultural system. In C. Geertz (Ed.), *Local knowledge: Further essays in interpretive anthropology* (pp. 73–93). New York: Basic Books.

Goldenberg, C., & Gallimore, R. (1991). Changing teaching takes more than a one-shot workshop. *Educational Leadership*, *49*(3), 69–72.

Green, J., & Dixon, C. (1993). Introduction to "Talking knowledge into being: Discursive and social practices in classrooms". *Linguistics and Education*, *5*, 231–239.

Green, J. L., Dixon, C. N., & Zaharlick, A. (2003). Ethnography as a logic of inquiry. In J. Flood, D. Lapp, J. R. Squire, & J. M. Jensen (Eds.), *Handbook of research on teaching the English language arts* (2nd ed., pp. 201–224). Mahwah, NJ: Lawrence Erlbaum Associates.

Hallinger, P., & Leithwood, K. (1996). Culture and educational administration: A case of finding out what you don't know you don't know. *Journal of Educational Administration*, *34*(5), 98–116.
Halpin, A. W., & Croft, D. B. (1963). *The organizational culture of schools.* Chicago, IL: Midwest Administration Center, University of Chicago.
Handy, C., & Aitken, R. (1986). *Understanding schools as organizations.* London: Penguin Books.
Hargreaves, A. (1992). Time and teachers' work: An analysis of the intensification thesis. *Teachers college record*, *94*, 87–87.
Hargreaves, A. (1994). *Changing teachers, changing times: Teachers' work and culture in the postmodern age.* London: Cassell.
Hargreaves, D. H. (1995). School culture, school effectiveness and school improvement. *School Effectiveness and School Improvement*, *6*(1), 23–46.
Hargreaves, D. H. (1999). The knowledge-creating school. *British Journal of Educational Studies*, *47*(2), 122–144.
Hodkinson, P., Biesta, G., & James, D. (2004). *Towards a cultural theory of college-based learning* [Paper]. Manchester: The Annual Conference of the British Educational Research Association.
Hodkinson, P., Biesta, G., & James, D. (2008). Understanding learning culturally: Overcoming the dualism between social and individual views of learning. *Vocations and Learning*, *1*(1), 27–47.
Hodkinson, P., & Bloomer, M. (2000). Stokingham Six Form College: Institutional culture and dispositions to learning. *British Journal of Sociology of Education*, *21*(2), 187–202.
Hofstede, G. (1991). *Culture and organizations: Software of the mind.* London: McGraw-Hill.
Hopkins, D. (1996). Towards a theory of school improvement. In J. Gray, D. Reynolds, C. Fitz-Gibbon, & D. Jesson (Eds.), *Merging traditions: The future of research on school effectiveness and school improvement.* London: Cassell.
Hymes, D. H. (1972). Models of the interaction of language and social life. In J. J. Gumperz & D. H. Hymes (Eds.), *Directions in sociolinguistics: The ethnography of communication* (pp. 35–71). New York: Holt, Rinehart, and Winston.
Kennedy, M. M. (1983). Working knowledge. *Knowledge: Creation, Dissemination and Utilization*, *15*(2), 166–185.
Knight, P. T. (2002). Learning from schools. *Higher Education*, *44*, 283–298.
Knight, P. T. (2002a). A systematic approach to professional development: Learning as practice. *Teaching and Teacher Education*, *18*(3), 229–241.
Knight, P., & Saunders, M. (1999). Understanding teachers' professional cultures through interview: A constructivist approach. *Evaluation and Research in Education*, *13*(3), 144–156.
Lave, J., & Wenger, E. (1991). *Situated learning: Legitimate peripheral participation.* Cambridge: Cambridge University Press.
Law, S. (1999). Leadership for learning; the changing culture of professional development in schools. *Journal of Educational Administration*, *37*(1), 66–76.
Leithwood, K., Jantzi, D., & Steinbach, R. (1999). *Changing leadership for changing times.* Buckingham: Open University Press.
Lieberman, A. (1996). Practices that support teacher development: Transforming conceptions of professional learning. In M. W. McLaughlin & I. Oberman

(Eds.), *Teacher learning: New policies, new practices* (pp. 185–201). New York: Teacher College Press.

MacGilchrist, B., Mortimore, P., Stedman, J., & Beresford, C. R. (1995). *Planning matters: the impact of development planning in primary schools.* London: P. Chapman Pub.

Masland, A. T. (1985). Organizational culture in the study of higher education. *The Review of Higher Education, 8*(2), 157–168.

Maslowski, R. (2006). A review of inventories for diagnosing school culture. *Journal of Educational Administration, 44*(1), 6–35.

Miller, L., & Lieberman, A. (1988). School improvement in the United States: Nuances and numbers. *Qualitative Studies in Education, 1*(1), 3–19.

Moen, A., Mørch, A. I., & Paavola, S. (Eds.). (2012). *Collaborative knowledge creation: Practices, tools, concepts* (Vol. 7). Cham: Springer Science + Business Media.

Murphy, J., & Hallinger, P. (1989). Equity as access to learning: Curricular and instructional differences. *Journal of Curriculum Studies, 21*, 129–149.

Newmann, F. M., Rutter, R. A., & Smith, M. S. (1989). Organizational factors that affect school sense of efficacy, community, and expectations. *Sociology of Education, 62*(4), 221–238.

Nonaka, I., & Takeuchi, H. (1995). *The knowledge-creating company: How Japanese companies create the dynamics of innovation.*Oxford: Oxford University Press.

Ogbonna, E. (1993). Managing organisational culture: Fantasy and reality. *Human Resource Management Journal, 3*(2), 42–54.

Ogbonna, E., & Harris, L. C. (2000). Leadership style, organizational culture and performance: Empirical evidence from UK companies. *International Journal of Human Resource Management, 11*(4), 766–788.

Opfer, D. (2016). *Conditions and practices associated with teacher professional development and its impact on instruction in TALIS 2013* (OECD Education Working Papers, No. 138). Paris: OECD Publishing.

Poekert, P. E. (2012). Examining the impact of collaborative professional development on teacher practice. *Teacher Education Quarterly, 39*(4), 97–118.

Priestley, M., Biesta, G., & Robinson, S. (2013). Teachers as agents of change: Teacher agency and emerging models of curriculum. In *Reinventing the curriculum: New trends in curriculum policy and practice* (pp. 187–206).

Prosser, J. (Ed.). (1999a). *School culture.* London: SAGE.

Prosser, J. (1999b). The evolution of school culture research. In J. Prosser (Ed.), *School culture.* London: Paul Chapman.

Putnam, R. T., & Borko, H. (2000). What do new views of knowledge and thinking have to say about research on teacher learning. *Educational Researcher*, 29(1), 4–15.

Rex, L. A. (Ed.). (2006). *Discourse of opportunity: How talk in learning situations creates and constrains.* Cresskill, NJ: Hampton Press, Inc.

Reynolds, D., & Packer, A. (1992). School effectiveness and school improvement in the 1990s. In D. Reynolds and A. Packer (Ed.), *School Effectiveness: Research, Policy and Practice*, 171–188. London, UK: Bloomsbury.

Rogoff, B. (2003). *The cultural nature of human development.*Oxford: Oxford University Press.

Sammons, P. (2007). *School effectiveness and equity: Making connections.* A review of school effectiveness and improvement research-its implications for practitioners and policy makers.

Schein, E. H. (2010). *Organizational culture and leadership* (Vol. 2). John Wiley & Sons.
Schein, E. H. (1992). *Organizational culture and leadership*. San Francisco, CA: Jossey-Bass.
Schipper, T. M., de Vries, S., Goei, S. L., & van Veen, K. (2020). Promoting a professional school culture through lesson study? An examination of school culture, school conditions, and teacher self-efficacy. *Professional Development in Education*, *46*(1), 112–129.
Schoen, L. T., & Teddlie, C. (2008). A new model of school culture: A response to a call for conceptual clarity. *School Effectiveness and School Improvement*, *19*(2), 129–153.
Schön, D. A. (1984). *The reflective practitioner: How professionals think in action* (Vol. 5126). New York: Basic Books.
Sparks, D. (2009). What I believe about leadership development. *Phi Delta Kappan*, *90*(7), 514–517.
Stern, G. G. (1970). *People in context: Measuring per- son-environment in education and industry*. New York: Wiley.
Stoll, L. (1999). *School culture: Black hole or fertile garden for improvement?* London: Paul Chapman.
Stoll, L., & Fink, D. (1996). *Changing our schools*. Buckingham: Open University Press.
Thomas, K. J., & Akdere, M. (2013). Social media as collaborative media in workplace learning. *Human Resource Development Review*, *12*(3), 329–344.
Yinger, R., & Hendricks-Lee, M. (1993). Working knowledge in teaching. In C. Day, J. Calderhead, & P. Denicolo (Eds.), *Research on teacher thinking: Understanding professional development* (pp. 100–123). London: Falmer Press.
Van Veen, K., Zwart, R., & Meirink, J. (2012). What makes teacher professional development effective. In M. Kooy and K. van Veen (Ed.), *Teacher learning that matters: International perspectives* (pp. 3–21). Abington, UK: Routledge.
Wenger, E. (1999). *Communities of practice: Learning, meaning and identity*. Cambridge: Cambridge University Press.
Williams, R. (1995). *The sociology of culture*. University of Chicago Press.

9 A Midwestern Elementary School in the USA

Overview of This Chapter

This chapter discusses school culture of a relatively new school in the US Midwest (3 years in operation at the time of data collection) in which faculty is actively involved in the construction of their professional relationships. The discussion of different aspects of school culture creates a unique image of this workplace in which the teachers are in the process of looking for ways to build their organizational culture. In addition to being open to new experiences, they have expectations that are grounded in patterns of their previous experiences. They seem to separate the social from the professional, thus missing some opportunities created by their colleagues and the principal to learn from each other informally. The administration seems to support teachers' professional growth; however, neither the principal nor the head teacher initiate any professional development events, as if leaving it up to the teachers to take care of their learning needs. In response, the teachers engage in formal and informal learning, depending on their individual motivation. The voices of teachers in this school contribute to the school culture by "singing solo" rather than making a choir. In addition, the missing mission of the school indicates an absence of effort in creating a well-tuned team inspired by the same goals.

> We learn mostly from bouncing ideas one off [of] another.
>
> (Kristi)

> We are doing stuff on our own.
>
> (John)

About the School

The school is situated in a fast-growing suburb of an industrial Midwestern US state. This suburban area, formerly farmland, is being filled with new single-family homes in subdivisions that are close to a small town, which two decades ago had a population of a few thousand people, and just one traffic light. A homogenous community of professional middle-class families with steady income populates the county. At the time of data collection, the participating elementary school was the newest in the district (having opened in 2003). Teachers came to this school from different buildings and districts. The teacher/student ratio was one of the highest in the district (23:1). Parents seemed to be interested in the high-quality education for their children that this school was aspiring to provide. They participated in school events and supported their children's involvement in after-school activities. The families appeared to trust the school and the teachers in meeting their educational standards and, at the time of this study, did not seem to exert pressure upon teachers to develop professionally.

The School's Missing Mission

District and school websites is typically the first place parents and community members go to find information used to make important decisions about their children's education. As such, that is where I decided to collect general data about educational goals and professional development strategies of the school; however, neither the district's nor the school's websites contained their educational mission statements. Both websites had the same design and contained structural and procedural information such as the county statistics of enrollment and high school graduation information by race as compared to the state's statistics, as well as calendars, schedules, and lists of teachers and administrators. One of the webpages showed test scores according to which the school occupied a position in the middle of the ranking list among district schools. This webpage highlighted the school's goal, "The goal is for all students to score at or above the state standard", which the school met.

> On the webpage, the school received high ratings and comments by parents.

For example:

> The school is very open to parents. Most teachers have good communication to [sic] parents on a regular basis. The kids love the teachers (most!).

Another parent commented,

> Great staff, nice people, and the playgrounds are great. I also like the fact that the staff treat [sic] the students like equals. They do not talk down to them but to them. That is a BIG deal to me.

My observations confirmed a friendly and open atmosphere in the building; however, there was less praise about their pedagogical choice of "team-teaching", which also seemed to be in line with my field notes:

> My son attended 2nd grade and had a great teacher. But in 3rd grade I am much less impressed. Watch out for "team teaching" here—it seems to be a way to put one teacher in charge of 60 students. Next year I am considering private schools instead.

Though most of the parents appreciated the school's efforts in meeting their expectations, the absence of the school mission at the time of this research seemed to imply that the school had not yet formulated its philosophy and specific goals. That could be explained by the novelty of the staff and faculty to the building. Moreover, I did not observe any efforts toward creating a mission for the school.

In the following sections, I explore how different structures (both architectural and administrative), school traditions, and professional relationships provide opportunities for teachers' informal learning in this school. I also analyze how teachers talk about these opportunities and how they use them for their professional growth.

The School Building Instills Separation

The school occupies a two-story building with lower elementary classrooms situated on the first floor and upper elementary on the second. Upon entering the building, everyone reports to the office (a common protocol in all American schools). When I arrived to meet the principal and the teachers, two attentive and smiling assistants were ready to answer any questions at the front desk. After several visits, they made me feel part of the school team, letting me know if the teachers I was working with were in the building, where I could find them, and asking me about my day, my work, and family. Often, I would find the principal in this area talking with the assistants or teachers and making himself available to visitors. The atmosphere of the school was friendly, inviting, and casual. The walls of the hallways by the classrooms were decorated with students' artwork and projects; by the office, a calendar, photographs, and stories from the recent events occupied a big space on the wall representing the work of the Parent–Teachers Association.

However, the architecture of the winged two-story building did not seem to encourage interactions between the teachers. Several teachers noted that it was more difficult here than in their former one-story buildings to get to know their colleagues and find out what they did in their classrooms. For example, Kristi expressed difficulty in getting to know her colleagues from other wings and other floors:

> We started doing *Morning Minglers* on Fridays, where teachers have breakfast **in their rooms**[1] and have other teachers come. That's more

> of a **relationship building thing and a get-to-know-you thing** because we are a fairly new building. Last year, we were also busy moving our classrooms over here and getting to know people that actually you are next to that we did not branch out into the building very much. We **did not have too much social time** to get to know people **on other floors** and **other wings** in the building. So, this year we are working more on that.

Further, she continued highlighting benefits of *Morning Minglers* for learning what other teachers did and talking with colleagues because there were very few other opportunities for interaction:

> It's **an opportunity to go to other classrooms and see what's hanging on the wall and what they are doing and also talk to some teachers that you don't have other opportunity to talk**. I think especially **with this building being two floors, it's difficult**. You know, **the lounge is upstairs**, and to be honest, **I often don't get up there**. During my lunch, I sit down here just because by the time you take it upstairs, there is no time for eating and we are often working during lunchtime.

She pointed out that as the teachers' lounge was on the second floor, she could hardly find time to go and have lunch there. In the next interview, Kristi expanded on her idea that this building was separating teachers:

> So I'd like to get to know people a little bit better. It's a little **bit difficult in this building** as well because being in the upstairs and the downstairs, there are people that I don't see daily, and **I don't even know whether they are here today** or not because **I just don't see them**. **They are upstairs, and I am downstairs**. Whereas in the building that I came from, it was an older building, smaller, everybody was on one floor. But you pass by people's rooms on your way to the copy room, or you pass by people's rooms [going] different places. Just the proximity of the classrooms—everything **that makes it a little bit more difficult**. I feel good about this year that as a staff, we've been **planning more things to get to know each other**.

I noticed that some teachers were interacting more often than others in the hallways and the administrative office. For instance, John, similar to Kristi, seemed to go out of his classroom only to visit his grade level colleagues, but even then, his colleagues would rather come to his classroom. Thus, his socializing was limited to chatting with his grade level colleagues in his classroom. By contrast, I saw Bob outside his classroom on many occasions interacting with teachers beyond his grade level colleagues as well as with students. That might mean that this architectural design could have restricted some but not others from getting to know their colleagues and use the environment to learn informally.

The Classrooms Reflect Individual Teachers' Styles

All the classrooms were spacious and brightly decorated. Materials that represented teachers' interests occupied most of the wall space. For example, colorful information about the school's spring camp took up the entire wall in one of the classrooms; in another classroom, a collection of souvenirs from different countries demonstrated the teacher's appreciation of other cultures; and in yet another classroom, a *Wordwall* was the first item people saw upon entering. Classrooms reflected teachers' styles, clearly defining their individual spaces and illustrating their academic priorities and personal interests. When the teachers gave me a tour of their classrooms, they sounded proud of their immediate work environment and satisfied with the administrative help they received in organizing their spaces. When asked what their ideal classroom would be, all of them told me that their current classrooms would be very close to their ideal.

The unique ways in which the classrooms revealed teachers' individuality served as illustrations in Virginia Richardson's (2003) commentary on the vivid culture of individualism in American schools:

> The American character, individualism, strongly affects the way in which many Americans—teachers and other professionals included—approach their work. In schools, it is abetted by the egg-crate environment and the practice of "closing the classroom door." Many classroom teachers would subscribe to the following view: "This is my space, and I am responsible for it. It is mine. It reflects me. I am the teacher here. This is unique and is therefore unlike any other classroom because of my uniqueness and my particular group of students."
> (pp. 402–403)

Further, she pointed to the tendencies in the educational policies that recognized the potentially negative effects of such individualism on teacher professional growth. To overrule individualism, national policies suggested standardizing curriculum to homogenize teachers' ways of thinking and "reduce the incidence of poor teaching and thus improve all teaching" (Ibid., p. 403). In personal conversations I had with her, Professor Richardson expressed her skepticism of this standardization trend, which the participating school also seemed to share. In the following sections, I describe how, by providing various opportunities for teachers' informal learning, the school tried to overcome the federal tendency for standardization of teachers' ways of thinking and doing.

Organizational Arrangements Encourage Collaborative Teachers' Learning

Valuing the process of teachers' learning from each other, the Midwestern school employed organizational arrangements to open its classrooms and create opportunities for collaborative teacher learning at their workplace. The school principal seemed to set the overall "tone", "pattern", or "attitude" for this development (Law, 1999) by encouraging and organizing opportunities for collaborative learning. Bob's answer to my question "What makes a school's culture?" was, "The principal has to do a lot with it. The principal sets the tone. The teachers react to the principal; he'd react to the teachers. So, if the principal's easy-going and friendly, the teachers tend to be that way. They follow him. And then the kids, in turn, will".

In this school, the principal scheduled classes in such a way that the teachers of the same grade level had common preparation time once a week. Many teachers in the school used this opportunity to collaborate and learn from each other. In addition, the principal supported teachers' participation in workshops and conferences. For example, Debbie, a reading specialist, compared this school to where she previously worked and explained the reasons for leaving that school:

> [Let's look at] the one in suburb of D. and here. This is much different than the one in the suburbs of D. They didn't give **any money for conferences**. There **wasn't really any special time**, because I was a (...) grade teacher. Teachers here have the same common prep. Everybody did things **on your own** [there]. You just **did it yourself**, these are your kids and **you shut the door** and that's it. So, there was not any formal training or informal. Informal would be going to somebody's classes. That is one of the reasons I left that district. If **they don't want to take any pride in their teachers and their learning**, I don't want to spend 25 years in that place. School is about learning.

In the same interview, she described ways in which this school organized teachers' professional learning such as having common preparation time at the grade level, inviting support teachers (e.g., reading, speech) to share different teaching strategies, and encouraging teachers' interactions with colleagues from other schools:

> The school here is set up with **specials[2] at the time** when grade levels can meet and sometimes they **invite me to the grade level teams** to just advise them about literacy, different strategies and how to teach the grade level content expectations. Another way is my principal

> [supports professional development], like tomorrow, I am **going to another school**, where the teacher does the same role. We get together and I help her with her kids and she helps me with my [sic].

Kristi, for example, extensively used her preparation time with her team every day, though spending time only with her grade level colleagues:

> Lunchtime, we **eat lunch together daily and [have] our prep time**. We have **all common preps** and **we've been together planning for the week** and it's usually, we spend about half of prep time saying, this is what we want to do and how we want to do it, and we split up and go, and do stuff to get it done for each other.

In this excerpt, Kristi defined the limits of her everyday interactions to communicating just with her grade level colleagues. She admitted "the PD [professional development] happen[ed] when I plan with the other [...] grade teachers"; however, it is important to be aware of the outcomes of such co-planning: does it stimulate teachers' individual learning and enrich each of the co-planners' abilities in teaching their students, or does it produce "cookie-cutter" lessons that aim at delivering the curriculum? Kristi seemed to be leaning toward the latter:

> And I like the fact that because we plan together all second grade teachers, you could **walk into ANY of our classrooms at that time and we'll probably be doing the same thing**.

Kristi's preference for commonly developed lesson plans, and my observations that teachers combined their classes so that one teacher could teach about 40–80 students at once, limited teachers' ability to interact with students and meet their needs for individualized instruction. In the class that I observed, Kristi introduced a math lesson to over 40 students from two same-grade level classrooms. She extensively used PowerPoint, flipping through the slides, explaining concepts and giving examples. I saw students having a hard time keeping their focus on the screen without having a chance to practice and interact for over 20 minutes. Together with the parent (quoted at the beginning of this section), I could see how such "co-teaching" would aim at covering curriculum rather than teaching students. In addition, Kristi did not seem to communicate much with other teachers in the building or outside it. Other teachers also described their patterns of interactions to suggest they were more self-servingly individualistic rather than collaborative. For example, John admitted, "for most of this year, **we are doing stuff on our own**".

Debbie also acknowledged that she was "**alone, isolated in this position**. There are no other reading teachers in the school"; however, she appreciated her flexible work schedule and met with other colleagues outside the school. She took advantage of the opportunities to learn "from other teachers throughout [the state]", and to "go to the [large city] area once a month and [...] get together with teachers in the same position": "**We watch lessons**, and **we talk about theory**, and **we go over how we can best help** the classroom teachers".

On the contrary, Bob did not position himself as a teacher in isolation. Rather, he talked about different opportunities that he used to learn through collaboration with his colleagues not only in the same grade level but also across the whole school:

> So now, we are trying **to collaborate with the (...) grade**. On one of your tapes, you'll hear John and I talking. We are **in the lunch room**. We were talking about things to be covered in the (...) grade because they were concerned about [State Standardized Test]. And you know, **we don't ever meet**. So, all the (...) grade happened to be there, and all the [next grade], so **we talked** about that, what needed to be taught and what needed to be covered. **They had a lot of concerns** that they have never had to deal with, so **we helped them out** that way.

In sum, the teachers in this school took advantage of the organizational arrangements that the principal provided. The principal played a leading role in organizing the teachers' schedules and spaces to offer multiple opportunities for teachers' informal learning; however, the teachers seemed to use these opportunities in different ways: some teachers extended their learning opportunities beyond the boundaries of the school; others took advantage of the school's organizational arrangements and initiated collaborative learning between teachers of different grades; and others confined their professional learning to collaboration only with their grade level colleagues.

Traditions Extend Contexts for Informal Learning, But Do They in this School?

The school's traditions reflected school culture and contributed to the opportunities for teacher learning in the building by creating occasions for informal interactions. When asked about their traditions, the teachers in this school talked about different calendar events that were planned by teacher committees. For example, March was a Reading Month. That tradition involved preparatory meetings where teachers exchanged ideas and organized all-school events.

Responding to my question about traditions, teachers referred to their district's traditions rather than those of their teacher teams. For example, answering my specific question about school traditions, Debbie, a reading specialist, focused on what could "shake up" teachers' thinking and learning *outside* the school, as if events at the school played no role in this process:

ELENA (E) Are there any traditions **in this school** that bring people together, that shake them up in a gentle way? How is it going **in this school**?

DEBBIE (D) We have **district PD days**. Teachers are required to do the five days; and that is part of the state (...) plan too. In these PD days for teachers, I am not sure if their needs are met during those PD days.

E Does it happen **in the school**?

D **It happens throughout the district**. They offer certain classes and you can pick your sessions. It's better this year because they broke apart different teams of teachers and you can pick your area of study for the day. The first year that they did, everybody did the same thing, so every elementary teacher was doing, for example, special education laws for the day; which is important too that they know special education laws, or every teacher is doing math. Well, I don't teach math. It's better this year (...).

E Yeah. **What about the school**? You have Friday *Morning Minglers* when you come in the morning, right? Do you come to them?

D Yes (nodding).

E I'm curious. I've learned about them from the teachers and they said, "Yeah, come and join us". I will do that. **Is it kind of PD also**?

D **No**, well, you never talk about school stuff (...). People are going on vacation, and different experiences. I don't think I talked very much about schools. **It's more of a social**.

E It's good, when they, know you, they can trust you, and later on they can share professional concerns with you. Are there other traditions **in the school** when you come together?

D We have **school improvement team**. We talk about school improvement issues. We gave different goals that each teacher tries to meet; the ones in reading, in writing, and in science. It's called on **from a center of accreditation**. Next year, I believe if we have the same goals, the PD days could be planned according to the school improvement goals, which would be great. So, there is a purpose behind these PD days.

E How about celebrating your birthdays here and other traditions that the team is doing [...]?

D We have a social committee; and the social committee plans various events. **I have not been able to make any of the events this year** because every time they seem to be planning **I am out at a conference**. So, I've not been able to make them. Like we have one next Wednesday and I am at a conference. They had one I think at the beginning of March, and in February; I was at a conference.

E What are those social events?

D They are like **a luncheon**. Everybody brings some additional food [...]

E And again when people socialize they don't talk about work.

D Not usually. Usually, if I have something to say, it's done through email. I prefer people not call me on my phone, because I cannot take the phone and I don't like checking voicemail.

In this excerpt, I repeatedly asked Debbie about the school traditions, and she kept telling me about her learning experiences outside the school. Apparently, Debbie chose to participate in professional events outside the school rather than in social events inside the building because she did not seem to view social events as learning opportunities. For example, when I asked Debbie if *Morning Minglers* were a kind of professional development, she categorically said, "No. (...) It is more of a social", juxtaposing professional development and social events as different kinds of experiences. Similar to Debbie, Kristi did not seem to see value in talking about social events in terms of teacher learning. She quickly switched to all-school calendar traditions and commented on their origin—brought from other buildings—rather than on their potential for teacher professional learning:

> (...) Doing the ***Morning Minglers***—that becomes somewhat of a tradition. And we have **an Art Fair in April** where the students display artwork throughout the building and parents come for an evening and the kids do musical performances throughout the night. And at the end of the year we have a little **Carnival**. [...] there are games and things that PTO puts on. We have our **Book Fairs** that happen a few times throughout the year where books are sold and we have **Santa Shop at Christmas** time. So, mostly, those are things that **other buildings do as well that were brought here to become a tradition** as well and we may do them in a little bit different way, different time of the year.

Kristi's short responses and quick switches to a different topic (in addition, see the following excerpt) suggested her lack of interest in the topic of *Morning Minglers*. Throughout her interview about these rituals, she made no mention of the events as learning opportunities.

The new tradition of *Morning Minglers* seemed to be viewed as a purely social event that had nothing to do with learning. It seemed to be gaining popularity rather slowly. Only when I specifically asked about their *Morning Minglers* would teachers talk about this new team tradition. I learned about the *Morning Minglers* rather late in the year and wanted to experience it; however, when I tried to attend one in April, I found out that it had been cancelled. Indeed, some of these minglers were cancelled because no one had signed up to host them. All the teachers seemed to have had one round of hosting already. It was not clear if the teachers continued to assign any value to social events at the school in general, and Friday *Morning Minglers* in particular. By the end of the year, their enthusiasm for *Morning Minglers* seemed to have dissipated; as Kristi said, they had "done their time". For example, Kristi did not even know when the next *Morning Mingler* was scheduled:

E So who's next for the *Morning Mingler*?
K Umm, **I don't even know**. I think the schedule may be hanging in the office.
E I was thinking about coming in there.
K You should.
E When is YOUR time?
K **We've already done our time**.

As I was familiar with the big celebrations at the end of the Lithuanian school year and how teachers worked together to generate creative ideas for celebratory scenarios that were different every year, I asked Kristi about the end-of-the-school-year traditions in her school. Kristi's reasoning for why they did what they did challenged my expectations:

E Any traditions for the end of the year?
K **No**. Having lunch for teachers last year. The principal provided it. Baby showers for teachers (*two teachers had babies, E.J.*-OK.). The last days are half-days, that is, Monday and Tuesday. **Everyone is anxious to get home**. And many people work hard, so they can **be done** by Tuesday afternoon, so they **don't have to come the rest of the week**.
E Is it the same from year to year?
K **Pretty much the same**. They will not be painting, so it's just cleaning the counters and taking some things off the walls. Usually, we have a calendar of events for the next year, but this year is negotiation of the contract. So, I haven't scheduled anything yet.

By pointing out that she was in a hurry to leave her workplace as soon as possible, Kristi seemed to differentiate between her time on the job strictly as "doing the job" and her time away from the building as time off from teaching. She was also convinced that everyone at this school related to their job the same way. Similar to Debbie, she did not seem to include social interactions as learning opportunities.

To conclude, traditions that could provide occasions for informal professional learning through social events do exist in this school. Teachers could make use of these social events to develop collegial relationships that could create and sustain professional learning opportunities; however, their initial enthusiasm for traditions such as *Morning Minglers* waned over the course of the year. For whatever reason, teachers began to view attendance of such events as a chore. They seemed to separate professional learning and socializing, and they did not maintain sufficient interest in spending time with their colleagues. The teachers were experimenting with traditions that would allow them to learn more about each other but their distinct separation of the social from the professional made it difficult to recognize social events as sources of valuable teaching knowledge.

Professional Relationships under Construction

Professional relationships create and reflect school culture and they produce an atmosphere that could expand or limit opportunities for informal workplace learning. In this section, I explore how teachers' professional relationships are mediums for teachers' learning through the four potential processes or "seeds" Hargreaves (1999) found for professional knowledge creation within schools: tinkering, transfer of knowledge, research of practice, and facilitation by middle managers. Tinkering, as Hargreaves (1999) noted, is common among professionals. It includes *ad hoc* unscientific, practical experimentation when teachers engage in the trial and error process in order to develop a greater variety of teaching tools for solving their classroom dilemmas (Huberman, 1992, Lampert, 2001). In this school, I did not find examples of tinkering as "an individualized embryo of institutional knowledge" (Hargreaves, 1999, p. 131). Teachers seemed somewhat reluctant to talk about their individual trial and error experiences—they seemed to view this process as tinting their identity and fervently protected their professional identity from any possible damage by revealing their mistakes. Rather, they would give examples of "collective tinkering". For example, Kristi commented on the work of their grade level "collective mind"—bouncing ideas off each other, trying them out, and observing how they worked in other classrooms:

> But even if we are getting ideas from books it is like we are sitting and "I read that somewhere. **Shall we try it?"** Talking it through and discussing it. Not even looking it up in the book. So, that's mostly **from bouncing ideas one off from another**. And **trying them out** and **certainly observing in other classrooms**. That was one good thing about peer coaching is going into each other classrooms because the goal was not to evaluate it.

According to Hargreaves (1999), when individual tinkering becomes more systematized—in other words, collective and explicitly managed, as was the case with this team of teachers (e.g., co-planning at a certain time every day)—it transforms into knowledge creation. Usually, this knowledge emerges from telling and sharing ("bouncing ideas one off [...] another") discussing "good ideas" and modifying them for implementation in their classrooms. In the previous excerpt, for example, Kristi reported that her team had applied a trial-and-error process to arrive at common knowledge creation.

The second "seed" of professional knowledge creation—transfer of knowledge—occurs when the information about one teacher's good practice becomes "part of [another teacher's] context of meaning and purpose and pre-existing knowledge" (Ibid., p. 132), with tinkering as an essential precursor. Kristi, for example, referred to powerful experiences at her former school where she learned from many colleagues, including a teacher who introduced peer coaching to that team:

> She would come and do an all-day workshop type thing with us. So, she was someone **we got to know well**. I think, there is a literacy leader in my old building, whom I learned a tremendous amount from because she provided us with **time away from the classroom** to actually have time to invest and **come up with literacy ideas**. And I think, that was really valuable—just **spending time away from the classroom**. A lot of things sound good, but actually at times **to implement them is difficult**. So I think she was a valuable teacher, and she provided us with that **time and access to things that we needed to incorporate the ideas** that we were hearing.

In this excerpt, Kristi pointed out factors that helped her learn from the guest teacher: getting to know her well and having time away from the classroom. The latter was necessary for processing and getting ready to incorporate new ideas. In addition, similar to Debbie, Kristi seemed to be learning from observing in other classrooms. Both teachers valued this kind of learning because they discovered practical elements that they could apply right away in their own teaching. Kristi, for example, found it useful to follow the language other teachers used when explaining something to their students:

> And I am constantly learning not just from our planning time but when we spend **time in each other's classrooms**, I am intensively learning the way **THEY are explaining things**. I often think when I am listening to them; and [T.], my team partner, she does the same thing. It's just nice because she'll say something and I'll think, **"Wow, it was really easy to understand! And it was not the way I was going to explain it, but it was probably a lot easier to understand."** And she says that she hears the same things when I talk. Sometimes she thinks, "Wow, that was really good the way she worded that".

Debbie's observations of her colleagues' teaching led her to form a framework for assessing if and how they transferred the knowledge that they have learned in professional workshops. She categorized three teacher stances for dealing with new knowledge, only one of which illustrated transfer—adapting attained knowledge to make it work in the teacher's own classroom:

> You go to a workshop, or you take a graduate level class and you hear lots of different ways to teach reading, or how to teach writing, or you go to hands-on math or science workshop and you are fired up to go back to classroom. And you try it, and **it doesn't work**, or it did not work out as best as you hoped to. **So you just give up and you go to your old ways**. There are those types of people. And there are other people that **continue to try and make it work however it fits your means**. So you take some pieces of it, which is good because **you are adapting the knowledge to make it work for yourself and your kids**. That's another type of person. And I'd say the third type of a person **thinks that he knows it**, and goes into the class just to fulfill the requirements of the state. They are not really "in class." They are just putting their time in.

These excerpts illustrate that some teachers in this school engaged in the process of knowledge transfer by co-planning and observing other colleagues' practices; however, this transfer did not seem to happen on a regular basis; for instance, to provide examples of such learning, Kristi referred to her learning practices in her former school. In addition, Debbie implied that not all the teachers in the building used these opportunities to learn.

Teachers' participation in formal research (both school-based and university-based)—the third "seed" of knowledge production in an organization—provides a pathway to knowledge conversion by offering opportunities for teachers to collaborate with other educators in constructing knowledge. This school, situated rather far from teacher training institutions, did not engage in supervising student teachers or any other systematic collaboration with universities; however, the teachers mentioned that they were working on developing a grade-level literacy curriculum for the district. This project provided them with opportunities to develop new ideas, pilot them in their classrooms, collect data, and report to the district about their findings.

The fourth seed of professional knowledge creation (Hargreaves, 1999)—effective use of middle managers who serve as "knowledge engineers"—provides a bridge from vision to its implementation. These middle managers serve as mentors for teachers in the process of knowledge creation. It seems that in US elementary schools, top managers (principals) and middle managers (head teachers) both play administrative roles in informing teachers and organizing their participation in professional development sessions. In this school, the head teacher (Kristi) clearly defined her role as an administrator:

> I'm a head teacher in this building. So when J. [the principal] is not here, **I have to be a principal** and that also means that **I plan all the assemblies for the building**. So, I joined the committee (Reading

> Month) knowing that part of March is also the assembly month, [to] let them know of what assemblies I have planned.

Kristi seemed to bring a lot from her administrative experiences to her teaching practice, specifically in classroom management:

> I think I **take a lot of THAT experience**, even though they are not children that are in my classroom. I can relate because **I had similar experiences with children in my own classroom**.

Head teachers seem to have specific responsibilities, most of which emerge when the principle is absent. School administrators usually do not lead professional development sessions, except for staff meetings; however, their role is crucial in creating appropriate conditions and providing support for teachers in the process of knowledge creation.

Though all components that Hargreaves (1999) suggests for evaluating vigor of knowledge production existed in this school, not everything went smoothly in the construction of the professional relationships. The majority of participating teachers expressed their regrets about some situations with their colleagues that did not contribute to collaborative knowledge creation. For example, Bob told me about his failed attempt of working in partnership with the neighboring teacher that resulted in closing the wall between the classrooms and having to deal with hurt feelings:

> And then when we **closed the wall**, it was like I being born. Even the resource teacher, who was friends with the other teacher, said, "When this wall was closed, he was like a new person." I think I became **more enthusiastic**. I went back to my old self, I think. I felt like a veil had been lifted off and **I wasn't under a spotlight**. And **I wasn't being critiqued** by another one, another teacher. And I think that helped a lot. So, then **I picked up**; then I became more enthusiastic about teaching. It went back to the way I used to run things.

Bob also experienced tension with colleagues because of his popularity among parents, which, peculiarly, made the job much more difficult for him:

> Well, the problem is that **I had a lot of requests for the next year**. Basically, my class was all filled up, and they still have to place some other kids. And **the [lower] grade teachers have difficult time** telling that. We are going to have 3 classes next year. **My class was filled with requests** and all these other kids just have to go between two other classes. So, **one of the other (...) grade teachers is really upset about that. And they've gone to the principal lately**. Their main concern is that there are not equitable heterogeneous groups (...). They think that I have all the high achievers, which I don't. I

still have resource room kids (…). Just, people around call and go just like, "What is going on?" They have an **issue with something ALL the time**. And they always find something. (…) **Or somebody is not talking to me**. It's just a lot of issues and I don't even want to think twice about it. Let it [blow over], and talk about something else. **That's what makes the job difficult**.

Debbie shared with me a different issue. Her feelings were hurt because she had offered help to a colleague who not only turned it down in a negative way but also talked about it behind her back:

D I have a questionnaire that I ask all the teachers to fill out. One teacher wrote **negative things**. **I took it personally**. But I learned a way to deal with the person. And I talked with other colleagues.

E Did you fix it somehow?

D I thought it was fixed. I was sitting in the chair lower than hers, in her study. She had a smile on her face when I left and thanked me. But **behind my back** (…). **I was motivated to help, but she did not want to change**. (…) I was trying to be only sensitive. But **she perceived it differently**. (…) Attitude affects everything.

Kristi also was not completely satisfied with the relationships in the building. She wished they were better and expressed hope that they would improve over time and that she would get to know her colleagues better:

> With the **staff, I would actually like that to be better**. I have a really good relationship with the three ladies I teach with, but in the building that I came from, I've been there eight years and have gotten to know everyone in the building really well. And in this building, [it] being a new building, (We've only been here for two years) **there are a lot of people that I don't know very well yet**.

In sum, this school team was actively involved in the construction of their professional relationships. New to the school, the teachers were in the process of looking for ways to build relationships with each other. In addition to being open to new experiences, they had expectations that were grounded in patterns of their previous experiences. They seemed to separate the social from the professional, thus missing the opportunities created by their colleagues and the principal to learn from each other informally. The administration seemed to support teachers' professional growth; however, neither the principal nor the head teacher initiated any professional development events, as if leaving it up to the teachers to take care of their learning needs. In response, the teachers engaged in formal and informal learning, depending on their individual motivation. The polyphonic voices of teachers in this school contributed to the school culture by "singing solo" rather than making a choir. In addition, the missing mission of the school indicated an absence of effort in creating a well-tuned team inspired by the same goals.

Notes

1 Here and further on in bold, I highlight phrases that are key to the meaning of the excerpt.
2 Specials in elementary schools are classes that are not taught by the classroom teacher such as Arts, Physical Education, and Music.

References

Hargreaves, D. H. (1999). The knowledge-creating school. *British Journal of Educational Studies, 47*(2), 122–144.

Huberman, M. (1992). Teacher development and instructional mastery. In A. Hagreaves & M. G. Fullan (Eds.), *Understanding teacher development.* London: Cassell.

Lampert, M. (2001). *Teaching problems and the problems of teaching.* New Haven, CT: Yale University Press.

Law, S. (1999). Leadership for learning; the changing culture of professional development in schools. *Journal of Educational Administration, 37*(1), 66–76.

Richardson, V. (2003). The Dilemmas of professional development. *Phi Delta Kappan, 85*(5), 401–411.

10 A Lithuanian School with Instruction in Russian Language

Overview of This Chapter

This chapter focuses on the school with Russian language of instruction in Lithuania. To stay consistent for comparative purposes, this chapter maintains the same sequence in re-constructing the school culture as the previous chapter. The school culture appears to be very different from the one in the Midwestern state: professional relationships in this school seem to be influenced by stressors from the outside (possibility of losing the job) and inside (pressure from the administration and parents). In order to keep all the teachers, the administration has to reduce teaching load, and thus, salaries. The polyphony of teachers' voices in this school seemed to be suppressed by the stance of the school's administration. The teachers try to conceal their uniqueness to fit the general tone and avoid standing out. Otherwise, they risk being negatively judged, which could result in losing their job. Thus, fiscal conditions, national educational policies, and administrative style in this school do not seem to create favorable opportunities for teachers' informal learning; however, the teachers seem to be highly motivated to use any opportunity for remaining in the profession and growing professionally.

> We are changing every four years.
>
> (Nadia)

About the School

For many years, this secondary co-education school has been considered one of the best in the city; however, this study took place at a particular time in the school's history when schools teaching in languages of national minorities were being closed every year, and this school was faced with proving its right to exist as a school serving national minorities (the Russian-speaking population of Lithuania). After Lithuania gained independence in 1991, many Russian-speaking families began enrolling their children in schools with Lithuanian language of instruction, so that they learned the state language academically (not colloquially) and integrated into the society that had passed strict laws about the knowledge and usage of Lithuanian language in public spheres.[1] Consequently, Russian schools started disappearing: each year, one or two were closed. Russian schools that managed to survive were under the additional pressure to propose something special that other schools did not offer. These circumstances continued for over a decade, and this school was not exempt from them. Teachers talked about insecurity and high competition for their jobs because teachers from the closed schools looked for jobs in remaining Russian schools.

Situated on a hill in an industrial part of a large Lithuanian city, this school attracted Russian-speaking students from all over the city because of its special curriculum (teaching English as a second language from the second grade), prestigious image, and high percentage of its graduates' acceptance to universities. In order to gain admittance to the school, children had to pass a test before applying for the first grade, and not everyone was necessarily admitted. Those who could read and displayed special academic abilities or whose parents were well known in certain social or political spheres had better chances of being accepted. Children, usually those of embassy personnel, from China, USA, Romania, Serbia, Ukraine, and other countries attend this school. Parents and the administration exerted a lot of pressure on teachers to meet the high expectations that parents had for this school.

The atmosphere of the school was influenced by its long and successful history. In 2016, the school celebrated its 70th anniversary. At the time of the data collection, a brief version of the school's history was located on the wall of the entrance hallway on the first floor and on the school's website. It highlighted major events, such as the school's foundation as an elementary school in 1946, right after the Second World War, and multiple changes of its status and name. The latest name change happened as part of the school reform during the years of regained national independence in 1999. This history of name changing reflected a bigger pattern of instability and social change that was typical for the region over the last 70 years.

Each principal headed the school for a long time and left a personal imprint on the school's culture. School alumni remained in touch and maintained an informal network, helping each other in life and in business, keeping friendships and even forming families. When reminiscing about their school years, they usually referred to a certain period, calling it by their principal's name.

The School's Mission, Goals, and Objectives Are Visible

On the wall near the entrance to the school, one could see a poster with the school's goals and objectives for the year. One objective was for the school to become the cultural "hearth" of the community. Alongside the traditional objective of improving the educational process, other objectives focused on culture: "Provide students with fundamental knowledge and a wide cultural worldview" and "Change the teachers' role: aim at teachers becoming consultants, advisors, assistants". A poster next to the goals listed the school's values: exhibiting high performance and developing, providing individual assistance, building direct connections with life, encouraging learning based on values and positive attitude toward work, and constructing partnerships between students, school, parents, and community.

The website highlighted the school's vision as "modern, open to change, grounded in humanistic and democratic values, employing new technologies, educational standards and methods". The website also included photos of the teachers and legendary principals from the 1950s, 1960s, and 1970s—a reminder of the "golden years", evoking sentiments for the time when the students' club "Gravity" encouraged expression of independent and creative thinking through writing poetry and songs, and staging performances. Nadia, a former member of the club, remembered that she learned how to organize big events from the leader of the club, who was her favorite teacher:

> **We organized huge events** (...) and **did everything ourselves**: scenery decorations, costumes, scenarios. Before the performance, we would stay up until two in the morning. The results were great! I was drawn to the school.

However, this club that once made the school unique, no longer existed to bring creativity and inspiration to everyday life of the students because the teacher who organized it left the school and the country. Instead, to compete with remaining schools that offered Russian as the language of instruction, the school focused on providing high academic quality and closely followed state requirements.

The Building Offers Few Places for Informal Learning

The 70-year-old, four-story school building was situated on the corner of two very busy industrial streets (one of the streets went from the airport all the way to downtown; the other one connected two huge big-box shopping centers). A security man dressed in black questioned every visitor. On my first day at the school, he attentively checked my camera bags and tripod. The next time, we exchanged friendly greetings and comments about the weather. Between class periods, he did not allow students outside the main entrance; however, after school, the students flooded the streets to walk or take a public bus home. Elementary students from this school were easily recognized in the streets of the city because of their school uniforms.

The hallways were usually empty and silent during class hours. Only janitors talked to each other by the teachers' lounge. When the bell rang announcing the end of the class period, the hallways were jam-packed with students and teachers trying to make their way to their next destinations. The school felt overpopulated, and Marija admitted that the school was overcrowded due to the educational policies in the country:

> **There are less and less children in the Russian schools**. Our **school is packed**.[2] That's why we don't have any spare classrooms. But our teachers don't have enough hours to keep full positions. That's a problem.

The participating teachers admitted that they had no time for interactions with other teachers. Nadia, for example, mentioned that they "exchanged a couple of words" when they took students to the yard during the "long break" (after two first periods there was a 20-minute break) or saw colleagues in the cafeteria:

> When we take kids **outside**, we can **exchange a couple of words** like, "What page are you on in Math?" On your own, you can fall behind. But in a bigger sense, **we don't have any time** [for interaction-] (...) **Interaction is scarce**. Sometimes we make a little circle and **talk in the cafeteria**. Our department meetings are every three months. If there is anything urgent, we stay after school.

Marija also emphasized the brevity of her interactions with colleagues in the building:

> My interactions with colleagues either from other schools or from this one are **momentary**—how do you deal with kids? What are you doing in your classroom now?

During specials, the teachers usually sat in the back of the class and checked students' workbooks. The teachers' lounge seemed to be more popular with middle and high school teachers. It was not the best place for interactions because there teachers prepared for their classes expecting it to be quiet. Elementary teachers rarely stopped by; they would come to check their schedule or make copies.

The school cafeteria seemed to be the place where teachers went to have a cup of tea and talk. Whenever I visited, my former secondary colleagues and I, along with a few elementary teachers, met there to talk. Our discussions often focused on the system of education in the United States, educational policies in Lithuania, and teachers' best practices. For example, Marija's comment about spending her time during specials (taught by other teachers) was consistent with what other teachers said:

> During specials, I usually **try to check workbooks**. Sometimes, **I go to the cafeteria** to have some tea and chat. (…) **I see the same teachers there** [Teachers from different grade levels had specials at the same time, and would come to the cafeteria to chat]. That is OK because many problems are similar among grades.

I did not notice teachers interacting anywhere else except for the cafeteria. Hallways seem to belong to administrators. In addition to janitors, they were the only people seen walking down the hallways during class time, stopping by some classrooms to talk with teachers or to make announcements. It seemed that it was not the architecture of the building, but the administration's stance that limited teachers' interactions.

The Classrooms Reflect Administration's Viewpoint

Elementary classrooms were all positioned on the first floor, on one side of a long hallway that stretched from the main entrance and the cafeteria past the offices of assistant principals, the teachers' lounge, and the central staircase leading to the second floor, and ended at small back stairs that led to the principal's office on the third floor. Each teacher taught the same cohort of students for 4 years in the same classroom. The classrooms that I visited (five out of eight) had a traditional (Soviet-type) setup: students' desks (usually made for two, often with chairs connected to the desk) were lined up in three rows facing a teacher's table, which was by the blackboard where most of the teaching usually happened. Four huge windows that faced one of the busy streets occupied the entire side of each classroom, and these windows filled the classroom with sunlight and street noise. Three remaining walls in the classrooms usually displayed little educational information, which had to be approved by the principal before finding its place on the wall. The Russian alphabet above the blackboard, a few mathematics or grammar posters on the sides, portraits of the famous Russian writers Tolstoy, Dostoyevsky, and Chekhov in the back, and a few flowers on the windowsills comprised a typical classroom decor. In some classrooms, educational posters were hand-made and looked worn out. No children's work, except for piles of workbooks on the windowsills and teachers' desks, was visible. The teachers explained that they could put up only something that was nicely framed and was aesthetically pleasing. The classrooms differed little from one another. It seemed that they had not changed much since the 1980s, when I worked in this school as a beginning teacher.

Organizational Arrangements Discourage Teachers' Collaborative Learning

Principals have always strongly influenced the learning culture of this school through a hierarchical administrative structure. Assistant principals who are responsible for elementary education, for academics in the higher grades, and for extracurricular activities, disseminated the principal's judgment of the school's progress and ideas for improvement to teachers for implementation. The teachers received instructions for what they had to correct rather than positive appraisal of their work. Teachers' self-assessments were never sought. For example, Nadia quoted their elementary department assistant principal: "Assistant principal would ask me, "*Why are your kids not reading to the standard?*".

The teachers felt bitter toward the way the administration disseminated information disregarding and depriving them of agency. Ana expressed her attitude toward staff meetings that took place during "the long break", which usually were called unexpectedly during teachers' preparation time to announce something unpleasant, and often not relevant to elementary teachers:

> Sometimes we have "5-minute" meetings. They could be **spontaneously** called. **They inform us** about what happened. For example, the high school students were caught taking cell phones from people on the streets. Often, we have such meetings before fall, winter or spring breaks. They are held during the long break. **Usually, there is nothing pleasant. Sometimes they involve the elementary department**, when we are expecting an audit.

The administration felt free to come into any classroom at any point to talk with a teacher (the school public announcement system was used only for special announcements by the principal or during the breaks between class periods). Such interruptions of teaching signified disrespect for teachers' work in this school. As the leader of the elementary department methods' committee and a member of the School Board, Marija experienced many distractions during her classroom time. She admitted, "Sometimes, the assistant principal comes in **right in the middle of a class**. (…) She knows that I am a responsible person, so she first tells me about an assignment [and expects me to disseminate that information to the other teachers]".

It seemed that the administration expected teachers to do what had to be done according *to them*, rather than providing flexibility and supporting teachers in creatively making choices and implementing their tasks. For instance, the teachers did not seem to be trusted with purchasing supplies that they needed for their classrooms ("Teachers don't get any money for supplies and books", Marija). Moreover, teachers were not encouraged to observe in their colleagues' classrooms or sign up for professional development seminars. If they chose to do so, they had to find a substitute teacher and often pay for the professional development themselves. Nadia commented on her limited opportunities for learning and lack of any choices:

> I am into a differential approach in grading students (...). However, my lessons still lack differentiation. **I wish I could observe** somebody or read literature. Sharing experience could help but **we don't have such a system. (...)** [I could go to professional development courses] only if there is an opportunity and I can **accidentally find a sub**, but **it is extremely difficult**. If only these seminars were after lunch... Sometimes, our administration invites somebody. But then, **we don't have any choice**.

Nevertheless, the teachers defined themselves as "fanatics", completely dedicated to their work and their students. That seemed to be the reason that they were still teaching in spite of little administrative support, lack of appreciation, and scarcity of equipment and supplies. In the focus group interview with the participating teachers, during which the teachers, eager to share their ideas, often interrupted each other, Nadia told a story of how she was very sick and still came to the event because her students took part in it:

N **We are fanatics**—go and work even when being sick.
A Yes, we put ourselves last so, that later...
N We were getting ready for the graduation party. I [was so sick that I] **crawled up** the stairs to the third floor and prepared everything—set up the curtain, attached everything to it, but **everything inside me was busting**. When I got home, I went to the medical center. My doctor looked at me—"you should go to the hospital". But I—**"No, I have the graduation party, I cannot go"**.

To conclude, organizational arrangements in this school discouraged teachers' collaborative learning. The hierarchical administrative structure seemed to be placing teachers at the bottom of the managerial triangle and assigning them the role of implementers of what the administration required them to do. Those instances when the elementary teachers had specials and did not teach seemed to be treated as preparation time, which they had to spend checking students' workbooks or getting ready for the next class. It did not seem that there was any comfortable place or time during school hours when they could share their experiences and learn from each other, however, fear of losing their jobs and their fanatical dedication to the profession inspired these teachers to grow professionally. Formal professional development being difficult to attain, the teachers found informal ways to exchange information and learn. In the next section, I describe how maintaining long-lasting school traditions provided opportunities for teachers to learn informally.

Traditions Provide Opportunities for Interactions

The school's website reflected that it valued its traditions. On the website, the long list of traditions was divided into three groups—State holidays and important dates (e.g., the Flag Day, A Citizen and the Constitution, the Independence Day celebration); the school's traditions (e.g., the Day of the Languages, the Teachers' Day, the School's Day, the Last Bell, Fashion and Music Show); and festivals by grade levels (e.g., in elementary grades, "The Colorful Leaf", "Santa's On the Way", "In the Fairytales' World"). By publicly listing the celebration of all the State holidays, the school seemed to be underscoring their patriotism and loyalty to the state as though trying to prove that they deserved to remain a part of the Lithuanian school system. By comparison, schools with Lithuanian language of instruction did not list celebrations of State holidays on their websites, though they did celebrate them (as I will note in the next chapter).

When I interviewed the teachers in this school, they were getting ready for the celebration of the Lithuanian flag. Elementary teachers were excited because they were responsible for a big part of the project and all were engaged. Nadia provided some details:

N The teachers of Lithuanian language took the flag, and we had projects dedicated to each color. "The yellow" is done already. Now, we have "the red" coming up, if we talk about traditions.

E Is there any time when you teachers get together?

N Of course, of course. **We all gather to do these projects**. Eventually, we all end up doing them together.

While Nadia noted that they do collaborate, the process of doing these projects did not seem to be well organized. Over a short period, the teachers had to devote all their available time to the project's implementation, including staying after school for hours. Marija explained the steps:

> The assistant principal reminds us. Usually, it is **at the last minute**. Then, we all jump up and do it.

Answering my question about the length of her workday, Nadia commented that implementing school projects in addition to her regular work took up the whole day, including even her dinner cooking time:

> Well, we can **discard only the time I sleep**. For example, now we have to prepare for the Red Day. We have to stage a play. That means, we have to write a script, make a phonogram and so on, but **we have**

> **only two hours per week of additional education**. So, **I am making pork chops and thinking**, "How could I make it work in this scene" (...) Last year, I was responsible for the Fat Tuesday celebration. So, I had to come up with the script and games for all the students of the grade level.

Marija also invested her personal time in organizing extracurricular activities: "Extracurricular activities provide me with opportunities. However, we are paid only two hours per week for that, but these activities usually take two hours per day".

Though the teachers worked additional hours when doing these projects, these instances might be one of a few opportunities for them to work together and share their ideas and experiences. They also mentioned another tradition as a way of learning from each other—at the beginning of the school, they exchanged lesson plans and resource books. They also got together to celebrate their colleagues' birthdays. Nadia admitted that even though they tried not to talk about work at these parties, they did anyway:

N We also **celebrate colleagues' birthdays**.
E Are you partying in the teachers' lounge?
N No, in the other room. We bring sandwiches, deserts. **Though we try not to talk about school, we always do**.

In sum, strong orientation to maintaining and developing school traditions provided the teachers with opportunities for interactions with each other. Preparation for traditional school events created occasions for informal learning; however, such interactions occurred in a stressful environment, when the teachers had to implement something conceived by the administration in a short timeframe, with limited resources, and under close supervision. In the next section, I analyze professional relationships as possible contexts for informal learning.

Professional Relationships Reflect the Stressful Atmosphere

Professional relationships, including tinkering, transfer of knowledge, research of practice, and facilitation by middle managers (Hargreaves, 1999), were different in the Russian school as compared to the Midwestern school in the United States. In an atmosphere in which the administration often publicly pointed out teachers' professional inadequacies but did not provide means for professional development, individual tinkering enabled the teachers to grow professionally. For example, Nadia picked up an interesting idea for making literacy projects with students while sitting in a Lithuanian language class checking her students' workbooks. She planned on trying it out. Marija told about her ways of finding out what works for drawing students' attention at the beginning of a lesson: "A couple of years ago, my children knew that if I was keeping silent, I wanted them silent too. But with this class, it does not work. I tried different ways (...) and found that clapping with them works the best".

The participating teachers in this school seemed to rely on beliefs and knowledge that developed through tinkering with their practice. For example, during my focus group interview with all three teachers together, Nadia referred to her belief that students benefited from doing homework. She was shocked when the assistant principal announced that there would be no homework assignments anymore. So, she tried to figure out how to maintain it without calling it homework.

Occasionally, the teachers made their individual tinkering public. For example, Marija talked about sharing her thoughts concerning "The Red Day" in the teachers' lounge. She seemed to appreciate an opportunity for bouncing ideas off the others:

> I approach each colleague in a different way. **We are very friendly among elementary teachers**. (...) After these holidays in January, I have been talking about "The Red Day," and there were teachers of English language in the room. One of them says, **"Why don't you** make a show "The Red Riding Hood?" **Great idea!**

Transfer of knowledge seemed to be happening on rare occasions, when the teachers had an opportunity to exchange information; however, Ana saw opportunities for interactions depending on personal rather than organizational factors. She brought up the issue of trust and pointed out that the degree of her openness depended on her colleagues:

> It is **important to interact with colleagues**, but not everyone is open. I do interact with colleagues but **it depends on a specific person**. (...) I am such a[sharing] person—whatever I learn new and interesting, **I would definitely share**. Maybe I don't always see an adequate response. Maybe a person is not interested in that theme. But **everything depends on my colleagues**. I know whom I can come up to and share. For example, I can always share with Marija. **It all depends on a person because people share their lived experiences, their mistakes**.

In this school, teachers did not participate in any research projects except for an internal audit that they were going through at the time of the study. The audit did not seem to provide them with tools and time for reflection and experimentation with their practice; rather it focused on evaluation of their performance.

The assistant principal for the elementary department and the leader of the elementary methods committee (Marija) were the middle managers, and played the role of "knowledge engineers" in this school. Three times a year, they led methods committee sessions where teachers made formal presentations about their best practices; however, the teachers did not express excitement about these sessions (they hardly ever mentioned these meetings). Instead, they seemed to view them as a requirement that did not relate to their everyday practice. Both of the middle managers also organized traditional calendar events (e.g., the Flag Day, festivals of the grade levels). The assistant principal "reminded" teachers of an approaching event, while Marija, the head of the committee, organized or, more often, did all the work ("I am not a leader. It is easier for me to do it myself than run around asking others"). In addition, the assistant principal observed lessons and debriefed the teachers. The teachers never mentioned anything about these observations and communication with the assistant principal. Over the last few years, the assistant principal for elementary education's responsibilities and time allocation have been cut down. The last time I interviewed teachers and looked forward to interviewing the assistant principal, I learned that her position had been eliminated.

In sum, professional relationships in the Russian-speaking school seem to be influenced by stressors from the outside (possibility of losing the job) and inside (pressure from the administration and parents). In order to keep all the teachers, the administration reduced teaching load, and thus, salaries. Nadia, for example, had a conflict with one of her colleagues because she asked for Music classes to add to her decreasing teaching load ("I am trying to be tolerant with everyone. However, I have a problem because of the Music classes. I have taken two hours of Music because my teaching load was too small"). The polyphony of teachers' voices in this school seemed to be suppressed by the stance of the school's administration. The teachers tried to conceal their uniqueness to fit the general tone and avoid standing out. Otherwise, they risked being negatively judged, which might lead to losing their job. To conclude, fiscal conditions, national educational policies, and administrative style in this school did not seem favorable for teachers' informal learning; however, the teachers seemed to be highly motivated to use any opportunity for remaining in the profession and growing professionally.

Notes

1 According to linguists and politicians of independent Lithuania, the Soviet bilingual (Russian and Lithuanian) policies damaged one of the oldest live languages (Lithuanian). As a defensive nationalistic reaction to Russian chauvinism—expressed, in this case, in the Soviet language policies—the Republic of Lithuania Law of the State Language (I-779, January 31, 1995) came into power. It states that to obtain or retain positions in public sphere, people whose native language is other than Lithuanian (the law is aimed at the Russian-speaking population), must pass a language exam to show linguistic

proficiency at a certain level. For more information, see http://www.minelres.lv/NationalLegislation/Lithuania/Lithuania_Language_1995_English.htm.

2 About 1,000 students in the building constructed to accommodate 600 students.

Reference

Hargreaves, D. H. (1999). The knowledge-creating school. *British Journal of Educational Studies, 47*(2), 122–144.

11 A Lithuanian School with Instruction in Lithuanian Language

Overview of This Chapter

This last chapter in Part III focuses on the school with Lithuanian language of instruction. To continue the discussion of school culture, the same sequence as in the previous chapters is used. This school features the unique culture that aspires for high professional standards and provides opportunities for learning and professional growth as well as collegial support, but does not tolerate lack of dedication and motivation for improvement. This culture displays the characteristic features of the family model of an organization in which the way of working is casual, flexible, and warm (multiple times, the teachers call the school their family, their home). The teachers care for one another, as illustrated by the ritual of sharing food and drinks at parties, sense of humor and camaraderie, and reassuring expressions of their commitment to their students. It also demonstrates attributes of the culture of collaboration (valuing individuals, interdependence, openness, and trust). The teachers in this culture expect each other to develop and to help their colleagues develop. The polyphonic voices of teachers in this school join in accord to create a unique performance in which every voice is heard and highly valued by the administration and the community. These cultural contexts empower the teachers to make many decisions including what, when, and how they are going to learn. The final part of this chapter offers conclusions in the form of a comparative analysis of the three school cases.

> Here, everything depends upon me.
>
> (Sigute)

About the School

The school was established as a combined effort of the City University and the City Department of Education to serve as a laboratory school for teacher preparation and experimentation with new methods. Initially, the school shared a building with a preschool in a middle-class district of a large Lithuanian city. Soon, this school was considered one of the best in the city. Because of its popularity and rapid increase in student numbers, the school team had to look for a bigger building. In 2002, after a Russian secondary school had been closed down, the school moved into that building—a standard school building that now served over 1,000 students ages 6–18, situated three blocks away from the Russian school. Students came from all over the city, and were accepted mainly based on their academic abilities (high academic potential), but it was also common for children from the families of famous people to attend. One of the features that attracted parents was an alternative curriculum that included a child-centered approach, English instruction starting from the second grade, and Drama instruction throughout the elementary years. Moreover, the students' high academic achievement on the city and state tests across all the grades was also a factor in its popularity. Consequently, the teachers constantly experienced pressure from parents to meet their high expectations.

Educational Priorities Clarify the Mission

The school's website was very business-like. It included schedules, lists of teachers and administrators, and so forth. Unlike the Russian-speaking school, it did not refer to history or traditions that were celebrated and observed. A list of three educational priorities appeared first on the site home page. The priorities followed from the statement: "The educational content and methods are defined by the changing needs of the modern society". These priorities were bulleted in the following order:

- Strong knowledge of foreign languages (beginning level of English from the second grade, advanced level from the fifth grade, and the second foreign language—Danish, German or Russian starting in the sixth grade);
- computer literacy; profiled education (the option of choosing the specialization);
- development of social skills (participation in international projects, collaboration with the University, and teaching Economics).

The school's mission was not spelled out explicitly, and these educational priorities seemed to take its place in explaining the direction for the school's development. Important state and district documents were also part of the school's website such as the latest educational laws, district goals, and Board decisions. In addition, the school took pride in their agreement with the City University that allowed it to work with student teachers and invited the school teachers to teach at the University. This form of collaboration sent the message that the school was interested in and open to innovation. At the time of the study, eight teachers worked hourly as university lecturers, sharing their expertise with student teachers, bringing novel ideas to implement in their classrooms, and sharing them with their colleagues at the school.

The Building Reflects the Students' and Teachers' Feeling of Ownership

The four-story building was built in the 1970s on the slope of one of the picturesque hills that surround the downtown area (the medieval part) of the city. All elementary classrooms were situated on the third floor, taking up the entire floor and sharing it only with the principal's and assistant principals' offices, the teachers' lounge, the library, and the technology center. Because of the school's popularity in the city, the building was overpopulated. According to the next stage of national school reform, the school was going to be divided into the basic school that would incorporate elementary and middle levels, and the high school. The elementary teachers expressed concerns about the possibility of being split. For example, Sigute voiced these worries, emphasizing that elementary teachers comprised a tightly knit team:

> We are **worried** about the school's destiny: it is going to be split in two. There are eighty teachers in the schools, and only twelve elementary teachers. **We would like to keep our team**. (…) We are going to have more than enough students. **During the first three days** [of the enrollment], **more students than we can accept have signed up already**. (…) **We are like a separate team—all together**.

Eventually, the City Department of Education decided that in 2007 the school would be physically reorganized into two: the elementary and middle school departments would stay in this building, while the high school would move out. The elementary teachers seemed to be pleased with this decision as they were to stay together as one team.

The building seemed to be full of life. The entrance hall, the staircases and the hallways were decorated with students' artwork and projects representing different events (e.g., field trips, sports competitions). On the third floor, one wall always hosted different art projects created by elementary students, and decorating this wall seemed to encourage interactions between teachers. Sigute, for example, commented on the way they collectively came up with ideas for these exhibits:

> In these exhibitions, for instance, now, we have "Trees." **I would not even say whose idea it is: one word from one teacher, another from the other one**—and we have it.

Everything in the school seemed to say, "It belongs to us all". Students, parents, and teachers felt at home there. In the interviews, the teachers explicitly talked about school being their home. Daina, for example, explained why she felt at home there:

> **The school for me is home**. (…) All, because, you know, I am dreaming [here]. I am not rushing out of here; I stay longer. It feels so good here (…) because here are many things: **what we make with children, and what I brought from home. Here, I feel at home**.

In addition, the teachers talked about their school with pride and affection. Similar to Daina, Ramute expressed her warm feelings about the school, calling it her "second home". She also hypothesized an important reason for the school's appeal to children, parents, and teachers—its authenticity:

> **School for me is the second home. I feel very well here**. We have our own classroom, and **we create our homes**. (…) **Our school is very stylish. And you can feel that it is not a put on show, but authentic**. (…) The majority of kids come from all over the city. That means that parents bring their children here **for some reason**. Another thing that we differ in is that we try to **make kids feel free here**, that they feel as though they are in a second home. We have a young team. That has an influence. **Our school is good, very good!**

Overall, the building reflected the students' and the teachers' feelings of belonging and ownership, which was visible in the interior decoration and noticeable in the teachers' reports of relations between all the members of the school community. Produced by students, teachers, and parents (I found out about parents' participation from talking with some of them), the physical environment reflected affection toward the school that the community expressed through creative collaborative projects.

The Classrooms Reflect Creativity and Experimentation

Each teacher in the school had her own classroom and taught the same cohort of students for 4 years in it. (This is the standard number of years of elementary education in Lithuania.) The classrooms reflected the teachers' involvement in different international projects (e.g., *Step by Step*, *Critical Thinking*, *Junior Achievement*, *The Project Method*). As participants of the projects, the teachers received training that was usually conducted by combined US-Lithuanian teams of trainers and included participants from the whole country. These experiences provided unique learning opportunities through interactive participation and sharing with colleagues from other schools and cities.

The set-up of spaces—desks put together for students' small-group activities—represented the child-centered approach that the team adopted from participating in one of the international projects. The teachers often changed the layout of the desks in their classrooms. Every classroom looked different from the others because it reflected the students' current work and the teachers' creativity. The assistant principal explained the reason for the classrooms looking so different by characterizing all the elementary teachers as being "extremely creative, young, and very knowledgeable about different teaching methods":

AP [They] are **able to demonstrate multiple methods during a lesson**, though they (...) also **know how and when [best] to use them**—what would be **the outcome when they use** [one or another]. (...) They don't just say, "Well, I know a lot of different methods and can use them whenever I want." Having experienced those methods in elementary school, children feel more confident. [They] have better social skills after following those methods, like the Project Method.

E How do you all know these methods? Why don't other schools [know them]?

AP Maybe because single teachers go to other schools. **But one soldier cannot win a battle. All twelve of ours go!** And then, **they all implement it**. And then having coffee together, they [talk], "I do it this way. But how about this and that? (...) How did you do that? May be you have materials [about it]?" **They share everything**; they hide nothing from each other because they are equally valuable.

Viktorija exemplified the assistant principal's statement: she demonstrated flexibility and awareness of different approaches when she talked about planning. She drew upon different resources depending on the subject matter, type of a lesson, and the children's interests as well as her own:

> It takes about 10–15 minutes to **think through the sequence** in order to prepare for Physical Education lessons. But if **I apply Critical Thinking** [method], I need to come up with tasks that would be attractive to the kids.

While every grade level followed the state curriculum and used state-approved textbooks for every subject, the teachers approached their lesson planning creatively and used innovative pedagogy such as small group activities, discussions, a project approach, peer assessment, to mention a few. Though they often included ideas that they learned in the seminars or from observing their colleagues, the classrooms reflected their own and their students' work. To further explore relationships between individual creativity and collectivity, in the following section, I analyze how organizational arrangements created contexts for the teachers to contribute their creativity in making collective decisions.

Organizational Arrangements Provide Teachers with Decision-Making Power

The administration of the school continued to maintain the spirit that was introduced by the first principal of the school. The current assistant principal for elementary education recollected how that the principal created the atmosphere of mutual respect, trust, and collegiality:

> Apparently, **that came from the principal**, because he behaved that way himself. He allowed kids to visit with him, call him by his first name, and share their problems. **The teachers picked that up**. And **that transferred to children**. And **he also introduced a nice tradition** of morning coffee. Teachers in our school **are never late** to their classes because they need to come and discuss events of the day with their colleague over a cup of coffee. **Our teachers liked it very much**. And the teachers themselves tried to come up with some nice surprises, and the principal, and the administration also did their best—someone would draw a funny face and write a caption in the teachers' lounge; another time bathroom scales would appear with a funny note. **Everyone would applaud and cheer!**

The new principal supported and further promoted this approach. The atmosphere of collegiality permeated all the relationships at the time of the study. Everyone contributed to the school organization. The principal seemed to have specific responsibilities that were well known to everyone in the building. For example, as Ramute reported, the principal provided necessary information and support for teachers to pursue their professional development:

> **We can go to any courses**, just find a sub and go. If the majority of teachers would like to hear about a certain topic, **our principal will make a workshop here**.

In another interview, Ramute commented on the principal's helpful and respectful way of informing teachers:

> We need to be thankful to our principal because **she knows how to get information to us quickly**. It is not anything fancy, just an email or a sheet of paper attached to the door.

Similarly, the assistant principal considered herself a coordinator and a colleague rather than a boss:

> **I don't feel that I am a boss**. And I don't think that the teachers who have their certificates could do anything wrong. I can see how they work, how they show their initiative. So, **I cannot imagine feeling smarter or superior in any way. We are just colleagues** and that's it.

I noticed that the teachers' team made many decisions on their own, which was the opposite from the Russian school a few blocks away. Thus, I wanted to verify my observation with Sigute. She confirmed my interpretation:

E Your team makes a lot of **decisions without administration**.
S Yes, yes. And often it happens that **we only inform our administration afterwards** that we decided so and so, if it is not any fundamental thing.

The teachers chose their own ways of professional learning and growth. For example, Sigute expressed dissatisfaction with professional development workshops and explained why this year the teachers signed up for fewer workshops:

> You go there expecting to get some new information, new ideas, new thoughts, patch some of your breaches, **but you don't get it. Or you get a minimum**, which you could get by just interacting [with colleagues, E.J.-OK]. So, we came to the conclusion that we are transitioning to that **informal communication**. (…) The principal always informs us about opportunities to participate in different projects and competitions. We also **observe** a couple of open **lessons**—there, you **always gain** something. (…) **Our team always has innovative ideas**.

Ramute, the leader of the elementary department Methods' Committee, played a coordinating role. She admitted that their schedule was so tight that they needed to use any spare minute to discuss ideas or problems that they encountered. Therefore, she seemed to prefer informal interactions with her colleagues that provided flexibility for scheduling such discussions:

> **We talk in hallways, during breaks**, though you can hardly feel the breaks because you are always in the classrooms. Now that the weather is better, **we go outside**. (…) During breaks, there is not much time, but if it is necessary, **I run around and say, "After the third period meet in my room**." Usually, **twenty minutes is enough** [to discuss an idea].

Different from both the American and the Russian schools, where teachers either had plenty of time scheduled for their interactions (the American school) or needed to use their personal time after school (the Russian school), these teachers found time to coordinate their ideas and actions in a way that was satisfying for their professional growth and enjoyable on the personal level as well.

In sum, in this Lithuanian school, the teachers felt empowered to do their job the best way possible by contributing their own creativity to collaborate. The organizational arrangements allowed them to make their own decisions about the means of achieving high quality in teaching. They chose what, where and how to learn, while the administration provided necessary support. In addition, they openly shared knowledge and materials, creating rich contexts for informal learning.

Traditions Bring the Teachers Together

Since the very first years of its existence, the school carefully created and maintained its traditions. The team of elementary teachers who started the school in 1993, in addition to all-school annual events, developed such staff traditions like coffee time before classes, holidays parties together (for Teachers' Day, New Year, End of the School Year, and teachers' birthdays). Each year, they came up with a theme and created costumes for these celebrations as if playing with their professional identities and trying on different variations. For example, one year for Teachers' Day, they dressed up as spies (sunglasses, wigs and dark pantsuits). At first, their students were puzzled because they had difficulty recognizing them, but the teachers told me that everyone had a lot of fun. Another year, for the End of the School Year celebration, teachers decided to dress in white. I asked the assistant principal why:

> I don't know why they do that. **They just like it**. [As if they say], **"We are elementary teachers; we have to be a little bit like kids ourselves; we have to be playful."** So, they like it. This time, they came up with an idea of wearing colorful socks. Last year, they had a white touch, and all dressed in white. And for the parents it is somehow [visible] that **in this school, something is always different than in others**. During the ceremony, they are invited up on stage [usually, these ceremonies take place in one of the city's theaters, E.J.-OK], the school buys them presents; **the principal shakes their hands and thanks them**.

The assistant principal explained that they wanted to be different—to be playful and original. It seemed that the teachers responded to the principal's praise of their work by being creative and showing that they were a team in accord. One year, they invited me to their New

Year party. Again, they were wearing costumes (an Eastern theme), and enjoyed talking about how they came up with the design and where they found details for their outfits. These examples showed that they enjoyed each other's company and liked to spend time together, and the positive atmosphere of these informal interactions carried over to professional relationships. In the following section, I analyze how professional relationships created cultural frames for informal learning, and how this close-knit teaching team displayed intolerance for teaching that did not match their distinct values.

Professional Relationships Provide Support and Freedom for Creativity

On many occasions, the teachers expressed satisfaction and enjoyment with their professional relationships. They seemed to be engaged in extensive learning from each other and collaborative knowledge creation. The drive for learning that motivated them to experiment in their classrooms (tinkering), borrow ideas from each other (transfer of knowledge), instruct student-teachers, and teach at the University was about to take them out into the "international waters" (**"Our school is different from others—we are interested in non-traditional methods**. I think we need to sail into **the international waters** now. **(…) Today after classes, we'll come together and discuss Socrates project** (Ramute).

The teachers had a special way of interacting that allowed them to know what each of them was doing in their classroom and to adopt colleagues' ideas in their own classrooms. Sigute compared these relationships to a family where everyone shared with others:

> I am feeling here **very well**. We are **like one family** (…). We are sharing everything. (…) Our **relationships with colleagues are very open**.

Ramute also provided a specific example of such sharing when she talked about what she had learned from observing in her colleague's classroom and how she was going to use another colleague's ideas that motivated students to read in summer:

> **We exchange more ideas** for Arts classes and about lessons in general, for example, about small groups' activities. Once, **I went to Grazina's** [I use pseudonyms to protect teachers' identities] **classroom**. She was working in small groups with her kids. I saw that she's got a sheet of paper on each table. She said that they are writing words and putting each letter in a separate box on the table. Later, in Math they were going to count and diagram how many of which letters there were.

> (…) Then, about reading: because we encourage our children to read as much as possible, **I have ideas for the next year already**. Again, **Aldona told me what her kids liked**. We encourage all the kids to read in summer. They have to read that many books. So, her kids made grand presentations of books that they have read. It could be a poster or a play if several of the kids read it. I will assign the same book to groups that live close to each other. **That book presentation is very effective**.

These teachers seemed to have social rituals for sharing, for asking for advice, for passing on new information. Ramute described a casual and quick way of receiving advice from others:

> Here **you can always run up to anyone for any advice**. Of course we talk in the evenings too. And these "run-ups" happen **before the classes, during the classes and after school**.

Because of the way the teachers interacted—openly and respectfully sharing their best practices and dilemmas—they felt confident and happy in their work environment. Ramute ascribed their trustworthy professional relationships to their intensive communication and being genuine with colleagues:

> **We talk among ourselves a lot**. That's why we may not have any ugly moments in communication. **If you don't like something, you just say so directly**. There have no behind-the-back talks (…) and **everyone feels good**.

In addition, Viktorija hinted at how that usually happened—talking a lot with her colleagues over the "coffee breaks": "Often, **we have coffee and chat** with each other. Recently, Ramute **stopped by to have a cup of coffee** and saw application forms" [and they all discussed how to apply to a new project, E.J.-OK].

In contrast to the American teachers, these interactions seemed to create an atmosphere in which everyone felt free to admit that they had dilemmas or questions. For example, Ramute described the way she felt about sharing her dilemmas—confident that she would get help if needed:

> Among elementary teachers—whatever you ask, **you'll get an answer**. If [a colleague] does not know, she will tell you, "Go there to X., she tried doing it." (…) **I feel very solid at work because I am not alone. I realized that earlier but now it is confirmed. We are a team of "bendraminciai"** [translates from Lithuanian roughly as colleagues who share the same philosophy, E.J.-OK]. **I am very happy that our team is like this**.

While reflecting on their professional relationships, teachers in the Lithuanian school defined their relationships to the profession, similar to their Russian counterparts; however, in comparison to the teachers from the Russian school, who talked about their fanaticism, these teachers defined their devotion to the profession differently—as coming from their nation's traditions investing their soul in everything they undertake. Sigute reflected:

> If we look at the colleagues from other countries—a teacher finishes the job and can forget about it. **It would not be like this here**. We are not likely to put out elders in nursing homes, **because we care**. The same with our work—**we invest all our soul in it**.

Their close ties to their profession were reflected in the way the teachers in this school constructed their school culture. Two out of the four teachers I interviewed, said that the school was their lifestyle and their home:

> Viktorija: **School for me is the second home** (…) It is life. (…) **It is my way of life**.

And,

> Sigute: I am the teacher who **is happy at work**. Why? **Because I feel that I belong here**. I like both the work and the results—when a kid did not know much, and now he is moving ahead. (…) **Here everything depends upon me**. (…) **School for me is my way of life because all my life is saturated with it**.

However, this distinctive school culture that celebrated long-lasting traditions, rituals of interactions and information transfer, the atmosphere of openness and trust within the community of learners was challenged when a new substitute teacher joined their team. Sigute told the story:

> We have a colleague this year. She is subbing. So, **she has problems with classroom management**. Other **teachers complain** that it is impossible to work because of the noise coming from her room. There were **different opinions about what could be done**. (…) Several colleagues went to **observe her lessons**, and the school psychologist went and **gave her advice in writing**. **Everything was friendly**. It's understandable that to get a graduating class for a new person is not easy. On the other hand, **we became a little bit upset** when **she did not take into consideration** any advice but only complained that it was impossible to get that class to work. She does not fit with our team. **We are good to each other, but when there is a problem, we say, "Why don't you do this or that."** Then you see that the person is trying. But **here—nothing happened**.

Apparently, the teacher did not suit the team's way of working. They told the administration about the problem. After multiple attempts to help her improve, the teachers invited her to a meeting and told her that she might think about leaving because her work quality did not correspond to the team's idea of quality teaching. Then, they informed the administration that she would be leaving, which was accepted.

This episode confirmed the existence of the unique school culture that aspired for high professional standards and provided opportunities for learning and professional growth as well as collegial support, but did not tolerate lack of dedication and motivation for improvement. This culture displayed the characteristic features of the family model of an organization in which the way of working was casual, flexible, and warm (multiple times, the teachers call the school their family, their home). The teachers cared for one another, as illustrated by the ritual of sharing food and drink at parties, sense of humor and camaraderie, and reassuring expressions of their commitment to their students. The school demonstrated attributes of the culture of collaboration (valuing individuals, interdependence, openness, and trust). The teachers in this culture expected each other to develop and to help their colleagues develop. The polyphonic voices of teachers in this school joined in accord to create a unique performance in which every voice was heard, and which was highly valued by the administration and the community. These cultural contexts empowered the teachers to make many decisions including what, when, and how they were going to learn.

Conclusions

In this part, I argue that in the dynamics of reform, schools find their focus in developing their educational policy and strategies, especially when the call for change requires them to perform more "effectively" (e.g., Taylor et al., 2000). Consequently, teachers are expected to develop professionally to meet new reform requirements and societal expectations.

To do so, teachers are expected to engage in formal professional development; however, I argue that research on teachers' formal in-service experiences has shown that their impact on teachers' practice is limited. At the same time, researchers maintain that the most powerful forms of teacher development are nurtured most directly and effectively inside the school (Leithwood et al., 1999). These findings call for a major reappraisal of school-based professional learning systems to bring into focus informal learning opportunities that are available for teachers at their workplace.

For this reason, this part focused on the examination of contexts in schools "that enable teachers to learn throughout their careers" (Eisner, 2000, p. 349) and ways teachers engage with these contexts in the process of professional learning. The leading proposition of the study that professional knowledge develops not only in the mind of the individual but is also cultural and intrinsic to the contexts within which the individual interacts, steer this inquiry of teacher learning toward examination of school cultures as contexts for learning.

Thus, in this part, I defined culture as a social phenomenon constructed through interactions between the members and the operational contexts of an organization. It is reflected in common knowledge of the members, who develop, share and use it to interpret the world within and outside an organization and generate social behaviors manifested through values, attitudes and different kinds of knowledge (Anderson-Levitt, 2002). This perception of culture led to an exploration of how specific characteristics of school cultures (school mission, traditions, physical environment, organizational arrangements, and professional relationships) foster opportunities for teachers' workplace learning, and how teachers in three schools relate to these cultures as learners.

The following summary of the three schools' cultures and the teachers' relationships with and within these cultures demonstrates that each school has a distinctive and different learning culture deeply intertwined with the school's and the country's historic and cultural development.

The Schools Revisited: A Comparative Analysis

The discussion of learning opportunities within the three school cultures (Lithuanian, Russian in Lithuania, and suburban American) demonstrated striking differences embedded in the institutional cultures. These cultural differences afforded teachers dissimilar opportunities for informal learning and professional growth. The fairly new American Midwestern suburban school was located in one of the fastest growing communities in the nation. Farmland, once supporting a rural, blue-collar population, has been developed into white-collar bedroom community subdivisions. Parental expectations for a good school to prepare their children to go on to 4-year universities were high. The Russian school, having had a long history as a privileged and highly regarded school, was in an uncertain turbulent situation at the time of the study, fighting for its survival as a school serving Russian-speaking national minorities in Lithuania that regained its independence from the Soviet Union and became part of the European Union. The Lithuanian school, though implementing almost the same curriculum as the neighboring Russian school, was an innovative school that was famous for its ground-breaking approaches to teaching, highly trained teachers, and warm collegial relationships within the school community.

No direct causal relationships between school culture and teacher learning are implied in this study. Identified dissimilarities between the schools' socio-cultural trajectories and their opportunities for informal professional learning are accounted for by unique differences in national, institutional, and individual histories and social developments. Each school's institutional organization, social cultures, and opportunities that teachers identified for learning should be regarded in the context of the unique developmental histories and present socio-economic and socio-political conditions in which they operated.

The School Mission Revisited

The different approaches to formulating and publicizing their school missions seemed to send clear messages about these schools' priorities and directions for development. The socially safe and confident stance of the American and Lithuanian schools was reflected in their website in that they appeared to find it unnecessary to include a mission statement there. The American school reported student academic achievement results as if responding to the current test-driven educational policies, implying they were in tune with current demands for improving student academic achievement. The Lithuanian school "translated" its mission into specific goals, which included both academic and social targets tied to the current needs of the society, sending a message to the community and parents about responding to the needs of the current societal development.

By contrast, the Russian school, by posting its mission on the web and replicating it in the main hallway, and by highlighting Lithuanian State holidays, seemed to claim its loyalty to Lithuania and its lawful place in the Lithuanian educational community. National educational policies seemed to put this school in a defensive position. Its concern for a steep decline in social status from one of the best schools in the city to an "unnecessary" institution with an uncertain future was evident in ways the school publicly presented itself. The three schools' differing approaches to highlighting (or not) their mission statements corresponded to each countries' different histories. The American socio-political situation appears relatively stable when juxtaposed with the upheaval in Lithuania's political and social landscape and the resulting shift in social stature for the Russian-speaking population in Lithuania.

In the following sections, I argue that the learning climate of these three organizations appeared to be consistent with the difference in historic and cultural developments. In the next section, I compare school traditions that reflect histories (national, institutional, and individual) in cultural representations of customs and beliefs shared by school professional communities.

Traditions Revisited

School traditions play a special role in creating informal learning environments.

They reflect the ways in which school communities shape and re-shape their shared beliefs and engage in informal professional learning over time. Communalism, which was cultivated in Lithuania during the fifty years of the Soviet regime, reflected in ways teachers engaged in traditional events.

Both the Lithuanian and the Russian schools cherished their old traditions (e.g., coffee time, the Teachers' Day celebration in the Lithuanian school and celebration of the state holidays in the Russian school); however, the Russian school seemed to express nostalgic feelings toward its history (as evidenced on its website), which went back to its "golden years" during the Soviet times when the school was highly regarded by educational authorities, students, and parents. At the same time, forced to fight for survival, the school focused on fulfilling state requirements by creating all-school events (e.g., celebrating the colors of the Lithuanian flag) and starting new traditions, which provided new contexts for teachers' interactions and learning. Meanwhile, fearing for their jobs, the Russian teachers who were overworked, over-controlled, and often distracted, tried to use any opportunity (e.g., celebrations of birthdays) for informal learning.

On the contrary, the Lithuanian teachers seemed to display a communal approach in observing school traditions. They did not separate all-school traditions (e.g., end-of-the-school-year celebration) and their team's social customs (e.g., coffee time)—the teachers recognized creative exchanges of ideas as opportunities for playfulness and good humor as they participated both in professional and social events that they used for developing, professionally replacing traditional PD with these informal learning occasions. Even though Russian teachers' all-school traditions were imposed and the Lithuanian school's were not, the events in both schools fostered teachers' creativity and encouraged informal interactions.

Conversely, the American school, which was operating only for a few years, was experimenting with different traditions that were mainly targeted at enhancing students achievement (e.g., the Reading Month). Teachers, fairly new to each other, whose individual values and interests guided their engagement in school events, seemed to separate the social from the professional, probably because they were still in the early stages of developing a professional school culture. As a result, they did not recognize social events as opportunities for their professional growth—they reported avoiding professional conversations during such events. Still, they looked forward to visiting other classrooms to observe what their colleagues were doing (e.g., during *Morning Minglers*). It seems that social traditions, breaking away from professional individualism, provided them with occasions to visit other classrooms in the school, which was rarely possible otherwise.

These different ways that the teachers related to their schools' traditions (created, initiated, participated, worked overtime to prepare, avoided, or withdrew) either created informal learning opportunities or discouraged them. In Lithuania, teachers' strong orientation to maintaining and developing school traditions provided teachers with opportunities for interactions with each other. By contrast, American teachers had yet to build a social professional community that moved them beyond individual views of learning opportunities. Preparation for traditional school events created occasions for informal learning in all participating schools; however, such interactions occurred in different atmospheres—stressful in the Russian school, appreciative, collegial, and creative in the Lithuanian school, and highly individualized and laid-back in the American school.

In sum, traditions provided occasions for informal professional learning through social events in all the schools; however, teachers related differently to school traditions. To expand informal learning opportunities, teachers could make use of these social events and develop collegial relationships that could create and sustain professional learning opportunities by viewing social events as contexts for informal learning. Remarkably, the Russian school culture demonstrated how even constricted opportunities for informal learning could not stop the teachers from learning informally to become even better teachers.

Physical Environment Revisited

Buildings and classrooms were designed and used differently in each of the three schools. The Lithuanian and the Russian schools occupied traditional four-story school buildings, which accommodated students from the first to the twelfth grades. In both schools, elementary classrooms were situated on one floor, allowing teachers to stop by their colleagues' classrooms and even have a cup of coffee together during recess (the Lithuanian school). On the contrary, in the newly built wing-shaped American elementary school, classrooms occupied two floors. According to the teachers' comments (in the American school), such structure created difficulties for communication with colleagues. In addition, a traditional view of classrooms as unique personal spaces did not seem to encourage colleagues to visit each other informally.

Classroom spaces seemed to play different roles in these three schools. In the American school, teachers decorated their classrooms in ways that expressed their personalities. They enjoyed full administrative support in providing them with necessary equipment and supplies. The teachers talked about their classrooms with pride and as being close to their ideal workspaces. They seemed to place value on creating spaces that reflected their unique identities, but in contrast, business-like common spaces in the American school (e.g., hallways, offices, the teachers' lounge, and reception) seemed to lack a special touch and felt unfit for learning. This contrast between classrooms and other spaces reduced teachers' informal learning environments to their own and, possibly, their closest neighbors' classrooms, though some teachers still used the whole school environment to interact with colleagues and learn.

For different reasons, the Russian school's classrooms also seemed to be the most important spaces for the teachers—their "shelters" from direct administrative supervision. The schoolyard and the cafeteria appeared to be the only other places where they could interact, at least briefly, while overseeing students during recess. Based on the data collected, the administration was not supportive of teachers' informal interactions and provided neither opportunities nor spaces for informal learning.

On the contrary, the Lithuanian school did not seem to have strict borders between classroom learning spaces and other school areas—all spaces seemed to reflect students' and teachers' creativity and initiative. The teachers seemed to feel free and welcome to visit other classrooms, stop by and talk in the hallways or discuss new ideas in the workroom and the teachers' lounge. The teachers were proud of their classrooms—they represented the realization of their imagination and resourcefulness and, as such, were intriguing for colleagues to visit. Thus, some physical environments, for one reason or another, seemed to restrict informal learning opportunities while others were more likely to expand learning spaces and encourage informal interactions between teachers.

Organizational Arrangements Revisited

The schools differed in their organizational arrangements for informal learning. The principal of the American school created additional opportunities for informal interactions by organizing the schedule to provide common preparation time for teachers of the same grade level. The teachers used this opportunity to learn from each other through collaborative planning. In addition, the principal supported and encouraged teachers' participation in workshops and conferences; however, the teachers did not report any events in which the principal or a head teacher would lead professional development activities for the colleagues—both positions seemed to be charged with only administrative responsibilities.

On the contrary, in both schools in Lithuania, the assistant principals for elementary education and leaders of the elementary Methods Committees (Marija and Ramute) were directly responsible for organizing their teachers' professional development. The Russian school administration enacted top-to-bottom management of teaching quality to prevent the school from a possible closure. Neither the principal nor middle managers provided support for formal professional development or valued informal interactions between teachers. Different from both the American and the Russian schools, where teachers either had plenty of time scheduled for their interactions (the American school) or needed to use their personal time after school (the Russian school), the Lithuanian school teachers found time to coordinate their ideas and actions in ways that were satisfying for their professional growth and enjoyable on the personal level across all elementary grades. The administration of the Lithuanian school found creative and quick ways for informing teachers about any possibilities for professional development outside the school. In addition, they maintained an atmosphere of trust and appreciation that encouraged and empowered the teachers to develop a tightly knit professional community with high professional standards. In sum, administrative arrangements in the schools reflected different leadership approaches and, thus, provided different opportunities for teachers' professional growth ranging from close supervision and evaluation (the Russian school), to accommodating and supporting teachers' professional needs (the American school), to empowering teachers to take responsibility for their work quality and professional growth (the Lithuanian school).

While initially I chose not to search for Law's (1999) five organizational elements of supportive professional development school culture, examples of some of these elements nevertheless emerged from my conversations with teachers and my participant observations. For instance, the teachers reported that the principal of the Lithuanian school effectively managed information/communication flows and provided them with information about professional development opportunities in a quick and informal manner. The principal of the American school developed a system for shared and open planning processes for the teachers to exchange ideas. The Lithuanian school seemed to develop open networking opportunities to facilitate mutual support and reflection.

The examples for two other organizational elements of supportive professional development culture—the operation of clear resource allocation procedures with focused aims and targets and the establishment of clear evaluation strategy used as a basis for ongoing review and development, were not identified and would require additional data collection to observe.

Professional Relationships Revisited

Different professional relationships in the schools created or failed to create favorable contexts for teachers' informal learning. The knowledge-creating elements of tinkering, transfer of knowledge, research of practice, and facilitation by middle managers illuminated relationships that were reflected in distinct and differing learning patterns that transpired in the schools (Hargreaves, 1999).

Professional relationships in the American school seemed to be friendly but not yet collegial. Isolation inherent to the profession (Lortie, 2002), enhanced by architectural and cultural factors, prevented teachers from sharing their professional experiences and dilemmas. In addition, tinkering, research of practice and facilitation by middle managers seemed to be overshadowed by one single element—simple transfer or borrowing of knowledge (Hargreaves, 1999). Nevertheless, some teachers in this school engaged in co-tinkering while co-planning and observing their grade-level colleagues' practices—picking up and transferring newly developed understandings into their practice; however, even that practice did not occur on a regular basis; teachers' reports seemed to imply that not all the teachers in the building used these opportunities for learning. Limitations in learning opportunities were also reflected in a single grade-level teachers' participation in curriculum development and piloting. Though the principal provided teachers with support and opportunities for informal learning, they seemed to use these opportunities in different ways: Some teachers extended their learning beyond the borders of the school; others took advantage of the school's organizational arrangements and initiated collaborative learning between teachers of different grades; and others confined their learning to collaboration only with their grade level teachers. One of their activities—curriculum development, seemed to engage the teachers in the research-like activity.

In the Russian school, a different pattern emerged. Professional relationships seemed to be influenced by stressors imposed from the outside (possibility of losing the job) and inside (pressure from the administration and parents). In order to provide jobs for all the teachers, the administration reduced their teaching loads and, thus, salaries. Nevertheless, the teachers engaged in individual tinkering, but due to the limited opportunities for interactions, they rarely engaged in knowledge transfer. In addition, they did not participate in research of their practice. A formal internal audit process at the time of the study focused on evaluation of teacher performance; it did not include teachers in the process by providing them with tools and time for reflection and self-evaluation of their practice. Though fiscal conditions, national educational policies, and administrative style in this school did not seem to favor informal learning, the teachers appeared highly motivated to use any opportunities for growing professionally, thereby surviving in the profession to which they passionately adhered.

The Lithuanian teachers seemed to engage in all four knowledge-creating steps. Reflecting on their professional relationships, teachers in the Lithuanian schools defined their close and passionate relationships to the profession, as did their Russian counterparts; however, in comparison to the teachers from the Russian school, who talked about their fanaticism, these teachers defined their devotion to the profession differently—as coming from their nation's tradition of caring. These teachers practiced tinkering by playing and experimenting with new ideas individually; they engaged in knowledge transfer through observations in their colleagues' classrooms and participation in formal professional development events, followed up with exchanging ideas. They engaged in research of their practice through hosting student-teachers, who fostered their reflections and collaborated with the University faculty; their middle managers encouraged teachers' professional growth by providing information about workshops, courses and projects, by organizing school-based professional development to meet immediate teachers' needs and by providing opportunities for informal learning.

To conclude, these three school cases reflected essential differences in the ways teachers related to and formed their school cultures. These differences were tied to the ways in which their school cultures created opportunities for their informal learning, which in turn appeared to be closely related to the historical and social contexts in the countries. In a relatively stable social environment, the American school provided rich administrative and structural opportunities for teachers to grow professionally in informal settings, which allowed teachers the freedom to choose their own ways of development. However, such openness and flexibility in the system did not seem to be sufficient to motivate teacher learning and growth, illustrating that while a school system can provide collaborative resources, a culture among the teachers that encourages and values collaborative learning is also necessary. Social threats to their job security from outside the school and pressures to comply with requirements inside the school limited Russian teachers' opportunities for informal learning. Administrators who enacted an authoritarian leadership style allocated few places or times for teachers' informal interactions. Though this situation did not seem favorable for teachers' learning, the teachers were highly motivated to grow professionally, and used any opportunity for their professional growth. The Lithuanian school culture, created during the recent exuberance inspired by Lithuanian independence, aspired toward high professional standards and provided ample opportunities for learning and professional growth as well as collegial support. The culture displayed organizational features characteristic of a family model. Teachers expected collaboration with each other to develop and help their colleagues develop. These collaborative contexts empowered teachers to make decisions, including what, when, and how they learned. This exclusive culture was intolerant of professionals who did not display dedication and motivation for improvement, accepting only teachers with highly devoted and creative approaches to learning. Teachers in the Lithuanian school, with its established institutional history and excellent reputation, were encouraged by the socio-political conditions of independence to affirm their current ways of learning collaboratively and to strive to increase that learning. Conversely, the same national socio-political conditions led teachers in the Russian school, with an even longer history and better reputation in the past, to switch their focus from learning to surviving. In the American socio-political culture, including extensive testing and accompanying suspicion of teachers' competence, teachers focused on satisfying requirements rather than attending to the construction of a collaborative culture for their personal and shared professional growth. These three cultures illustrate complex relationships between broader social environments, organizational development and teachers' efforts to grow professionally within complex contexts.

Implications and Further Anthropological Investigation of Workplace Informal Teacher Learning

Educators who engage in research, practice or policy-making can benefit from the design and outcomes of these three cases. For educational researchers, these studies offer approaches for further exploration of relationships between school culture and workplace informal teacher learning. Bringing to the forefront teachers' representations of their informal learning trajectories and professional development allows for an in-depth analysis. An insider perspective illuminates various dimensions of school culture that creates a web of meanings, which is qualitatively unique in each school. It also casts light on relationships of school cultures to particular local cultures, which, in turn, is part of broader national socio-political structures and developments. Further examination of each cultural characteristic (school philosophy, physical environment, organizational arrangements, traditions and professional relationships) could be useful for identifying how specific features of each characteristic relate to informal learning opportunities. Additionally, these findings raise questions for further consideration, such as: What motivates teachers to pursue informal learning opportunities at their workplace? How does their informal learning translate into practice? What is the relationship between informal and formal learning? Keeping informal teacher learning the focus of systematic investigation reminds teacher educators and policy makers about the crucial role of informal learning in teachers' professional growth and, consequently, in the success of educational change.

For teacher educators, this study provides a view of an area that has not been valued as professional development. This study suggests that preparation of future teachers could be improved by stressing the importance of creating and making use of informal learning opportunities. Once in the schools, teachers could benefit from assessing and developing informal collaborative learning. By acknowledging the importance of this method of career-long professional development, they could enhance their own and their colleagues' learning and contribute to building and sustaining the infrastructure necessary to maintain such development for themselves and future teachers in their schools.

The characterizations and illustrations of the best practices in various school cultures presented in this part could inform teachers, teacher educators, and school administrators in their efforts to create and improve learning cultures in their schools. By understanding how culture is built from many interrelated elements, participants could construct a community that would nurture opportunities by providing stimulating social contexts for teachers' professional change. Such socio-cultural infrastructures and cultures are needed for continual and consistent implementation of educational reforms and to better respond to the needs of ever-changing societies.

References

Anderson-Levitt, K. M. (2002). *Teaching cultures: Knowledge for teaching first grade in France and the United States.* Cresskill, NJ: Hampton Press, Inc.

Eisner, E. (2000). Those who ignore the past .... *Journal of Curriculum Studies, 32*(2), 343–357.

Hargreaves, D. H. (1999). The knowledge-creating school. *British Journal of Educational Studies, 47*(2), 122–144.

Law, S. (1999). Leadership for learning; the changing culture of professional development in schools. *Journal of Educational Administration, 37*(1), 66–76.

Leithwood, K., Jantzi, D., & Steinbach, R. (1999). *Changing leadership for changing times.* Buckingham: Open University Press.

Lortie, D. C. (2002). *Schoolteacher: A sociological study* (2nd ed.). Chicago, IL: The University of Chicago Press.

Taylor, B. M., Pearson, P. D., Clark, K., & Walpole, S. (2000). Effective schools and accomplished teachers: Lessons about primary-grade reading instruction in low-income schools. *The Elementary School Journal, 101*(2), 121–165.

Part IV

National Educational Cultures and Teacher Informal Workplace Learning

Part IV

National Educational Cultures and Teacher Informal Workplace Learning

Economic and cultural globalization as well as the creation of the European Union (EU) is challenging the historic framework in which education systems were originally established in both Europe and the United States. Though in the European Union, education is the responsibility of individual Member States, the current common goal for all members is to shape a new European identity.[1] In the United States, differently from the EU, raising educational achievement especially at the lower end of the spectrum became a number one priority as reflected in the recent educational initiatives such as *No Child Left Behind* Act and *Race to the Top* that shifted the traditional commitment from contextualized and practical education toward an academic knowledge- and outcome-oriented one. These federal initiatives also yielded consistent educational goals, accountability measures, the adoption of common learning standards—all of which were tied to various federal education funding. However, the implementation of these common initiatives in the individual US states was inconsistent due to their independent governance rights and different state priorities. These federal and state transformations were also motivated by continuous discontent with the United States standing in the international comparisons of student achievement (e.g., Merry, 2013; Schleicher, 2019) and the realization that "discourse in education policy has become increasingly global and that international organisations such as the OECD appear to have a growing authoritative role in that sector" (Rautalin et al., 2019, p. 515), posing a challenge for educational research in defining the forces at work in national educational systems. In the present-day context, current research provides more and more evidence that national systems of education are experiencing a growing international influence and are adopting separate features of other educational systems (e.g., Godon et al., 2004; Tan, 2019). Cross-country comparison and exploration of educational phenomena in the international contexts allows for highlighting features of educational systems that would be difficult to see in a single system. A cross-national comparative perspective used in this part as the last layer of the "nesting doll" design is crucial in achieving the goals of this book and finding out how teachers interact with the informal learning opportunities afforded by the national educational cultures, especially those that are changing swiftly, such as Lithuanian and the United States.

About Part IV

The goal of this part is not to describe the universality and specificity of educational culture in Lithuania and the United States. Such direction would invoke an educational policy perspective. Instead, this part aims at listening to how teachers' voices reflect educational developments in each country as related to their professional growth. To hear teachers-as-learners' voices is especially important now, as society on both sides of the Atlantic is changing rapidly, and professionals and lay people need to learn constantly in order to keep abreast with the ongoing economic, political, and social developments. Under these conditions, non-institutionalized informal learning is taking place in everyday life on a broad scale. For example, the need to stay abreast of new technologies like cell phones and telecommunications tools and software necessitates an almost constant learning curve, where teachers (and professionals in many other fields) are tasked with needing to learn new applications, vocabularies, and content each day in order to stay digitally connected. This is especially true in the workplace, where learning happens both incidentally and intentionally as individuals must adapt their behavior to the changed conditions and develop knowledge of the innovations that have been introduced. As this increased workplace learning becomes more prevalent and commonplace, educational institutions adopt new attitudes to learning that occurs outside planned professional development events. Peter Jarvis (2000) noticed that gradually, "public education institutions are beginning to accredit workplace learning, and with it [comes] the accreditation of prior experiential learning—learning from prior experience for educational qualifications" (p. 349). Such workplace informal learning plays a significant role in educators' professional growth. Earlier in this book, we have discussed how individual teachers engage in such learning and how their workplace cultures create or stifle informal learning opportunities. In this part, it is important to investigate how education systems create opportunities for teachers' informal learning in their workplace and how teachers view and interact with these opportunities.

Specifically, in Part IV, I combine contextual knowledge of the societies and cultures in which these teachers live and work with the analytic concepts of the field of teacher education and tools of discourse analysis (Sutton & Post, 2006) to explore how national educational cultures create contexts for teachers' informal learning at their workplace. In doing so, I keep national educational cultures in the background and bring teachers' perceptions and actions to the foreground. I employ critical discourse analysis because it "can illuminate problems and controversies in the world" (Gee, 2014, p. 10) by scrutinizing the individual and focus interviews with Lithuanian and American educators conducted for this study to compare how these professionals construct their identities as learners and how the systems in two countries position teachers to learn informally.

To define ways in which national educational systems shape teachers' professional identity as informal learners, I start by comparing how the Lithuanian and the American national systems each construct a culture of teacher professional learning by highlighting main tendencies in education and by bringing in the teachers' perspectives including their perception of their own professional pre-service preparation and in-service professional development.

Though both Lithuanian and US systems of education possess common features, at the same time, they retain characteristics that are embedded in dramatically different historical developments and, thus, are specific to each country. In the subsequent chapters, I describe historic and current educational contexts in these countries and then analyze how educational systems create contexts for informal teacher learning and how teachers perceive and respond to those contexts. I do this by applying the comparative analysis of the national educational cultures on four major elements each of which is discussed in a separate chapter:

1. Educational systems: centralized and planned versus decentralized;
2. Teacher and students programming: 4-year looping versus single-grade/year teaching;
3. Professional development and evaluation system: market-driven structure versus structures for motivating teachers;
4. Stability of society: teacher identities in a culture that is stable versus a culture that has undergone a radical change and is still changing.

Perspectives on Teacher Identity Formation

In answering the question of how teachers as learners interact with national educational systems and learn informally, it is important to consider what constitutes teachers' professional identity, what learning environment their national educational systems provide for them, and how teachers interact with their professional environment in constructing their identities. Therefore, professional identity is one of the key concepts in this part. It yields a rich understanding of the relationship between self and contexts of practice and learning (Akkerman, & Meijer, 2011; Ashmore & Jussim, 1997; Baumeister, 1986; Britzman, 1992; Beauchamp, & Thomas, 2009; Day et al., 2005; Deaux, 1992, 1993; Foucault, 1988; Gleason, 1983; Hartung, & Subich, 2011; Mandell, 2007; McCall & Simmons, 1978; Stryker, 1987). Among different perspectives on teacher professional identity (Barrett, 2005), Rudolf Van den Berg's (2002), who defines teachers' professional identity as "the result of an interaction between the personal experiences of teachers and the social, cultural, and institutional environment in which they function on a daily basis" (p. 579), best reflects the approach of this book. This definition underlines an interactive, contextual, and informal nature of identity construction. Moreover, identity theorists point to a fluid nature of the process because we experience constant pressure "to examine and re-examine our identities against the flux of unstable representations around us" (Howarth, 2002, p. 145). Mockler (2011) adds a temporal dimension claiming that a teacher's professional identity is "formed and re-formed constantly over the course of a career and mediated by a complex interplay of personal, professional and political dimensions of teachers' lives" (p. 518). As a result, different aspects of identity intertwine and define each other in a continuous process of interaction, which, according to Baxter (2011), includes competing demands on individual rights, time and energy, and loyalty expressed in the conflict between following self-interests verses others' interests.

The changing nature of social environment and the long-term nature of identity development call for a dialectical approach to processes of identity formation in a social context. Such formation, according to Habermas (1993), usually happens through "communicative action", when we can only know ourselves and recognize others when we have come to terms with, and reflect upon, our structural "embeddedness" in formal and informal structures. Consequentially, the "embedded" subject is one who communicates, negotiates, and acts upon difference in relation and response to meaningful social interactions with others (Jurasaite-Harbison, 2012). This perspective of an on-going process of negotiation with self and environment argues for teachers' professional identity as being shaped by social and structural relations that exist within individual, schools', districts', national, and cross-national social contexts. Therefore, in identifying aspects of teachers' identity construction, such as teachers-as-learners, in this case, we have discussed individual and school contexts moving to define social environments constructed by national professional culture.

The Role of Culture in Identity Construction

Culture plays a special role in identity construction (Pike, 2000). It defines relevant actors and the choices that are available to them in this process. Simultaneously, culture works toward individuals framing cultural groups that form to meet their demands for identity construction. In this sense, culture could be defined as "Janus-faced" (Laitin, 1999, p. 290) in its role in developing both individual and group identities. People are both guided by the symbols of their culture and use their culture to gain and maintain power and (professional) stability. This perspective illuminates the reciprocal nature of relationships between culture and social and professional groups (teachers, in this case). It also helps to explain, for example, the differences identified in the previous chapters between the identities of teachers who belong to the titular nation and national minorities in Lithuania after the fall of the Soviet Union. When analyzing identity development, it is important to keep in mind that in Lithuania, as in other countries of the region, these identities are shaped by the formation of the newly constructed state that defines the policies of citizenship and cultural strategies toward nation-formation in ways that are intended to distinctly separate its Soviet past from the qualitatively different present. This was especially true at the time the research for this study was conducted, with Lithuania's independence from the Soviet Union only spanning a little more than a decade and a half at that time. New legislation positioned national minorities as different from the titular nation (and in some cases, deficient). For instance, a new law re-instituted the state language (Lithuanian) and required (and still requires) all non-Lithuanian teachers to pass the state language exam by a certain deadline at not lower than level B (ability to communicate, read, and write in the state language); failure to do so results in loss of eligibility to teach. This state decision causes additional tension for non-Lithuanian educators, underscoring the existing cultural gap between titular and non-titular nations in the country. In such extraordinary times, as Lithuania currently still experiences, the process of identity construction and re-construction accelerates, as "people take advantage of their multiple cultural repertoires and refashion their identities to make them relevant to the crisis they face" (Latin, 1999, p. 292). Together with changes in constructing a new national identity, globalization processes and regional developments, such as Lithuania becoming part of the EU in 2004, increasingly bring in common-to-other EU member countries tendencies, which influence the developmental trajectories of national educational systems in general, and teacher identity formation, specifically.

In looking at various cultures, especially those featured in this study, current comparative research points to the emergence of global similarities on different levels of national educational structures. For example, scholars notice global similarities in the official curriculum systems across different nations and cultures: in elementary schools, one-third of time in a week is devoted to language arts, and about one-sixth of it to mathematics (Boli et al., 1986; Meyer et al., 1992). Scholars also point to an analogous nature of classroom teaching (Anderson-Levitt, 1987), to similar basic structure of teacher–student interaction (Sharan & Sharan, 1991), and to interaction between students (Vasquez & Martinez, 1992) seen across classrooms across the world.

Nevertheless, when researchers discuss teaching as a cultural enterprise, they tend to highlight national differences rather than similarities. Numerous studies illustrate that national teacher cultures are significantly different. For instance, a few comparative studies present evidence of numerous national differences in teacher–student interactions, handling of conflicts between students, different teaching philosophies, and teacher responsibilities seen in the US and German classroom analysis that the

Spindlers pioneered (Spindler & Spindler, 1982, 1987). Others include comparative studies of preschools in Japan, China, and the United States (Tobin, 1999; Tobin et al., 1989); an exploration of teaching first-graders to read in France and the United States (Anderson-Levitt, 2002); a study of elementary education in the United States, Japan, and China (Stevenson & Stigler, 1992); a study of bilingualism in Germany and Israel (Moin et al., 2011); international comparisons of teacher preparation (Adamson, 2012); classroom discipline and student misbehsavior in Australia, China, and Israel (Lewis et al., 2005); and students' mistake-handling in Italy and the United States (Santagata, 2005).

While the studies listed here highlight teaching and classroom differences across different cultures, actual observed cultural differences are not as straightforward—either in these studies, or others that are connected to educational research. There are other studies, which through comparing two cultures, note transnational similarities and national differences in teaching and learning to teach (e.g., Pöllmann, 2008; Shimahara & Sakai, 1995). Kathryn Anderson-Levitt (2002) suggested that examination of different elements of teaching cultures such as, for example, the interpretation of events and examination of values, might bring different results. She saw the origin of these contradictions exemplified in getting different results from similar studies and in the different stances of researchers: some interpretations drew on transnational professional culture while others employed value judgments that might have been rooted in the researchers' national cultures.

Research on teaching yields another layer of discussion when viewed within comparative international contexts. Researchers claim the existence of national patterns of teaching based on their argument that teaching *within* countries is more consistent than *across* countries (Stigler and Hiebert, 1999). On the contrary, Gerald LeTendre et al. (2001) argued against the prevalence of national patterns of teaching, instead favoring commonalities of lessons among countries as the indicators for larger global patterns of teaching. Such a debate can be used to confirm that teaching and teacher identity construction are complex processes with multiple dimensions to consider.

In contrast to the deliberation of within- and across-countries' similarities and differences in teaching as well as their influence on students' learning, comparative studies of teacher knowledge often identify commonalities rather than differences in teacher thinking. Researchers have found that teachers in different countries develop the same kinds of professional knowledge (Ben-Peretz et al., 1986; Blömeke, & Delaney, 2012; Blömeke et al., 2013; Clark & Peterson, 1986; Grimmett & MacKinnon, 1992), shared teaching culture (Ben-Peretz & Halkes, 1987), and similar ways teachers and parents talk about children (Edwards et al., 1996). However, few studies investigate *ways of developing* teachers' professional knowledge in different countries and how those ways of development relate to their professional identity. In earlier publications, I, along with Lesley Rex (Jurasaite-Harbison, 2007; Jurasaite-Harbison & Rex, 2010) illuminated cultural and individual differences in learning patterns of elementary teachers in Lithuania and the United States. The findings in both publications called for further investigation into the ways national educational cultures and institutional (school) cultures influence teacher informal learning. Responding to this call, in Part IV of this book, I investigate how national educational culture influences teachers' informal learning and ask: ***what features distinguish educational cultures in two countries in terms of constructing teachers' identity as learners, and how do teachers interact with national educational cultures in shaping of their identities as learners?***

Comparing Teacher Learning in Different National Cultural Contexts

This part focuses on identifying the broadest context of the "nesting doll" design and hypothesizing about cultural mediation of relationships between the informal teacher learning and opportunities for it in different national educational cultures. It explores how teachers construct and act upon an important part of their professional identities—teachers as learners. I analyze national cultural contexts for teacher learning by using comparative analysis of two educational systems and employing both synchronic and diachronic perspectives (Chrisomalis, 2006), and moving between etic (my interpretations) and emic approach, which emphasizes the voice and agency of the learner in specific cultural contexts of learning (Zhu, & Bargiela-Chiappini, 2013). This comparative analysis provides insights into the culture of teacher learning "through explaining the behavior of educational systems" (Grant, 2000, p. 309) as teachers experience it. The synchronic lens allows for generating categories for cross-cultural comparisons, while the diachronic view provides historical context for cultural patterns.

The comparative framework on the synchronic plane involves analysis of specific components of national educational systems that are relevant to teachers' informal learning, such as national education goals and policies, teacher pre-service training and accreditation, system of professional development and ways educational systems structure teachers' work. I also consider the implications of these factors for informal teacher learning. This analysis involves both primary (interviews) and secondary sources (educational legislation, official documents of departments of education, national statistical data).

As primary sources, I used two elite interviews (Marshall & Rossman, 1999): one with a high official from the Lithuanian Ministry of Education and Science and one with the team of teacher trainers from a highly regarded non-governmental organization (further, NGO) in Lithuania. In addition, I used individual and focus group interviews with the participating teachers to investigate how they perceived their opportunities for professional growth in both countries. Unfortunately, similar data were not available to contextualize the US Midwestern teachers' voices. Statistical data served this purpose in addition to the American participants' perspective regarding the extremely flexible system of professional development in which the teachers' and the school's choices were honored first.

To examine the teachers' perspectives and describe the meaning that the teachers assigned to the phenomenon of learning informally within their education systems, in these four chapters, I continued analyzing semi-structured phenomenological interviews (Marshall & Rossman, 2014) with the seven elementary teachers in Lithuania (Ana, Marija, and Nadia in a Russian school, Daina, Sigute, Ramute, and Viktorija in a Lithuanian school) and the four elementary teachers in the United States (Kristi, Debbie, Bob, and John). The series of interviews with each teacher focused on the exploration of the teachers' past and their current learning experiences that included their pre-service and in-service learning. The goal of these interviews was also for each of the teachers to define their own essential informal learning experiences.

In addition to the individual interviews, in the focus group ethnographic interviews with the group of teachers in each Lithuanian school, I was interested in how the participants perceived and interacted with culture to elicit meanings that they ascribed to events and behaviors. These interviews contained three main types of questions: descriptive, structural, and contrast. Each interview took place in the participants' schools during the time when they were not teaching (e.g., during "specials", when Music, Physical Education, Art, etc., teachers worked with their students); each interview lasted approximately 40 minutes. We explored the nature of teachers' learning in their workplace, their role in professional development and the impact of recent educational change on their professional growth. The interviews were video-recorded and transcribed in English, Lithuanian, and Russian. Later, I coded them in their original language using the grounded theory approach (Strauss & Corbin, 1997; Mills et al., 2006) and critical discourse analysis (Gee, 2014) to allow categories to emerge from my interaction with teachers and, further, to look for the relationships between these categories. Finally, I translated excerpts that best represented the emerging patterns to include in this part—the analytic process that I used in the previous parts of the book, but with a different focus guided by a different set of research questions. Reiterative reading of the transcripts enabled me to refine the identification of specific aspects of teacher learning in the contexts of different educational cultures. I also noted the gaps in the participants' accounts; for example, in one cultural site they mentioned some aspects that were completely omitted by participants from other cultural sites. I had intended to engage in this same process with the teachers in the US school; however, they were unable to find a common time to meet for a focus group interview.

The Broad Context: National Educational Cultures and Teacher Informal Learning

In the following pages, I depict broad national/regional contexts that are characterized by the general tendencies across educational systems of the United States and Lithuania. I look for relationships between national educational goals, policies, curriculum and assessment, and teachers' professional identity. My goal is to identify how these cornerstone features of national education relate to teachers' professional growth, what opportunities they offer for elementary teachers' pre-service preparation, in-service training and professional development, how they structure teachers' work to support (or not) their engagement in informal learning, and how teachers perceive their opportunities for professional growth within these specific national contexts.

National Educational Cultures in the United States and Lithuania

At different times in history, education systems of the United States and Lithuania have influenced each other, borrowing ideas and systemic elements from one another. For example, American education emerged from adopting ideas and structures from the European tradition, which continues to serve as the foundations of Lithuanian education. Since gaining independence in 1990, Lithuanian education has been undergoing continuous reforms in which it has adopted many progressive ideas, models, and practices that originate from the United States. For instance, early childhood and elementary education teachers in Lithuania started using a student-centered approach with its roots in Deweyan constructivism; in higher grades, Lithuanian teachers apply critical thinking and the project approaches, which also come from the United States. These examples demonstrate an on-going dialogue between the systems that influence each other.

At the same time, educational systems in these two countries have been developing in very different historic and socio-economic environments. While Lithuania historically has a centralized education system, in the United States, education is mostly governed at the state level, with the exception of a few federally mandated statues (e.g., Title IX, the Individuals with Disabilities Education Act). As such, there are vast differences in key educational facts from state to state such as funding, curricula, ethnic make-up of student population, approaches to the second language acquisition, and so forth. For example, according to the US Department of Education and the National Center for Education Statistics (2021), 54.9% of students enrolled in California schools in 2019 identified as Hispanic as compared to the US average of 27% in that same year. Education funding in the United States is also complex, with allocations for public education drawing from a mix of federal, state, and local funding sources, including tax dollars. As such, local allocation of funds differs widely from state to state (e.g., in 2020, Utah spent $7,179 per elementary/secondary student while New Jersey spent $10,140, and New York spent $23,091). Considering these differences across the states, I focus on describing the education system in one Midwestern state, whose overall general population is about 10,000,000 (in 2020), and in which K-12 students comprise 66% White, 18% Black, 8% Hispanic, 3.1% Asian or Pacific, and 4.9% multiracial. In addition, this state spends about $12,000 per student, which is close to the national average.[2]

In comparison, during the last years since Lithuania broke away from the Soviet Union and declared independence, it underwent tremendous political, economic, and social change—dealing with the economic blockade by the collapsing Soviet Union, banning the Communist Party, fighting to preserve Lithuanian language through passing restrictive laws about the state language and Lithuanian citizenship; transforming all spheres of economy by moving from planned to market, and democratizing the political, legal, educational, and health systems. In 2020, Lithuania had a population of about 2,800,000 (almost four times less than the above-mentioned Midwestern state) comprising 84.2% Lithuanians, 6.6% Poles, 5.8% Russians, 2.4% Byelorussians and other nationalities. As compared to the average of 3.22% of GDP spent on education in the United States in 2016 (3.49% in the Midwestern state), Lithuania in 2016 spent 2.5% of GDP on education allocating $6,100 per student in elementary schools, which is one of the lowest among OECD countries (OECD, 2017) and about twice as less as in the Midwestern state. Student-teacher ratio in Lithuania in elementary education in 2003 was 13:1, which was lower than in most of the EU countries and the Midwestern state (17.5:1). According to the data of the Ministry of Education and Science of Lithuania, there are 15,022 elementary schools that include state, municipal, and private schools. This number does not include elementary departments in secondary schools. In 2013 in the country, there were 17 schools with Russian language of instruction that decreased to 12 in 2018. The average salary of Lithuanian teachers was one of the lowest among EU countries totaling to about $14,000 per year as compared to the Midwestern state average of over $61,000.

A Sketch of Recent Education History

For more than a decade in the United States and Lithuania, there has been a deliberate effort to reform education systems to align them with the highest standards in education and transform them into world-competitive organizations; however, on the diachronic plane, these tendencies often have taken different directions. For example, in the Sputnik era, the Soviet system of education (Lithuania being part of it) together with the whole society experienced "the thaw" (e.g., curriculum changed to soften its ideological grip and to exclude any references to the personality cult of Stalin; schools became mixed-gender; foreign languages, psychology, and culture became a significant part of the curriculum, etc.), while education in the United States went through a different kind of reform. As Robin Alexander (2001) noticed, in the United States, curriculum planning was heavily systematized along the lines of behaviorism in the first part of the 20th century. As the country was undergoing significant civil rights reforms in the 1950s and 1960s, US education was thusly impacted through the desegregation of government-designated "Black" and "White" schools with the Supreme Court's 1954 decision on the *Brown Versus Board of Education* case. In the decades that followed, many in the public education sector continued this civil rights focus, examining persistent inequities in American education for students of color, while others sought reform for students with disabilities, and still others examined educational disparities among children living in poverty (e.g., Hughes et al., 2013; Milner, 2020).

While states maintain their educational governance, in recent decades, American education was shaped by a number of federal Acts that called for reform to raise educational standards, particularly to increase student achievement and access to high quality education for traditionally marginalized or underserved populations that largely comprised Black and Hispanic students, as well as those in high-poverty households and students with disabilities. Namely, this began with the 1983 report *A Nation at Risk* examination of lack of reading success, followed by the Bush Administration's 1991 six *National Education Goals* for the year 2000, which was extended by the Clinton administration's 1994 *Educate America* Act, and was succeeded by the 2001 *No Child Left Behind* Act followed by *Race to the Top*. These represent the federal government's continuous attempt to improve education in the United States (though not always successfully) by increasing accountability, implementing a set of nationally held education standards (i.e., Common Core Learning Standards), providing more centralized approaches to states, school districts and schools, and offering more choices of alternative models for parents and putting reading first (Meier & Wood, 2004; Peterson & West, 2003). In addition, in 1990, the 1975 Education of Handicapped Children Act was amended and reconceived and renamed as the Individuals with Disabilities Education Act, followed by additional amendments in 1997 and 2004, further ensuring that all students with disabilities and learning difficulties have access to free, public education. Subsequent to these various pushes for greater inclusion and equity in US Public Education, the Trump administration reverted the social justice agenda and promoted an approach to undocumented children education with a so-called "Malignant Standard" that refused them the same rights and protection that are provided to all other children (Sáenz, 2020). This most recent legislation is contrary in spirit to the others that precede it, and while it removed access to education for a distinct population of students, it did not replace or overturn any of the other existing legislation.

The history of Lithuanian education in the years of independence (since 1990) represents a continuous effort to reform the education system at all levels. This reformation period could be divided into three relative phases: (1) 1990–1997, (2) 1998–2002, and (3) 2003 (Lithuanian Ministry of Education and Science). The first phase aimed at centralized transformation of the content (curricula, textbooks, pedagogy), democratization of educational process (moving from reproductive to interpretive pedagogy), extension of opportunities for learning choices, integration of students with special needs into general education, and introduction of the system of attestation and granting qualification categories to teachers and school administrators. The second phase involved solving problems brought about by the rapid development of the economic, political, and social aspects in the country. As a result, a compulsory education period increased from 8 to 10 years of schooling embracing the kindergarten year; an enhanced conception and structure of the educational system was designed to ensure continuous universal education. With the decreasing number of students, the financing of schools was restructured by introducing the principle of the "student's basket", according to which the amount of funds allocated for a school depended on the number of students in this school. In the third phase, the Parliament of the Republic of Lithuania approved the National Education Strategy 2003–2012. The Bill (Provisions of the National Education Strategy, 2003, pp. 3–4) defined the mission of education in Lithuania as follows:

1. To help an individual to understand the contemporary world, to acquire cultural and social competencies and to become an independent, active, and responsible person who is willing and able to learn and create a life of his own and life of society;
2. To help an individual to acquire a vocational qualification corresponding to the level of modern technologies, culture, and personal skills, and to create conditions enabling life-long learning, which encompasses continuous satisfaction of cognitive needs, seeking to acquire new competencies and qualifications that are necessary for the professional career and meaningful life;
3. To ensure balanced and knowledge-based development of the economy, environment and culture of this country, domestic and international competitiveness of the economy, national security and evolution of the democratic society, thus strengthening the creative powers of the society;
4. To guarantee continuity of culture nourished by the nation and the country, continuous process of creation, protection of identity, as well as to foster the open and dialogic nature of the culture.

Notably, among the eight strategic goals for Lithuania that education was expected to help achieve, at least four focus on the development of culture and national identity, making it a number one priority: (1) to find place in the culture and economic area of the West; (2) to develop the democratic culture of the country; (3) to nurture cohesive civil society; (4) to preserve the national identity (Provisions of the National Education Strategy, 2003, p. 4). Since 2004, in contrast to these goals, new tendencies appeared in Lithuanian education, which were influenced by the EU education and training policy (Ertl & Phillips, 2006). As a member of EU, Lithuania had to align its educational policies with the general goals of the European educational system by 2010. Specifically, Lithuania was compared to other EU countries in five strategic areas on which EU focused its educational policies:

1. Reduce the average number of early school leavers (dropouts) to 10%.
2. Increase the share of graduates in mathematics, science and technologies aged 20–29 per 1,000 of population of the relative age range to 15%. Alteration rate—20.74%.
3. Increase the share of those aged 22 who have successfully completed upper secondary education to at least 85%.
4. Reduce the share of those aged 15 with low reading proficiency to at least 20% as compared to 2,000. TIMSS data (2003): In Lithuania since 1999, the share of students with low achievements in science has decreased by 40%, and in math—by 21%.
5. Ensure that at least 12.5% of the adult population of employable age (25–64 years of age) participate in lifelong learning.

To attain these goals, Lithuania incorporated the outlined areas into the National Education Strategy, which was also influenced by OECD strategy and the Bologna process. Newly elected government developed a 2013–2022 National Education Strategy that included the reform of higher and tertiary education and training. It set out goals "to turn the education system in Lithuania into a sustainable foundation for the development of national welfare and to raise a young independent and innovative generation that will lead the country". Specifically, it outlined the following priorities:

- Establishment of educational community, where professional teachers and lecturers are reflective, constantly developing and work in a highly effective manner;
- To develop an educational culture driven by data analysis and self-evaluation, that in turn will ensure effective interaction among stakeholders in education;
- To ensure that learners (pupils, students, and young people in general) have the best opportunities to realize their individual potential in full by ensuring accessibility and long duration of education and equal possibilities to all learners, by providing the effective pedagogical and psychological aid to pupils who experience learning difficulties;

- To establish a system of incentives and equal conditions of lifelong learning opportunities, a system that gives effective aid in choosing a career path or to combine one's choice with the labor market needs.

(Valstybinė švietimo 2013–2022 metų strategijos [The National Education Strategy for 2013–2022], 2013)

To conclude, educational development trajectories in Lithuania and the United States demonstrated both similarities and differences. The countries have been and are undergoing rapid and turbulent changes, though in different spheres of education. In addition, the whole country of Lithuania is changing on all levels—moving from the Soviet system that permeated it for more than 70 years to a modern system that is aligned with the European Union. Under these conditions, teachers experience uncertainty, job insecurity, decreasing self-efficacy and appreciation by administration and society. In the United States, excessive student testing that is tied to the evaluation of teacher quality and constant introduction of new strategies and methods of teaching (Buchanan, 2015) demonstrate distrust in teachers' professionalism and undermine their professional identities. Nevertheless, teachers in both countries maintain passion for teaching and learning.

In the following chapters of this part, I analyze the opportunities afforded by the educational systems in these countries through the teachers' perspective using four cultural elements of educational systems mentioned above.

A Note on the Use of Discourse Analysis in This Part

The ensuing chapters use critical discourse analysis (Gee, 2014) to identify cultural patterns/forces at work and ways the teachers construct their identities as learners in the contexts of their national/regional educational systems. The texts in this part are analyzed based on the premise that generation and interpretation of categories involve a dialectic process. Both the researcher and participants display cultural knowledge that is expressed linguistically; the analysis provides interpretations of what particular cues index, and what types of specific content and enacted events engage in the context (Wortham & Rymes, 2003). This dialectic process involves "regimentation" (Silverstein, 1993, 1998) of indexical cues by available cultural types of events. It means that when speakers and hearers presuppose that a particular type of event is going on, the expectable script for that type of event comes to regiment many indexical cues. Members of any society explicitly and implicitly recognize complex sets of types of events. Gregory Urban (1996) calls such presupposed pattern or cultural type of text or script a "metadiscourse", similar to what Gee calls Discourses with capital "D". Metadiscourses are the explicit and implicit framings used in a given society for understanding social events as coherent. Thus, they are publicly circulating devices for interpreting or regimenting interactional events. The circulation of metadiscourses explains the "contextually-situated, interactional establishment, maintenance and renewal of social relations in societies" (Silverstein, 1993, p. 35). The social events, relationships, and identities characteristic of a society are made recognizable by the metadiscourses that typify them (Urban, 1996). The concepts of "metadiscourses" and "regimentation" are useful for the following analysis for illuminating a larger social and cultural background that participants bring in to their everyday interactions. By applying "contextualization cues" that metadiscourses constrain and signal indexically to a particular context, the analysis of the language-in-use reveals how participants of the interaction position themselves in a situation. In this part, it reflects how teachers negotiate metadiscourses in identifying themselves as learners in everyday informal situations at schools, how other educators and educational officials relate themselves to the metadiscourses in interpreting opportunities for teacher informal learning, and how the teachers represent their embedded-in-metadiscourses learning in their interactions.

In the following chapters, I provide a broad-stroke picture of educational cultures in Lithuania and the United States and of ways in which teachers construct their professional identities when interacting with national educational cultures. Further, I triangulate the results of the teachers' interview analysis with the elite interviews, with the teachers' focus group interviews, and official educational documents.

Terms and Qualifications

Though the educational systems in the countries in focus are constantly in flux, in the United States, the educational system is highly decentralized, and its financing is much more dependent on the resources of the schools' geographic area as compared to the Lithuanian educational system. Standards in American schools can vary greatly from state to state, and within each state. Thus, any reference to "American education" in general needs to be bounded by qualifications. To overcome the approximate character of such generalizations, by using the terms "American education" or "American teachers", I either describe very general national tendencies or use these descriptors to differentiate the US teachers from those in Lithuania. On the contrary, in Lithuania, comparatively centralized system of education, the standardized system of pre-service teacher training and in-service teacher attestation allows for a more unified picture of "Lithuanian education" and "Lithuanian teachers". However, in this research, I also make a distinction between teachers serving different ethnic groups (Lithuanians and Russian-speaking population in Lithuania). Therefore, it is important to note that the meaning of these terms is highly contextualized within the subsequent chapters.

Notes

1 In the Council on 5 May, 2003 the Member States agreed upon a series of "Reference Levels of European Average Performance in Education and Training (Benchmarks)" against which their systems would be measured.
2 Because the data collection for the study occurred earlier (2005–2006), it is not easily available now. Thus, to illustrate my point of significant differences between the states, I use the latest available data.

References

Adamson, B. (2012). International comparative studies in teaching and teacher education. *Teaching and Teacher Education*, *28*(5), 641–648.

Akkerman, S. F., & Meijer, P. C. (2011). A dialogical approach to conceptualizing teacher identity. *Teaching and Teacher Education*, *27*(2), 308–319.

Alexander, R. (2001). *Culture and pedagogy: International comparisons in primary education*. Malden, MA: Blackwel.

Anderson-Levitt, K. M. (1987). The classroom environment study: Teaching for learning. *Comparative Education Review*, *31*(1), 69–87.

Ashmore, R. D., & Jussim, L. (Eds.). (1997). *Self and identity: Fundamental issues* (Vol. 1). Oxford: Oxford University Press.

Barrett, A. M. (2005). *Teacher identity in context* (Doctoral dissertation). University of Bristol, London, UK.

Baumeister, R. F. (1986). *Identity: Cultural change and the struggle for self.* New York: Oxford University Press.

Baxter, L. A. (2011). *Voicing relationships: A dialogic perspective*. Los Angeles, CA: SAGE.

Beauchamp, C., & Thomas, L. (2009). Understanding teacher identity: An overview of issues in the literature and implications for teacher education. *Cambridge Journal of Education*, *39*(2), 175–189.

Ben-Peretz, M., & Halkes, R. (1987). How teachers know their classrooms: A cross-cultural study of teachers' understandings of classroom situations. *Anthropology and Education Quarterly*, *18*(1), 17–32.

Ben-Peretz, M., Bromme, R., & Halkes, R. (1986). *Advances of research on teacher thinking*. Lisse: Swets & Zeitlinger.

Blömeke, S., & Delaney, S. (2012). Assessment of teacher knowledge across countries: A review of the state of research. *ZDM*, *44*(3), 223–247.

Blömeke, S., Suhl, U., & Döhrmann, M. (2013). Assessing strengths and weaknesses of teacher knowledge in Asia, Eastern Europe, and Western countries: Differential item functioning in TEDS-M. *International Journal of Science and Mathematics Education*, *11*(4), 795–817.

Boli, J., Ramirez, F. O., & Meyer, J. W. (1986). Explaining the origins and expansion of mass education. In P. G. Altbach & G. P. Kelly (Eds.), *New approaches to comparative education* (pp. 105–150). Chicago, IL: University of Chicago Press.

Britzman, D. P. (1992). The terrible problem of knowing thyself: Toward a poststructural account of teacher identity. *Journal of Curriculum Theorizing*, *9*(3), 23–46.

Buchanan, R. (2015). Teacher identity and agency in an era of accountability. *Teachers and Teaching*, *21*(6), 700–719.

Cardelle-Elawar, M., Irwin, L., & Sanz de Acedo-Lizarraga, M. L. (2007). A cross cultural analysis of motivational factors that influence teacher identity. *Electronic Journal of Research in Educational Psychology, 13–15*(3), 565–592.

Chrisomalis, S. (2006). Comparing cultures and comparing processes: Diachronic methods in cross-cultural anthropology. *Cross-Cultural Research, 40*(4), 377–404.

Clark, C., & Peterson, P. (1986). Teachers' thought processes. In M. C. Wittrock (Ed.), *Handbook of research on teaching* (3rd ed., pp. 255–296). New York: Teachers College Press.

Day, C., Elliot, B., & Kington, A. (2005). Reform, standards and teacher identity: Challenges of sustaining commitment. *Teaching and Teacher Education, 21*(5), 563–577.

Deaux, K. (1992). Personalizing identity and socializing self. In G. M. Breakwell (Ed.), *Social psychology of identity and the self-concept* (pp. 9–33). London: Academic Press.

Deaux, K. (1993). Reconstructing social identity. *Personality and Social Psychology Bulletin, 19*, 4–12.

Edwards, C. P., Gandini, L., & Giovanni, D. (1996). The contrasting developmental timetables of parents and preschool teachers in two cultural communities. In S. Harkness & C. M. Super (Eds.), *Parents' cultural belief systems* (pp. 270–288). New York: The Guilford Press.

Elmore, R. F. (2000). *Leadership of large-scale improvement in American education.* Washington, DC: A. Shanker Institute.

Ertl, H., & Phillips, D. (2006). Standardization in EU education and training policy: Finding from a European research network. *Comparative Education, 42*(1), 77–91.

Foucault, M. (1988). *Technologies of self.* Boston, MA: University of Massachusetts Press.

Gee, J. P. (2014). *An introduction to discourse analysis: Theory and method.* Routledge.

Gleason, P. (1983). Identifying identity: A semantic history. *Journal of American History, 69*, 910–931.

Godon, R., Juceviciene, P., & Kodelja, Z. (2004). Philosophy of education in post-Soviet societies of Eastern Europe: Poland, Lithuania and Slovenia. *Comparative Education, 40*(4), 560–569.

Grant, N. (2000). Tasks for comparative education in New Millennium. *Comparative Education, 36*(3), 309–317.

Grimmett, P. P., & MacKinnon, A. M. (1992). Craft knowledge and the education of teachers. G. Grant (Ed.), *Review on Research in Education, 18*, 385–456.

Habermas, J. (1993). *The thesis of communicative action* (A. McCarthy, Trans.) (Vol. 2). Boston, MA: Beacon Press.

Hartung, P. J., & Subich, L. M. (2011). *Developing self in work and career: Concepts, cases, and contexts* (pp. viii–245). American Psychological Association.

Howarth, C. (2002). Identity in whose eyes? The role of representations in identity construction. *Journal for the Theory of Social Behavior, 32*(2), 145–162.

Hughes, S., Noblit, G., & Cleveland, D. (2013). Derrick Bell's post-Brown moves toward critical race theory. *Race Ethnicity and Education, 16*(4), 442–469.

Jarvis, P. (2000). Globalisation, the learning society and cooperative education. *Comparative Education, 36*(3), 343–355.

Jurasaite-Harbison, E. (2007). Teachers as learners: Individual aspects of informal professional learning. *Teacher Education (Mokytoju Ugdymas)*, *9*, 44–60.

Jurasaite-Harbison, E. (2012). Workplace learning in informal contexts: Transnational comparison of teacher professional growth in Lithuania and the United States. In M. Ginsburg (Ed.), *Preparation, practice, and politics of educators: Problems and prospects in comparative perspective*. Rotterdam, Netherlands: Sense Publishers.

Jurasaite-Harbison, E., & Rex, L. A. (2010). School cultures as contexts for informal teacher learning. *Teaching and Teacher Education*, *26*, 267–277.

Laitin, D. D. (1999). The cultural elements of ethnically mixed states: Nationality re-formation in the Soviet successor states. In G. Steinmetz (Ed.), *State/culture: State-formation after the cultural turn* (pp. 291–320). Ithaca, NY: Cornell University Press.

LeTendre, G. K., Baker, D. P., Akiba, M., Goesling, B., & Wiseman, A. (2001). Teachers' work; institutional isomorphism and cultural variation in the U.S., Germany and Japan. *Educational Researcher*, *30*(6), 3–16.

Lewis, R., Romi, S., Qui, X., & Katz, Y. J. (2005). Teachers' classroom discipline and student misbehavior in Australia, China and Israel. *Teaching and Teacher Education*, *21*(6), 729–741.

Lithuania Resolution: Provision of the National Education Strategy, 2003–2012. (n.d.). No. IX-1700, 4 July 2003, Vilnius. Retrieved January 12, 2021, from http://planipolis.iiep.unesco.org/en/2003/lithuania-resolution-provisions-national-education-strategy-2003-2012-no-ix-1700-4-july-2003

Lithuanian Ministry of Education and Science. (n.d.). Retrieved January 12, 2021, from https://www.smm.lt/web/lt/

Mandell, D. (2007). Use of self: Contexts and dimensions. In D. Mandell (Ed.), *Revisiting the use of self: Questioning professional identities* (pp. 1–19). Toronto Ontario: Canadian Scholars' Press Inc.

Marshall, C., & Rossman, G. B. (2014). *Designing qualitative research*. Thousand Oaks, CA: SAGE.

McCall, G. J., & Simmons, J. L. (1978). *Identities and interactions* (Rev. ed.). New York: Free Press.

Meier, D., & Wood, G. (Eds.). (2004). *Many children left behind: How the No Child Left Behind Act is damaging our children and our schools*. Boston, MA: Beacon Press.

Merry, J. J. (2013). Tracing the US deficit in PISA reading skills to early childhood: Evidence from the United States and Canada. *Sociology of Education*, *86*(3), 234–252.

Meyer, J. W., Kamens, D. H., & Benavot, A. (Eds.). (1992). *School knowledge for the masses: World models and national primary curricular categories in the twentieth century*. Washington, DC: Falmer Press.

Mills, J., Bonner, A., & Francis, K. (2006). The development of constructivist grounded theory. *International Journal of Qualitative Methods*, *5*(1), 25–35.

Milner IV, H. R. (2020). Fifteenth annual AERA brown lecture in education research: Disrupting punitive practices and policies: Rac (e) ing back to teaching, teacher preparation, and brown. *Educational Researcher*, *49*(3), 147–160.

Mockler, N. (2011). Beyond 'what works': Understanding teacher identity as a practical and political tool. *Teachers and Teaching*, *17*, 517–528.

Moin, V., Breitkopf, A., & Schwartz, M. (2011). Teachers' views on organizational and pedagogical approaches to early bilingual education: A case study of bilingual kindergartens in Germany and Israel. *Teaching and Teacher Education*, *27*(6), 1008–1018.

National Center for Educational Statistics (NCES). (n.d.). Retrieved January 12, 2021, from https://nces.ed.gov/programs/coe/indicator_clr.asp

OECD. (n.d.). Retrieved January 12, 2021, from http://www.oecd.org/education/

Peterson, P. E., & West, M. R. (2003). *No Child Left Behind?: The politics and practice of school accountability*. Washington, DC: Brookings Institution Press.

Pike, G. (2000). Global education and national identity: In pursuit of meaning. *Theory into Practice*, *39*(2), 64–73.

Pöllmann, A. (2008). National attachment among Berlin and London head teachers: The explanatory impact of national identity, national pride and supranational attachment. *Educational Studies*, *34*(1), 45–53.

Rautalin, M., Alasuutari, P., & Vento, E. (2019). Globalisation of education policies: Does PISA have an effect? *Journal of Education Policy*, *34*(4), 500–522.

Sáenz, G. (2020). America's second-class children: An examination of president Trump's immigration policies on migrant children and inquiry on justice through the Catholic perspective. *The Scholar: S. Mary's Law Review on Race and Social Justice*, *22*(1), 143–191.

Santagata, R. (2005). Practices and beliefs in mistake-handling activities: A video study of Italian and US mathematics lessons. *Teaching and Teacher Education*, *21*(5), 491–508.

Schleicher, A. (2019). *PISA 2018: Insights and Interpretations.*Paris: OECD Publishing.

Sharan, S., & Sharan, Y. (1991). Changing instructional methods and the culture of the school. In N. B. Wyner (Ed.), *Current perspectives on the culture of the school* (pp. 143–164). Cambridge, MA: Brookline Books.

Shimahara, N. K., & Sakai, A. (1995). *Learning to teach in two cultures: Japan and the United States*. New York: Garland.

Silverstein, M. (1993). Metapragmatic discourse and metapragmatic function. In J. Lucy (Ed.), *Reflexive language*. New York: Cambridge University Press.

Silverstein, M. (1998). The improvisational performance of "culture" in real-time discursive practice. In K. Sawyer (Ed.), *Improvisation*. Norwood, NJ: Ablex.

Spindler, G. D., & Spindler, L. (1982). Roger Harker and Schonhausen: From the familiar to strange and back again. In G. D. Spindler (Ed.), *Doing ethnography of schooling* (pp. 20–46). Prospect Heights, IL: Waveland Press.

Spindler, G. D., & Spindler, L. (1987). Cultural dialogue and schooling in Schonhausen and Roseville: A comparative analysis. *Anthropology and Education Quarterly*, *18*(1), 1–16.

Stevenson, H. W., & Stigler, J. W. (1992). *The learning gap: Why our schools are failing and what we can learn from Japanese and Chinese education*. New York: Summit Books.

Stigler, J. W., & Hiebert, J. (1999). *The teaching gap*. New York: Free Press.

Strauss, A., & Corbin, J. M. (1997). *Grounded theory in practice*. Thousand Oaks, CA: SAGE.

Stryker, S. (1987). Identity theory: Developments and extensions. In K. Yarley & T. Honess (Eds.), *Self and identity: Psychological perspectives* (pp. 89–103). New York: Wiley.

Sutton, M., & Post, D. (2006). Comparative education, area studies, and the disciplines. *Comparative Education Review*, *50*(1), 125–149.

Tan, C. (2019). PISA and education reform in Shanghai. *Critical Studies in Education*, *60*(3), 391–406.

Tobin, J. J. (1999). Method and meaning in comparative classroom ethnography. In R. Alexander, P. Broadfoot, & D. Phillips (Eds.), *Learning from comparing* (Vol. 1: Contexts, classrooms and outcomes, pp. 113–134). Wallingford: Symposium Books.

Tobin, J. J., Wu, D. Y. H., & Davidson, D. H. (1989). *Preschool in three cultures.* New Haven, CT: Yale University Press.

Urban, G. (1996). *Metaphysical community.* Austin, TX: University of Texas Press.

Valstybinė švietimo 2013–2022 metų strategijos (The National Education Strategy for 2013–2022). (2013). *Approved by the resolution of the seimas of the republic of Lithuania No. XII-745 of 23 December 2013.* Vilnius: Švietimo ir mokslo ministerija. [Online] [05.09.2016]. Available at https://www.e-tar.lt/portal/legalAct.html?documentId=b1fb6cc089d911e397b5c02d3197f382. (In Lithuanian)

Van den Berg, R. (2002). Teacher's meanings regarding educational practice. *Review of Educational Research*, *72*(4), 577–625.

Vasquez, A., & Martinez, I. (1992). Paris-Barcelona: Invisible interactions in the classroom. *Anthropology and Education Quarterly*, *23*(4), 291–312.

Wortham, S., & Rymes, B. (Eds.). (2003). *Linguistic anthropology of education.* Westport, CT: Praeger.

Zhu, Y., & Bargiela-Chiappini, F. (2013). Balancing emic and etic: Situated learning and ethnography of communication in cross-cultural management education. *Academy of Management Learning & Education*, *12*(3), 380–395.

12 Centralization versus Decentralization in Educational Systems

Overview of This Chapter

This chapter focuses on the discussion of cultural similarities and differences as they relate to educational goals, policies, curriculum, and assessment practices in Lithuania and the United States. Though educational systems are in continuous flux depending on the prevailing political inclinations, tendencies toward centralization or decentralization of educational systems seem to create specific contexts for teacher informal workplace learning. When discussing educational goals, policies, curriculum, and assessment systems, teachers from both countries commented on how educational standards, curricula, and their planning provide opportunities (or not) for their informal learning. The teachers in Lithuania (a more centralized system) seem to have all subjects' content written and planned out for them. Their role is to choose teaching methods that fit the needs of their students and communities the best; they report that they are eager to learn new, more effective teaching methods and look for specific activities to teach the content to their students better by involving them more actively in the learning process. The role of the teachers in the Midwestern US school (a decentralized system) is to create a curriculum around the benchmarks for each subject, and plan it out for the year—the task that allows them to exercise their creative freedom and opens informal learning opportunities, but also puts a lot of pressure and takes up almost all their non-teaching time at work.

Goals, Policies, Curriculum, and Assessment

As mentioned in the introduction to this part, despite geographical, economic, political, linguistic, and historical differences between education in the United States and Lithuania, there are cultural similarities that are visible at the state, institutional, or classroom levels. In both countries, basic education is free and compulsory (excluding a small percentage of private schools). Basic education has similar components, such as official goals for education, official curriculum systems, social organization of educational institutions, and the architecture of the buildings (school buildings are easily recognized); however, most of the cultural similarities seem to end here.

Different historic, economic and social developments account for major cultural differences between the United States and Lithuanian schools featured in this study. For example, since one of the main goals of American schools is to prepare students for life in American society, educators stress the development of social and communication skills, which are increasingly considered as essential workplace skills; thus, American schools devote classroom instructional time to socialization and collaboration. This can be seen in the common Core State Standards (Council of Chief State School Officers, 2010), which tout the larger goal of "college and career readiness" and was originally adopted by many states as part of NCLB and continued with Race to the Top. "Collaboration" is a key feature in numerous English Language Arts (ELA) and Math standards across all grade levels, and especially in the Speaking and Listening strand of the ELA standards. While NCLB, IDEA, and other legislations discussed in the introduction of Part IV of this book aimed for high expectations for all learners, regardless of their historical achievement levels or other factors, there are still a number of districts and schools across the country that have held onto antiquated academic traditions like tracking, where there are different academic goals for different tracks of students. In schools that still follow this approach, the internal division of tracking aims to meet specific learning needs of academically diverse student populations separately, holding them to different expectations for academic growth. This further challenges high achieving students to prepare them for universities, but only offers basic education to those who cannot maintain the same level of academic growth (Grant, 2000). Curriculum choices are mostly at the district and sometimes school level, with inequities seen as school and district budgets are largely determined by state and local taxation sources. So, school districts with a higher mean salary are likely to receive larger funding per student than districts with lower mean salaries. By contrast, the Lithuanian system of education, in some respect, seems to retain some traits of the Soviet[1] educational system (Elliott & Tudge, 2007; Minina, 2017), which has been systematically analyzed both on its own and in comparison to other countries (Alexander, 2001; Kerr, 1994; Muckle, 1990; Nikandrov, 1995). While holding onto such traditions as using the same textbooks and similar methods of instruction throughout the country, Lithuanian education also focuses on teaching values that are rooted in educational philosophy that was developed during the times of Lithuanian independence. It also aligns its teaching approaches with tendencies that are prominent in the European Union. Even with the recent push toward decentralization (e.g., schools and teachers within schools can choose non-traditional curricula that are based on pedagogical systems of Montessori, Waldorf, Suzuki, and others), financing of education now is provided by local governments, and decisions seem to be constrained by a few choices of textbooks and additional educational materials, which are commissioned and revised centrally by the Ministry of Education and Science.

The centralized approach to education in Lithuania versus the decentralized approach in the United States can be traced in how the **educational goals** reflect the idea of national identity and its role in education. Having experienced domination by neighboring countries throughout the last several hundred years, and recently, consolidating its independence within the context of the European Union, Lithuania focuses its educational goals on humanistic education, freedom, and democracy as well as traditional values of family and motherland, which saturate the educational content.

On the contrary, as Robin Alexander (2001) observes the United States, "which by virtue of a rather different constitution is denied a national educational system, has used that constitution [...] to shape not the content of education but its conduct and organization at community level" (p. 155). Thus, in the United States, with the minimal federal involvement in education, educational goals mainly focus on meeting the expectations of a state, district, and community. With the country's strong focus on diversity, national and ethnic identity construction, usually, is the area in which family and community values play the leading role. In contrast, Lithuanian educational goals, as related to national identity, are aligned with the constitution and with what the nation expects from the younger generation.

National **curriculum**, which also reflects centralization–decentralization divide between the two countries, plays an important role in educational culture because it reflects values of the society, such as national priorities and objectives. For example, while literacy is given the highest priority in Lithuania and the United States, instructional subjects are grouped differently, and different amounts of time are allocated for them. Based on the data from the Lithuanian Ministry of Education, Science and Sports, Table 12.1 represents instructional time allocated for elementary grades in Lithuania (with a slight difference between schools with national minority (Russian, Polish) language of instruction, which amounts to 22–26 hours per week for grades 1-4. This does not include time for recess (commonly, 10-minute breaks between 45 minutes periods) or snack time (commonly, 20 minute-break that follows two first periods).

Differently from Lithuanian schools, which count only time for actual lessons and gradually increase **instructional hours** during the 4 years of elementary school, American schools are described in terms of hours of direct student instruction per year and time spent at school. There is almost no increase of direct instructional time across the first 4 years of elementary schooling. For example, in the Midwestern state elementary schools (grades 1–6), direct instruction should account for at least 1,098 hours spread across 180 days per year or about 30.5 hours per week (IES/NCES, 2021). The instructional time includes recess (breaks) and transition time between classes, but does not include lunch period.

Table 12.1 Instructional time recommended by the Ministry of Education for Lithuanian schools and non-Lithuanian schools (hours per week)

Grades	*1*		*2*		*3*		*4*	
	LT	*N-LT*	*LT*	*N-LT*	*LT*	*N-LT*	*LT*	*N-LT*
Lithuanian language	10	–	10	0–3	10	4	9–10	4
World science	–	10	–	9–10	–	10	–	9–10
Native language	–	–	–	–	–	–	–	–
Mathematics	4	4	5	4–5	5	5	4–5	4–5
Foreign language	–	–	–	–	–	–	2–3	2
Arts and crafts	2	2	2	2	2	2	2	2
Moral education (religion or ethics)	1	1	1	1	1	1	1	1
Music	2	2	2	2	2	2	2	2
Physical education	3	3	3	2–3	3	2	2–3	2
Total allocated instruction	**22**	**22**	**23**	**23**	**23**	**26**	**23**	**26**
Reserved lessons (optional)	–	–	3	3	3	3	3	3
Additional education	3	3	3	3	3	3	3	3

This table illustrates an argument that in elementary schools in the United States and Lithuania literacy is given the highest priority, instructional subjects are grouped differently, and different amounts of time are allocated for them, which reflects values of each society, such as national priorities and objectives. The table also demonstrates a slight difference between Lithuanian and non-Lithuanian schools in Lithuania, which amounts to 22–23 and 22–26 hours per week for grades 1–4, respectively. Differently from Lithuanian schools, which count only time for actual lessons and gradually increase instructional hours during the 4 years of elementary school, American schools are described in terms of hours of direct student instruction per year and time spent at school

This structure accounts for some difference in time spent in the workplace between Lithuanian and American schools. In Lithuania, elementary students are usually dismissed about two hours earlier (at about 1 PM) than their peers in the United States, so that they can pursue extracurricular activities both at school and outside of school, and still have time left in the day for rather extensive independent academic homework. In the United States schools that I observed, elementary students often received homework as punishment—if they did not finish their classwork. Centralized efforts to introduce Common Core State Standards across the United States encountered resistance on the local level and were adopted in the majority of the country after federal funding was tied to the adoption of the common guidelines (Gilday, 2020; Rothman, 2011).

To conclude, Lithuania's approach for a centralized but moving toward decentralization educational system seems to regulate certain components of education such as setting educational goals, designing and coordinating curriculum, and allocating instructional time. Teachers in Lithuania are expected to implement educational policies in the classrooms through creatively choosing and applying appropriate and effective teaching methods. In comparison, a decentralized system in the United States leaves it up to the communities, districts, schools, and teachers to decide upon specific educational goals, curriculum design, and the use of instructional time, positioning teachers to carry out tasks that they may not be trained to perform (e.g., designing a curriculum, setting strategic goals), which might put additional pressure on teachers and impact their professional identity. In Lithuania, elementary teachers spend less time with students, though it is dedicated to intensive academic work in the classroom. The American teachers' time with students takes up a longer part of the day, is less regimented in terms of in-classroom programming, allowing for more flexibility for completing lessons and other educational tasks. In both countries, specialists (Arts, Music, and Physical Education) could teach about 30% of the curriculum. In the following section, I bring in teachers' perspective in relation to standards, curriculum, and planning.

Standards, Curricula, and Planning: Elementary Teachers' Viewpoint

In the interviews, teachers in the Midwestern US and Lithuania schools reflected on the length of their workday and their responsibilities differently. To plan and prepare for the next day and to grade students' work, Lithuanian teachers usually used time after classes. Some of them worked additional hours (for extra pay) in the extended-day groups (elementary students have an opportunity to stay at school and do their homework with a certified teacher until their parents finish their workday). To extend education and learn more about their students, teachers used after-school time or weekends to take students on field trips. For example, Ana, a teacher from the Russian school in Lithuania, commented about taking her children to a weekend concert (in all subsequent excerpts, I add emphasis in bold to highlight contextualization cues):

> That was on the weekend. **It is not my teaching time**, but my parents are so inert. (…) I try to do many extracurricular activities with my children (…) **so that I could learn about the children outside the school**.
>
> **I was surprised** that in the concert, those who attend the Music School listened less attentively than those who did not.

Ana did not seem to regret spending her personal time with her students because she saw it as a learning opportunity and assigned a special value to it for learning about her students after school. In contrast, Kristi, an American teacher, perceived her work time differently. She did not seem to be inclined to spend any extra time on the job:

> I'm **out of here** at 4 o'clock. (…) **I love my job. I think this is a very very important job. What I do is as important as any job is, but it's a JOB**. And I understand that. You know, a big part of my life is here, but a **bigger part of my life is at home**. So, I leave at 4 o'clock. And I don't come super early either. I am here **early enough**. (…) I don't get to work when the bell rings. But most of the planning that I do, and the work that I do, **happens during my prep time and my lunch time here at school**. Some teachers spend their time in the lounge eating, that's fine. At one point in my life, I did that too. Now, I spend my lunchtime down here [in her classroom—E.J.-OK] working.

Kristi clearly defined that for her, teaching was a job and the bigger part of her life was at home. Other American teachers made comments along the same lines, drawing on the metadiscourse about socially acceptable hierarchy of values in which a job never occupied the highest position. Rooted in generally accepted social stance, this difference in teachers' attitudes toward spending their personal time on work stood out as one of the characteristic distinctions between the American and Lithuanian educators.

Generally, teachers in the United States, where proposed curricula benchmarks are determined at the school or district level in accordance with the state and federal guidelines, have multiple resources and freedom to select or construct curricula that meets the academic needs of their students. All 50 US states have some form of official curricular documents and specific centralized learning standards for English, math, and science alongside with some form of statewide testing policy; all of which need to be submitted to the US Department of Education in order to receive federal education funding (United States Department of Education, n.d.). In addition, the Common Core aimed at providing some consistency across the country in terms of curricula content. Nearly every state put these standards in place, although they do vary in terms of specificity, areas covered, and format.

The teachers related to standards in different ways: some routinely used standards and benchmarks in their planning process and recognized standards' value in keeping them focused. John saw standards as a stimulating factor for him and his students to strive for higher performance:

> I mean, you cannot move on into junior high without knowing how to multiply or to divide, or read. It's just doesn't seem right. Those kids cannot go that far. I know, it happens. But **I like the standards for that reason**. And I also like the standards because **you need somebody to push you that much more**. You know, **if you don't have someone pushing, just like me**. If I don't have to do it for a class, for college, there are a lot of lessons that **I would have never made**, if my class **requirement wouldn't have told me to do it**. And I think **the standards do the same thing**: as people get used to things—kids are doing very well at one level, well, **it's time to take it up a notch, to make it a little bit more challenging and they kind of push you to do that**. And at the teacher end sometimes it's difficult because then you look and say, "My kids cannot do this!", you know, but eventually they end up doing this.

In this excesrpt, John emphasized the power of standards to push and challenge him in making an effort to bring students to a certain level. He used the verb "to push" three times to underscore his perception of the role of standards, in which he expected standards to challenge and push him to perform professionally better. He defined contexts of his work by depicting standards and requirements acting upon him ("if my class requirement wouldn't have told me to do it" and "the standards do the same thing").

American teachers who participated in this study related to curricula in many different ways. Some participating teachers expressed their frustration about things that they would like to teach, but because of curricula constraints, they had no time to focus on. Bob commented,

> **I don't think that we have enough time to teach what WE really like to teach** even if it would benefit the kids. We have so much stuff that we have to cover, that we **are told** that we have to cover.

Others felt more comfortable with some curricula, such as Math and Science, because these curricula were more detailed and included supporting materials. The open nature of other curricula (e.g., Literacy and Social

Studies) did not seem to help those teachers do a better job planning or teaching as their pre-service training does not prepare them to create their own curricula. For example, John shared,

> I'd say for ME, **having a lot of my curricula set up for me** [would be the best]. Maybe it's just an impression of myself, but I don't feel I am very creative, or very generating a lot of new ideas. I can, what I think I do good is when I have something set out in front of me, I know what it's supposed to be, I can do it, but then I can throw my actual ideas. Right now, we have only 2 or 3 curriculums that are kind **of planned out**. I really like those. I feel that I can do a better job WITH those rather than what I had to do BEFORE I had those, which meant create things all the time, which I felt I was not doing a great job. (…) But for my classroom **I would like to have all areas set out that way**. Then I can look at it and say, "I know what I need to do now. I can do this on this day." **I can do my planning a lot better**.

Even though some curricula were detailed and tailored to meet the uniform standards (at least at the state level), they significantly varied in format, content, and supporting materials from state to state and from district to district. For this reason, the US elementary teachers in the study spent considerable amount of time individually or in teams planning everyday activities for students. These planning sessions usually generated professional discussions that stimulated teachers' informal learning. The teachers in Lithuania seemed to have all subjects' content written and planned out for them. Their role was to choose teaching methods that fit the needs of their students and communities the best. In my observations and private conversations with the teachers in Lithuania, they were eager to learn about new, more effective teaching methods and looked for specific activities to teach the content to their students better by involving them more actively in the learning process. The role of the teachers in the Midwestern US school that was framed by the decentralized nature of education in the United States was to create a curriculum around the benchmarks for each subject, and plan it out for the year—the task that allowed them to exercise their creative freedom and opened informal learning opportunities, but also put a lot of pressure and took up almost all their non-teaching time at work.

In the following chapter, I analyze another national contextual difference—time allocated for teachers to get to know their students and its relationship to teachers' informal learning.

Note

1 The occupation of Lithuania by the Soviet regime lasted for over 50 years (1940–1991). According to the agreement signed between Lithuania and Russia, Russian troops left Lithuania by August 31, 1993.

References

Alexander, R. (2001). *Culture and pedagogy: International comparisons in primary education.* Malden, MA: Blackwell.

Elliott, J., & Tudge, J. (2007). The impact of the west on post-Soviet Russian education: Change and resistance to change. *Comparative Education*, *43*(1), 93–112.

Gilday, C. L. (2020). Controversy and the common core. A book review of common core: National education standards and the threat to democracy. *Democracy and Education*, *28*(1), 12.

Grant, N. (2000). Tasks for comparative education in New Millennium. *Comparative Education*, *36*(3), 309–317.

Kerr, S. T. (1994). Diversification in Russian education. In A. Jones (Ed.), *Education and society in the new Russia* (pp. 47–74). Armonk, NY: M. E. Sharpe.

Minina, E. (2017). 'Quality revolution' in post-Soviet education in Russia: From control to assurance? *Journal of Education Policy*, *32*(2), 176–197.

Muckle, J. (1990). *Portrait of a Soviet school under Glasnost.* London: Macmillan.

National Center for Education Statistics. (2021). Retrieved January 12, 2021, from https://nces.ed.gov/programs/statereform/tab5_14.asp

Council of Chief State School Officers. (2010). *Common core state standards.* Washington, DC: Authors.

Nikandrov, N. D. (1995). Russian education after Perstroika: The search for new values. *International Review of Education*, *41*(1–2), 47–57.

Rothman, R. (2011). *Something in common: The Common Core Standards and the next chapter in American education.* Cambridge: Harvard Education Press.

United States Department of Education. (n.d.). Retrieved January 20, 2021, from https://www2.ed.gov/about/offices/list/ous/international/usnei/us/standards.doc; https://www2.ed.gov/about/overview/focus/what.html

13 Teaching Children versus Teaching Curriculum

Overview of This Chapter

This chapter highlights the elementary teachers' viewpoint on difference in time allocated to teach students (4-year looping versus single-grade teaching), how these models relate to the teachers' pedagogical knowledge, and how they influence teacher professional learning. As a result of having a looping system in Lithuania and a single-grade teaching programmatic approach in the USA, the teachers in Lithuania view their students from a developmental perspective and get to know them very well, which results in tailoring their instruction to their students. The American teachers learn about their students from test results and, thus, characterize them in terms of their membership in a higher- or lower-achieving group, which results in teaching their grade curriculum rather than specific students.

Getting to Know Students and Evaluate Their Progress: Testing Versus Looping

Teachers are not able to teach effectively if they do not know their students. One of the important contextual differences between the two systems seen in this study lies in how teachers in the Lithuanian and the US schools learned about their students' academic potential and what meaning in that respect they ascribed to assessment as a tool for identifying where their students are in terms of academic progress. The Lithuanian and the Midwestern US systems of education positioned teachers to get to know their students in different ways, which, in turn, engaged teachers in contrasting way of learning informally.

Testing as a Way of Learning about Students

In the US schools, teachers did not seem to apply common standards in ongoing formative assessments. On the contrary, required summative state tests (e.g., Illinois Standards Achievement Test and Prairie State Achievement Examination; or Michigan Education Assessment Program

(MEAP), or North Carolina End of Grade Tests (Grades 3–8) and tests to define certain levels of each student's performance (e.g., reading tests to determine students' reading level such as Reading Inventories) are standardized. Nationally, standardized testing has been an ever-growing industry, which has dramatically expanded in the 1960s and continued to grow with the provision of the latest testing initiatives. In addition to such programs as the National Assessment of Educational Progress (NAEP, 2021), which typically tests students at the ages of 9, 13, and 17, states develop tests for the core subjects to measure the achievement of the state benchmarks. For example, MEAP measures students' achievement in Reading and Math in the fourth grade and Science in the fifth grade. Further still, many schools employ the use of standardized (often research-based verified) reading and math screeners and diagnostic assessments in early elementary grades to determine if students are developing foundational reading and math skills on pace with standards and developmental expectations.

With the ever-expanding accountability measures, participating American teachers seemed to spend much of their instructional time "teaching for the test" and administering different assessments designed to predict performance on and/or serve as a practice for the official test. They also seemed to have a reason and motivation for why they needed to do that. Debbie, a literacy specialist, offered her opinion,

D **We have tons of assessments** that they do. For example, kindergarten, it's up on my board here. Kindergarten would do writing prompts, a retelling, concepts (…), hearing sounds and words, developmental reading analysis, letter-sound analysis. That's all put onto a spreadsheet, and then we take kids and code them by "these are the kids making it" and "these are the kids not making it and need additional intervention".

E Right, and are you doing all these tests or teachers? (…)

D A classroom teacher does it. **The district finds days when they can get a substitute** and **they pull the kids out** in the hallway and they do the testing.

E Does this happen usually in late September?

D No, **throughout the year**. So they are testing in the fall, they test in November, and they test in spring. So four major times in the year, they test because **it's the assessment that guides your instruction**. You cannot just go in and start teaching a lesson. **You have to figure out what the kids know, what are their strengths, what are their weaknesses, and then build on their strengths, so they feel capable and competent as a learner**.

Providing an example of teachers' ways of learning what students knew and what their strengths and weaknesses were, Debbie described a complicated testing procedure which elementary teachers had to follow in order to tailor their instruction to their students' academic needs: run tests, put them on a spreadsheet, and code the result to determine a student's reading level, and then work with those students to meet their academic needs, and test again. All these steps seemed to take place during the instructional time—a classroom teacher would run tests with individual students while a substitute teacher would teach the class. It would seem that such a scenario might hinder the cohesiveness of the teaching and learning process in the classroom—even more so, if it happened throughout the school year, students who were tested, would be missing classes, and classroom teachers would not be enacting their main responsibility—teaching their students. In addition, it seemed like teachers put an equal sign between the assessments and testing the school was using, directly linking their knowledge about students to testing outcomes. Rather than using additional measures or approaches to learn about their students' academic growth and overall development, or holistically observe and support their students' progress and engagement in the learning process, the teachers relied solely on the results of these barrage of formal assessments to learn about their students. In addition, they seemed to gain limited (and not always accurate) knowledge about their students from running these standardized tests even while testing their reading or math content knowledge and skills several times a year because some students may not be good test-takers.

In contrast, in Lithuania, there are national standards for all subjects; however, assessment in Lithuania is not nationally standardized, except for the final years of each schooling level (the fourth grade, the ninth grade, and the twelfth grade). These final tests are identical for all the students in the country. They are compiled and issued by the Ministry of Education and Science and administered and graded by school committees. In other grades, teachers have considerable freedom in how they assess students' progress. For example, Sigute commented about the informal way, in which she and her colleagues put together a reading test,

> We **forgot** that we still had to do a reading test with our first graders. So quickly, **not even having any text yet**, we **ran to one another [asking] who did what before**. Once we found a text, we ran back to the assistant principal, because she had to give this test. She also (...) forgot. (...) So, we offered our help.

The fact that both the teachers and the assistant principal forgot to prepare and to give the test provided a clue to the larger contexts in which this situation occurred: Testing did not seem to be of any significance for either the teachers or the school administration. Assessment in the form of testing did not seem to be driving instruction in the Lithuanian schools. If not testing, what was driving instruction? How would Lithuanian teachers learn about their students' abilities and progress?

Looping

The single-year or specific grade levels programmatic approach in the United States and teachers looping with their students over 4 years in Lithuania contributed to significant differences between the educational systems in the two countries. It also served a foundation for a different teaching philosophy. Though looping has been tried out and studied in the United States (Cistone & Shneyderman, 2004; Goodson, 2020; Little & Dacus, 1999), all the participating American teachers were specialists in a certain grade level (and even, had a preferable subject area to teach within their grade level). The Lithuanian teachers taught most of the subjects to the same group of students through all 4 years of their elementary education and often discussed their students' progress with special subjects' teachers. This gave teachers and students in Lithuania an extended period to learn about each other's teaching/learning styles, personalities, and expectations (Hufton et al., 2003). In addition, students in Lithuania traditionally stayed in the same building for 8 more years, and elementary teachers had an opportunity to follow their development and meet with their upper-grades' teachers, which allowed for a smoother transition for students between the levels of education.

By contrast, in the United States, teachers do not usually work with one set of students for more than a year, with some exceptions for 2-year teaching. Consequently, teachers have to spend significant amount of time getting to know their students at the beginning of each school year. Kristi, for example, commented on her dilemma of getting to know her students in order to teach them "from where you get them",

> You have to start from where they are at that moment. And you cannot **assume that they are going to know something**. **Just as you cannot assume that they are not going to know anything, because they may**. You have to teach them from where you get them. So, it takes some time, **three weeks or** so. But I think with some kids it's **most of the year**. Because just when you think you know them, **they surprise you in some way**.

For Kristi, it usually took about three weeks to get to know her students well enough to be able to teach; however, she doubted that she could get to know some of her students even by the end of the year. That might mean she was not able to tailor her instruction to respond to specific educational needs of some children. Though a system of frequent testing and data collection was designed to help their current teacher to teach effectively and their next teacher to start tuning teaching to the academic needs of the students, these tests did not seem to provide accurate or sufficient information about students and their learning. Kristi had to build her instructions on assumptions and anticipations as other teachers did too. Such discrepancy between teachers' assessments and real students' abilities seemed to be rooted in the system of single grade-level teaching and the corresponding professional development, when most of their professional development events were organized by grade levels. Consequently, teachers became experts in their grade level, putting grade-level curricula rather than interactions with students to enhance their learning in the center of their professional growth. Thus, the teachers in the study seemed to be positioned to mainly focus on learning about how to better teach their grade level curriculum but not learn more about their students' academic progress and development. In addition, even though students in the United States school stayed in the same building for 5–6 years of elementary schooling, their teachers usually had little opportunity to follow the development of their students even over this period.

By contrast, the teachers in Lithuania concentrated on learning to teach their students better, because their system of education put them in the position of getting to know their students in-depth over the years. Teachers played an active part in their education and development, and followed upon their students beyond elementary schooling years into the middle and high school. Interviews with Lithuanian teachers illustrated that looping became an important context for informal teacher learning. For example, Daina described her teaching in loops as a creative process,

> With each loop, **I work differently, absolutely differently**. Life is providing us with themes, so even a story from a textbook I use very differently. Now, it is very different: there are many teaching materials. **If I want, I can do this, or that, give them this or that**.

Evidently, in Lithusania, the teachers were taught to recognize these patterns in teacher preparation programs and were expected to be pedagogically capable of responding to a wide variety of developmental patterns that they observe in their classrooms. Such structure also required recollection and review of their own and colleagues' relevant teaching and learning experiences and building on those experiences to create more effective approaches.

As a result, the teachers in Lithuania usually described their students as being at a certain stage of development, whereas American teachers characterized their students in terms of their membership in a higher- or lower-achieving group (Hufton et al., 2003). Thus, the highly personalized relationships between teachers and students in both Lithuanian elementary schools developed through looping over 4 years, enabled participating teachers to tailor their teaching to the specific educational needs of their students and work together with families on enhancing their academic achievement.

In the following chapter, I explore if and how systems of professional development and evaluation differ in supporting teachers' professional growth and alternative ways of learning. I do so by considering contrasting ways in which the systems of education position teachers to teach curriculum in one case, and to teach students in another and to test students or to assess their progress over time accordingly.

References

Cistone, P., & Shneyderman, A. (2004). Looping: An empirical evaluation. *International Journal of Educational Policy, Research, and Practice: Reconceptualizing Childhood Studies*, *5*(1), 47–61.

Goodson, H. (2020). Looping in education. *Education*, *141*(2), 79–82.

Hufton, N. R., Elliot, J. G., & Illushin, L. (2003). Teachers' beliefs about student motivation: Similarities and differences across cultures. *Comparative Education*, *39*(3), 367–389.

Little, T. S., & Dacus, N. B. (1999). Looping: Moving up with the class. *Educational Leadership*, *57*(1), 42–45.

NAEP. (2021). Retrieved January 20, 2021, from https://www.ets.org/k12/assessments/federal/naep/?WT.ac=k12_36148_overwrite_naep_170105

14 Market-Driven Structure of Professional Development and Evaluation versus Structures Motivating Teachers' Professional Growth

Overview of This Chapter

This chapter discusses teachers' informal learning opportunities for professional growth through the comparison of professional development (PD) in US Midwestern state and Lithuania. As was argued before, formal professional development and teacher assessment often does not satisfy teachers' learning needs and leave teachers with a necessity to learn informally at their workplace. This chapter examines forces (market and centralized) that are at work when PD is designed and offered to teachers and opportunities that are afforded to teachers in the context of these forces at work. The teachers offer their perspective on how they relate to the organized PD—in both countries expressing dissatisfaction with their PD events. Consequently, the systems of PD underwent changes. In Lithuania, changes are implemented on the national level. The centralized and planned Lithuanian PD system includes teachers' attestation—a component that motivates teachers once every few years to reflect upon their practice and present it for a formal review in order to receive a higher professional category, which has been revised to make it more effective. In the Midwest, the districts' authorities acquire and coordinate PD events; in the researched district, PD events seem to be organized and re-organized to better meet teachers' professional needs; however, teachers do not express much enthusiasm about their PD sessions.

It seems that it is commonplace in the United States to treat PD as a commodity and a policy implementation tool, and design PD training opportunities based on commissioned topics that stem from new educational policies. This top-to-bottom approach fails to respond to specific teachers' needs, creating a gap between teachers and PD providers. To take into consideration teachers' interests and needs, PD providers need to relate to teachers' everyday dilemmas that help them perform their roles effectively. This chapter demonstrates that the focal systems of PD in the schools in the Midwestern state and in Lithuania seem to be very different. In the United States, the PD system seems to be guided by the market forces, while in Lithuania it is planned; it offers teachers the attestation process within which a positive review of their practice leads to achieving a higher qualification that comes with a higher pay.

Pre-service Preparation and Professional Development: The Teachers Feel Similar

The systems of teacher preparation also differ in the two countries, which is important to note as it creates different needs for workplace teacher learning. Another feature of the decentralized approach to education in the United States is that processes and requirements for teacher certification vary from state to state, with many certifications not honored in other states (Education Commission of the States, 2020; Sass, 2011). To become a teacher in the United States, a candidate needs to receive a state-level teaching certificate, which is earned after completing a teacher education program at a certified university, and in many states, certification exams are also required. Future teachers enter programs with rather limited knowledge in how to teach various content areas, and often take courses that either align to their interests (e.g., literature, biology), or address their own insecurities (e.g., including poor spelling, fear of Math, and confusion in Geography) in addition to general survey courses of teaching methods (Ingersoll & Strong, 2011). Certification is also required for different grade levels, content/subject areas, and specialties like special education, and English language instruction. It is important to note the option for National Board Certification, which features more rigorous requirements than that required of many states, and which can be used as a qualification for teaching in many states (National Board for Professional Teaching Standards, 2020). After having taught in a public school for 3 years, I have seen teachers earn tenure and may continue teaching for as long as they choose; however, tenure guidelines and requirements also vary from state to state, and in many cases, district to district. Many states require that teachers complete a certain number of hours of PD (which differs from district to district) within a certain time frame in order to maintain their certifications. Perhaps most consistent across the board is that salary increases are tied to years of service and education credits earned over what is required, which is a common salary approach for government or civil service employees across the country.

In Lithuania, a candidate enters a 4-year teaching program at an accredited university or college with a specialization (a preschool, an elementary or a subject teacher) from the very first year. Candidates come to teacher education programs with solid high school level content knowledge. Thus, instead for taking courses in content areas (Math, Language, Science, etc.), they take psychology and teaching methods courses. After completing all the requirements, a teacher candidate graduates with a bachelor's diploma and permission to teach at school.

The PD incentive is built into the process of teacher attestation, which includes several career steps. In-service teachers start their professional career at the level called “a teacher”. After 2 years of successful teaching, they may apply for a “senior teacher” category. In 2–3 more years, after presenting a written analysis of their innovative practice and teaching exhibition lessons (otherwise called “open lessons”) for the district officials and colleagues, they may apply for the “teacher-methodologist” category. Each category increases their paycheck. In addition, all teachers are required to take extensive PD courses no less than every 5 years of their teaching on their own schedule.

The operating PD systems closely relate to discourses on teacher professionalism (Day, 2012; Day & Sachs, 2005; Goepel, 2012; Grundy & Robison, 2004; Hilferty, 2008). It looks like the two countries exhibit what Sachs (2001, 2003) identified as two dominant discourses of teacher professionalism—managerial and democratic discourses, which represent different standpoints toward educational policy and practice. Managerial discourses, according to Sachs, directly inform viability of teacher standards and accountability as they are currently enacted in many countries, including the focal Midwestern school in the United States. On the contrary, democratic discourses of professionalism rely on teacher professional judgment, which, as Preston implied (1992), involve a certain level of professional autonomy. The democratic discourse is characterized by “privileging the nuance of judgement over the ‘one-size-fits-all’ approach of standardisation [that] requires a level of trust to be placed in teachers that they will act ethically, in the best interests of their students and their society” (Mockler, 2012, p. 41). The teachers in the Lithuanian school serve as a vivid example of a democratic discourse: they are trusted and highly appreciated professionals, who exercise power in making decisions in their school and beyond (e.g., teaching at the university, writing textbooks). Paradoxically, there are social and political forces on different societal levels that could change the trajectory of this discourse. The teachers in the Russian school in Lithuania exemplify these forces at work discussed in the previous part, which create a tense and hostile context for their professional growth as compared to their colleagues in the Lithuanian school. Thus, I would refrain from defining each system as enacting strictly one or another discourse.

Though the systems of teacher preparation and training in the United States and Lithuania seemed to be significantly different, the teachers in both countries similarly reflected on the professional value of their preservice education. They contrasted it with their workplace learning, especially informal, underscoring the significance of such learning. Likewise, they commented on their experiences as beginning teachers and on the social value that society ascribes to their profession along the same lines. For example, Ana, a Russian teacher in Lithuania, distinguished her pre- and in-service experiences by pointing out that pre-service education offers only the basics and it is necessity to continue learning,

> **The University gave me the basics**. [However], **practice and deeper understanding of children required [me] to revise everything**. I believe that there should be many different methods. A teacher chooses what is best for her and her students. Usually**, I do not stop at what we have**. Here is a specific example: now, we are in the *n* grade. I look at the [higher] grades and try to give more than in the textbook. I look 2–3 years into the future. **That is why I have to work on my qualifications constantly**.

Ana saw the gap between her university training and practice in how she had to develop a deeper understanding of children. Debbie, an American teacher, also expressed concerns about the breach between knowledge that teachers received in college and knowledge that they needed for doing their job:

> They [professors] really **don't teach how to teach a child to read** at the university level. **They give you the basics**. But to really analyze and provide instruction—THAT **was given to me by another reading teacher**. And she would sit down, and she would be my coach and watch me.

Using almost the same wording, both teachers expressed their limited knowledge and skills that they developed in pre-service training (it gave them the basics) and confirmed that they learned the best and the most in their workplace—from practicing teaching and communicating with colleagues. Kristi seemed to have found an effective combination of theory and practice, which she discovered when taking courses and working in her own classroom at the same time underscoring the value of being able to put theoretical ideas into practice:

> I guess thinking back on what was the most valuable—TEACHING experience just because when I was doing my undergraduate work, there wasn't a lot of time for practicing. I did my student teaching and I had time when I was in the classroom. But other than that, **you are learning something and are NOT able to put it into practice**. But at least **teaching full time and at the same time I was taking those master's classes—anything I did learn I was able to put into practice at that moment**.

She claimed that learning occurred when she was able to bring new ideas to her classroom and implement them. In another excerpt from the same interview, Kristi told a story about her interactions with a pre-service teacher. She noticed a big difference between being a pre-service and an in-service teacher in terms of their thinking (as a side note, I can share that I notice that change from thinking like a student to thinking like a teacher in my undergraduate students by the end of their fifth or sixth semester),

> I said, "The last time I had to do a bibliography was probably for a master's class and I got my masters in '98." So, it's been a number of years and I graduated from college in '93 with my undergrad certificate. So, I said, "it's honestly, **a different way of thinking**." You have to switch modes and think in this way because it was not something that I could just easily answer her [student-teacher's] question. But I know for fact that if I was still in that situation, still in college taking those classes, it wouldn't have been something that I even had to think about. It would have been something that I just automatically answer. **But I couldn't just switch modes like that anymore**. And I found it really interesting because I thought, "You know what, I felt in a way out of it."

In sum, the teachers in both countries differentiated between pre- and in-service professional education and training, stating that they needed to learn how to teach in their first teaching position. They claimed that they learned how to teach and become comfortable with it only after the few first years of practice and by constantly working on improving their qualifications on the job. This important observation demonstrates the significance of workplace learning. Learning from their own and their colleagues' practice, then, became key in their professional growth. In the following section, I analyze how the structure and content of professional development created contexts for teachers' informal professional learning.

Systems of Professional Development: Attestation versus Fragmentation

The structure and content of PD in Lithuania and the United States seems to be different. As the teachers shared with me, the Lithuanian PD system was organized on three levels: state, district, and institutional. On the state level, PD was tied to the system of continuous attestation. Teachers were required to take courses and write practice-based papers every 2–5 years. On the district level, there were regular facilitated PD days, when teachers who taught the same subject met and discussed national strategies, goals, guidelines, and curricula innovations, and observed and discussed master-teachers' lessons. At the institutional level, teachers who taught the same subject or grade level engaged in discussions facilitated by the head of

Methods committee. To stimulate their professional improvement, they typically discussed innovative teaching methods and issues in teaching, shared their experiences and worked on collaborative projects that aimed at specific issues of their practice. Elementary teachers were considered one group; they did not split by subject areas. In most cases, on the district and school levels, PD sessions happened when teachers did not teach (in the afternoon, during fall, winter, and spring breaks).

Special legislation was passed to institutionalize PD system in Lithuania. The Parliament Bills (2003, 2005) and the Ministry of Education and Science Acts (2021) defined the nature, structure, goals, main concepts, and implementation of teacher PD in Lithuania. Recently, the teacher attestation system was modified. Educational authorities noticed discrepancies between teachers' professional categories and students' academic achievement (Kaminskiene, 2006), and consequently set out new goals to organize continuous growth of teacher professional competencies and, thus, improve the effectiveness of the educational process (The Ministry of Education and Science Act, 2021).

In addition, in Lithuania, there is a broad network of NGOs (non-governmental organizations) that conduct workshops for teachers in specific approaches and methods (e.g., the Center for Modern Didactics focused on Literacy and Critical Thinking, the Center for Teaching Methods provided training in child-centered methods). Usually, they use interactive, student-oriented training methods that are more attractive to teachers. In the focus group interview with educators from one of the NGOs, the participants highlighted the importance of informal interactions during their workshops:

GENIE **Learning happens also during coffee breaks** at the workshops, when anyone can ask questions and have conversations. **Though at a formal training, but it happens during informal interactions**.

SANDRA When we get ready for our workshops, we always have **a goal of having discussions in small groups**. Sometimes that could change the whole workshop.

Both Genie and Sandra (teacher trainers) seemed to value informal learning that happened through interactions. They set a goal of incorporating special time for such interactions during their training activities.

In the participating school from the US Midwestern State, PD was usually guided by the state goals for education (5 days per year required), introduction of new curricula, and needs and interests of teachers; however, it differed from district to district and from school to school depending on the priorities of the Boards of Education, available funding, and trainers. Debbie's comment comparing her current PD experiences with her former district's approach illustrated a range of policies and politics in providing formal opportunities for teachers' professional growth. The lack of an organized system of PD was the reason for her departure from her former district:

> This is much different than the one in the suburbs of D. They **didn't give any money for conferences**, there wasn't really any special time, because I was a *n* grade teacher. Teachers here have the same common prep. Everybody did things [there] on your own. You just did it yourself, these are your kids and **you shut the door** and that's it. So, there was not **any formal training or informal**. That is one of the reasons I left that district. **If they don't want to take any pride in their teachers and their learning, I don't want to spend 25 years in that place**. School is about learning.

At the district level, some teachers did not consider PD sessions particularly helpful ("I am not sure if their [teachers'] needs are met during those PD days", (Debbie); however, Debbie further reflected that the situation was improving that year because the sessions were restructured to provide teachers with a choice, and thus, better served their professional needs:

> **It's better this year** because they broke apart different teams of teachers and **you can pick your area of study** for the day. The first year that they did, everybody did the same thing, so every elementary teacher was doing, for example, special ed. laws for the day, which is important too that they know special ed. laws, or every teacher is doing math. Well, I don't teach math. It's better this year. Every year things get better.

The teachers from both countries expressed the need for workshops that would provide them with practical ideas that they could apply in their teaching. For example, Kristi was happy to learn how to make spreadsheets:

> I've attended this year a very good technology PD. (…) So, that's something that I enjoyed this year because **it helped me to be a little bit better at it**. We need to make sure we do lots of assessments and keep scores of assessments; teach from the assessment because we need to turn in those scores periodically during the year. So, something that I learned at technology PD is **how to make spreadsheets**.

To conclude, teachers from both countries expressed dissatisfaction with their PD events. Consequently, the systems of PD underwent changes. In Lithuania, changes were implemented on the national level. The centralized and planned Lithuanian PD system included teachers' attestation—a component that motivated teachers once every few years to reflect upon their practice and present it for a formal review in order to receive a higher professional category, which was also revised to make it more effective. In the Midwest, the districts' authorities coordinated PD events—each district seemed to implement its own approach. In the researched district, PD events seemed to be organized and re-organized to better meet teachers' professional needs; however, teachers did not express much enthusiasm about their PD sessions. In the following chapter, I discuss how teachers engaged in informal learning to compensate for the lack of formal PD and how informal learning was viewed on the national level.

References

Day, C. (Ed.). (2012). *The Routledge international handbook of teacher and school development.* Abington, NY: Routledge.

Day, C., & Sachs, J. (2005). *International handbook on the continuing professional development of teachers.* New York, NY: McGraw-Hill Education (UK).

Education Commission of the States. (2020, June 24). *50-state comparison: Teacher license reciprocity.* Retrieved January 24, 2021 from https://www.ecs.org/50-state-comparison-teacher-license-reciprocity/

Goepel, J. (2012). Upholding public trust: An examination of teacher professionalism and the use of Teachers' Standards in England. *Teacher Development, 16*(4), 489–505.

Grundy, S., & Robison, J. (2004). Teacher professional development: Themes and trends in the recent Australian experience. In C. Day & J. Sachs (Eds.), *International handbook on the continuing professional development of teachers* (pp. 146–166). Berkshire: Open University Press.

Hilferty, F. (2008). Teacher professionalism and cultural diversity: Skills, knowledge and values for a changing Australia. *The Australian Educational Researcher, 35*(3), 53–70.

Ingersoll, R., & Strong, M. (2011). The impact of induction and mentoring programs for beginning teachers: A critical review of the research. *Review of Educational Research, 81*(2), 201–233.

Kaminskiene, V. (2006). *Metodinis darbas ir atestacija* [Action research and attestation, in Lithuanian]. Retrieved February 15, 2007, from http://www.pprc.lt/MetodineVeikla/?page=naujienos/defalt.asp

Ministry of Education, Science and Sport of the Republic of Lithuania. (2021). *Legal information.* Retrieved January 20, 2021, from https://www.smm.lt/web/en/legial-information

Mockler, N. (2005). Trans/forming teachers: New professional learning and transformative teacher professionalism. *Journal of In-service Education, 31*(4), 733–746.

Mockler, N. (2012). Teacher professional learning in a neoliberal age: Audit, professionalism and identity. *Australian Journal of Teacher Education, 38*(10).

National Board for Professional Teaching Standards. (2020). *Guide to national board certification* [PDF file]. Retrieved January 24, 2021, from https://www.nbpts.org/wp-content/uploads/Guide_to_NB_Certification.pdf

Preston, B. (1992). *Teacher professionalism: Implications for teachers, teacher educators and democratic schooling.* Paper presented at the *AARE Annual Conference.* Deakin University, Geelong, December 1992.

Sachs, J. (2001). Teacher professional identity: Competing discourses, competing outcomes. *Journal of Education Policy, 16*(2), 149–161.

Sachs, J. (2003). *The activist teaching profession.* Oxford: Oxford University Press.

Sachs, J., & Mockler, N. (2012). Performance cultures of teaching: Threat or opportunity? In C. Day (Ed.), *Routledge international handbook on teacher and school development* (pp. 33–43). Abingdon, NY: Routledge.

Sass, T. R. (2011). *Certification requirements and teacher quality: A comparison of alternative routes to teaching* (CALDER Working Paper No. 64). American Institutes for Research.

15 Teacher Identities in a Culture That Is Relatively Stable versus a Culture That Has Undergone a Radical Change

Overview of This Chapter

This chapter highlights the teachers' voices as they reflect on the dynamics of societal changes while re-constructing their professional identities. Professional learning here is conceptualized as "identity work" (Mockler, 2012). The discussion compares social and political developments in Lithuania and the United States inferring that the construction of professional identities takes different trajectories in these countries. In response to the dramatic changes in Lithuania, teachers' professional learning curve steeply increased, causing their identities to change. Teachers frequently have to implement new requirements quickly, often without any training. Under these circumstances, they heavily rely on workplace learning, which stimulates the development of heightened reflectivity and self-awareness in perceiving themselves as learners. The American teachers are slightly changing their identities in the new school, bringing something from their previous workplaces and leaving something behind. As learners, they do not seem to feel any outside pressure to involve in any PD beyond the required hours per year. The chapter closes with a conclusion section that summarizes the findings in Part IV: The findings call for reconceptualization of teachers' professional development to recognize, acknowledge, and accredit professional knowledge, which teachers develop informally through interaction with colleagues and reflexive practices, in which every day learning becomes a reality of professional growth rather than a theoretical concept constructed by researchers.

Formal and Informal Learning Contexts in a Stable Culture Versus a Culture That Has Undergone a Radical and Rapid Change

Viewing teacher professional growth as identity work keeps the focus both on the individual and on the social dimensions of learning. Though the dimensions are closely interrelated, for the analytic purposes, I focused more on the individual aspects of professional learning in Part

II, and school cultures as contexts for workplace learning in Part III. Part IV, and this chapter specifically, emphasizes systematic, societal aspects of such learning with, as Mockler (2012) noticed, "the ongoing 'becoming' of teachers" (p. 42) in the center of the process. Thus, this process is more about the formation and mediation of teachers' professional identity in the society, which develops at the intersection of context (societal, institutional, and personal) and experience (both personal and professional).

In the last decades, the United States and Lithuania experienced radically different developments in educational systems, which can be characterized as stable and radically changing, accordingly. In the United States, the educational system typically experiences shifts with the change of the political leadership at both the national and local levels that introduces new initiatives aligned with the new political climate. As these shifts occur, teachers' identities will slightly change to embrace and implement new policies.

In Lithuania, over the last 30 years of independence from the Soviet regime, the educational system (and the whole society) has experienced radical change and continues to evolve rapidly. The three stages of educational reform mentioned in the Introduction to this part required teachers to constantly re-evaluate their values, beliefs, approaches, and instructional strategies. In addition, the law requiring passing the state language exam[1] put extra pressure on non-Lithuanian teachers, as those who did not meet new language proficiency requirements were in danger of losing their jobs. This law indirectly encouraged other nationalities to send their children to schools with Lithuanian language of instruction to integrate into the society smoothly instead of their native languages (e.g., Polish, Russian, Hebrew), which caused reduction of student population and subsequent closures of many national minorities' schools. Teachers in those schools that remained open (as the Russian school in this study) experienced constant threat of following the fate of their colleagues and losing their jobs.

Because of these and other policies in Lithuania, in addition to a huge influx of non-governmental organizations assisting with implementation of democratic approaches at all levels of education, the teachers' professional learning curve steeply increased and their professional identities were undergoing change. Teachers often had to implement new requirements rapidly without any training. For example, one of the new challenges for elementary teachers at the time of the data collection was the introduction of the idiographic evaluation system. According to this system, elementary school students were not graded anymore. Teachers had to come up with alternative ways of evaluating students' achievement and provide students with consistent feedback.

To implement this requirement, the teachers in the Russian school initiated a project aimed at finding out about the best practices of the idiographic evaluation. Nadia, for example, visited another school looking for positive examples. Her goal was to find out how her colleagues in that school evaluated children without grading. After her visit, she remained skeptical about the idea of ideographic evaluation in general and the practices of her colleagues in particular. She commented:

> Ideographical evaluation **is grading anyway**. In one Lithuanian school, they develop their own **grading book**. Every day, students self-evaluate [their performance] by coloring a box. One poor boy had all the boxes brown.

In the Lithuanian school, Ramute also seemed confused by the students' ideographic evaluation. She did not seem to possess enough knowledge to implement this national requirement. Therefore, she looked for seminars about this evaluation system:

> I always sign up when they talk **about methods**. There, I meet other teachers; we share and discuss. They go there deliberately, not for a check. This year, I have not signed up for anything yet. The closest [PD] is in February, **"Students' Evaluation in Elementary Grades**." We cannot give grades, **but what can we do**?

She looked specifically for workshops that would help her learn more about methods of assessing students without assigning grades; however, in the middle of the school year, she remained without resources to help her deal with the dilemma of evaluating her students' progress. It seemed that teachers in Lithuania were positioned to come up with their own methods of alternative evaluation. The teachers in the Lithuanian school preferred to sign up for seminars, while their colleagues in the Russian school chose to learn from best practices of other teachers.

This situation illustrates how changes in educational policies position teachers to engage in learning, in other words, how metadiscourses influence the direction of teacher learning. The problem of eliminating the grading system was at the top of their minds as the teachers from both participating schools shared their need to figure out what to do instead. Removing the grading system from elementary grades in Lithuania put teachers in an intense learning situation where they had to look for resources and find out alternative ways of evaluation. To help teachers, the Ministry of Education and Science offered workshops; however, openings in such workshops were very limited because they enrolled teachers from the whole country, often giving preference to teachers from smaller towns and remote locations that have less access to resources. This situation created unique contexts for informal learning, which the teachers used to collaborate and share their findings in informal ways.

State and Teachers Assign Different Value to Informal Learning

The Lithuanian teachers discovered a surprising pattern: when they prepared a spreadsheet representing their PD hours over the past 5 years (requested by the administration), it showed a decrease in their formal learning. Sigute, who was responsible for collecting this data, found out that the number of hours for all elementary teachers in her school has been dropping every year. She brought this finding up for discussion with the group of her colleagues:

> When we gathered, [I asked], "Why is it decreasing? Have you brought me all your certificates?" And we talked that in reality over the years, we have taken so many [workshops], that there is **not much new** out there anymore. (…) So, we realized that we were **transitioning toward informal learning**.

This pattern of decreasing PD credits over the years showed them that informal rather than formal PD was the main vehicle in their professional growth. In contexts where formal PD could not keep up with radical and rapid change, teachers accommodated their professional needs by engaging in informal learning activities, such as hallway and over-lunch discussions with colleagues, visits to other classrooms, and collaboration on projects.

The NGO mentioned earlier, an innovative training center that offered alternative workshops on child-centered methods in pre-school and elementary classrooms, also viewed informal learning as an essential part of teachers' professional growth. For example, Genie commented:

> Teachers learn **from each other in informal settings**. (…) One of the priority directions of the EU is to find ways **to give credits for informal learning**. (…) One teacher might have many formal certificates, but he is not a good teacher. Another teacher is better but he does not have that many certificates. Parents know [who is a better teacher]. **That means that informal learning is more important than formal**.

In contrast, the Ministry of Education and Science seemed to undervalue informal learning for teachers' professional growth. A Ministry official expressed her concern about the time teachers spent talking, claiming that their conversations produced no result:

> (…) I am a little worried because our teachers **spend a lot of time talking**. But nothing comes out of this talking because such **conversations are irresponsible**, therefore [teachers] don't have to take

> anything into consideration or change in their work. (…) If you ask a teacher what she has learned and how, what would she say?

Such meta-discursive framing of teachers' professional behaviors implied that teachers could not be trusted and therefore needed supervision and guidance over their own learning (O'Neill, 2002; Quicke, 2000). Disagreement between the Ministry and other educators on the value of informal learning for teachers' professional growth seemed to be reflected in the ways national level educational authorities designed and managed the system of PD. Often, teacher educators in Lithuania did not account for teachers' specific needs but rather constructed their PD themes to explain changes in educational policies. They focused on what they thought teachers needed to know, rather than on helping teachers solve professional dilemmas that they encountered in their practice. Consequently, teachers, as is in the case of the focal schools, experienced difficulty in finding workshops that would satisfy their professional needs.

To conclude, teachers commented on PD events with disappointment in both countries. They pointed out multiple reasons for their dissatisfaction with the formal system of PD: low quality of presentation, outdated themes, inconvenient schedule (in Lithuania, often workshops took place after school or on weekends), and high fees that schools did not always cover. Therefore, teachers compensated for the lack of effective or relevant PD by constructing their own professional learning in informal settings. Having discussed external contexts that shape teachers' identities as learners in both countries, I turn to internal identity work. The next section, in which I explore teacher learning as part of teachers' professional identities, illustrates how teachers' identities are constructed in the national contexts, and how they relate to teachers' informal learning.

Teachers' Identity as Learners: Cultural Aspects

One of the significant factors in teachers' identity construction was the way society defined their social and professional roles. Teachers' identities in Lithuania were constructed on the basis of teacherly roles that combined academic and pastoral responsibilities, in which education and upbringing were closely intertwined. Teachers as professionals helped children develop intellectually, and at the same time contributed to families' work in upbringing.

In contrast, in the Midwestern schools, "the two [were] separate and teachers [were] fighting to keep them that way. One [was] the province of schools, the other of parents" (Alexander, 2000, p. 234). In addition, the fragmentation of the academic tasks and the imposition of structural constraints upon the ability to interact with students over an extended period (e.g., teaching the same-grade) resulted in a depersonalized school environment (Hufton et al., 2003). Specifically, such alienation influenced relationships between teachers and their students. Thus, American teachers' identities were constructed based on their roles as instructors and curriculum deliverers. Teachers seemed to prefer to be considered professionals whose sole responsibility was to develop students' academic skills.

The way the participating teachers in both countries referred to their students reflected this difference in their professional identity. For example, in my conversations with teachers in Lithuania they referred to their students using the words "kids" and "children" and never used "students". The teachers in the Midwest constantly used the official term "students" and only once in a while used "children" or "kids". These differences in expression of teachers' identities related to the ways the national education systems positioned their teachers in terms of their professional growth and the ways teachers perceived themselves as learners.

In Lithuania, teachers' professional growth (measured by credit hours of PD) seemed to be directly related to their attestation level and salary. National goals and teacher standards served as guidelines and inspiration for teachers' development; however, as the official from the Ministry of Education and Science (currently, the Ministry of Education, Science and Sports) noted, current economic and social factors slowed down or even hindered teachers' learning to embrace change. Her definition of Lithuanian teachers' identity as learners represented a meta-discursive perspective characteristic of the general societal understanding of factors that prevented teachers from becoming agents of change rather than subjects of reform. The Ministry official underscored the main factor—teachers' insecurity:

> **(...) Our teachers are insecure**. There are many reasons. One is that with the change of the society, **many teachers did not manage to change** neither emotionally, not intellectually. (...) Not only some teachers have not changed, but those **who evaluate them haven't changed** too. Maybe, a teacher has changed, but that evaluator has not. So the teacher feels very insecure. All those changes, such as joining the EU and all kinds of transatlantic [projects]—though we want to be together with others but we have to move so fast that that **rapidity, haste also makes us insecure**. One more thing is **the decrease of children and the optimization of the educational system**, I mean the job security. Our society changes and **children are different**. And teachers don't understand that they have to change. Children are not going to change. THEY have to work with those different kids. (...) That is why our teachers are insecure. We have a very **strong hierarchical system**. And if you stand on this [higher] step, your voice is important but it is also not safe. Because we need more time and desire to establish democratic relationships. That's why **change is slow**.

In this excerpt, the Ministry official claimed that many teachers failed to change and those who evaluated them failed to change as well. Nonetheless, in the same interview, she complimented Lithuanian teachers as compared to teachers from other countries, and defined elementary teachers in Lithuania as highly responsible professionals:

> (…) Our teachers are very responsible as compared to foreign teachers because they [foreign teachers] have everything. But they don't appreciate it, **and they look at their job as tradesmen**.

However, being responsible in a highly hierarchical system could also mean being complacent with the status quo. Thus, in the current Lithuanian context of insecurity, responsibility, though typically a positive professional feature, could also impede professional growth and change.

Further, the Ministry official pointed out other positive features, such as the high quality of Lithuanian teachers' professional preparation and their creativity:

> (…) Many notice our teachers' creativity as compared to American teachers. We don't have many things, but [we have strong] preparation in methods and good textbooks. Over there, everything is ready to go, and a teacher has only to play it out, and fulfill. But we have **to live everything out together with children**.

The teachers' comments that the school was home for them and that teaching was their vocation rather than profession, as well as their generous dedication of personal time to their professional work and their curiosity and drive to solve professional dilemmas—all these features accorded with the official's perspective. In my private conversations with American teacher educators, when they came to Lithuania to help with teacher training, they also expressed amazement at Lithuanian teachers' knowledgeability, ingenuity, and creativity.

By contrast, in the Midwest, after teachers completed their Master's degree, they did not seem to have any external motivation to go to PD workshops or teacher conferences. They felt that they were qualified professionals. In addition, they did not seem to be aware of any specific teacher standards or other regulations that would require them to grow professionally after they acquired tenure. As a disclaimer, I need to say that the conversations with American teachers took place in 2005–2006. Today, with the introduction of teacher evaluation in every state, I might have received a very different response from my interviewees. John, for example, at the time of the interview did not know about any teacher standards or any goals for teacher development that he would have to fulfill:

E Are there any **teacher standards** in the United States?
J **Not that I know of**. You mean like to be a teacher, or to stay a teacher?

E To stay a teacher or to proceed to a certain level?

J You know **we don't have that**. What we have as far as I know is: you just need a college degree to pass the state tests and get certificate, you teach for four years and then you can get tenure. And then after that it's kind of up to you to further yourself.

Kristi, who agreed that she had accomplished her formal education, admitted that informal learning was as important to her as the formal one (similar to the teachers from the Lithuanian school). She positioned herself as being "post-formal-learner". Like John, she did not seem to have any obligations to participate in professional development events except for the district requirements of 5 PD days per year:

> **The learning I do informally is as important as the one I do formally**, especially, when I am **past formal learning**. Occasionally, I take vocational courses or do professional development that my district requires me to do. But the **majority of the learning** that happens now for me **happens in the classroom**.

Interestingly, all Lithuanian and some American teachers expressed and defined a specific internal aspect or "a drive" to be constantly engaged in learning and professional growth as an important factor for learning. Ana, for example, described how she learned by setting up a goal and pursuing it:

> (...) **I put up a goal and go toward it**. There are still many moments that **I need to work on**. (...) **I know everything what is going on in Russia** [in education] from the Internet.

Working in the school with the Russian language of instruction, Ana seemed to be interested in educational developments in Russia that could inform her work. She desired to provide consistency and better support students from embassy families that eventually would return to Russia.

Debbie also described her "drive" for professional growth through constantly taking courses: "Well, I'm **always taking courses**, may be 10–12 credits a year". Moreover, later, she added a story about how she had followed a famous specialist to a different state to learn from her:

> You can get that training in [this state] but [the teacher trainer] went to Ohio State to train all the professors there. That's why I went to Ohio State (...) and got the training there. **So I think, it's determination, responsibility, risk-tak[ing], motivation—those are all key factors in learning**.

In sum, though social developments and related educational policies in Lithuania and the United States seemed to position teachers to grow professionally in different ways (a centralized, structured, goal-oriented, and externally motivated system of PD in Lithuania and an open-ended, almost requirement-free, and flexible PD system in the United States), most of the teachers in both countries expressed dissatisfaction with the existing system of PD. They argued that they learned most of all informally in their classrooms or by interacting with their colleagues.

Conclusions for Part IV

This part illustrated ways in which Lithuanian and American education systems organized teachers' professional learning and growth differently. Comparative analysis highlighted patterns within the contexts of PD provision. Relationships between state-run teacher training institutions, NGOs that offered alternative teacher training, and teachers seemed to be coordinated in Lithuania, where teachers were both positioned and motivated externally and internally to seek higher levels of professionalism. In the United States, such relationships were determined by minimum local requirements, and mostly left for the teachers to define. In addition, the quality of opportunities for effective learning varied from state to state and from district to district (Bransford et al., 1999).

Teacher identities as learners also appeared to differ significantly in Lithuania and in the Midwestern US state. Teachers perceived their work differently: for the American teachers in this study it was a regular job, while for the Lithuanian teachers it was a vocation. Curricula and assessment reforms created contexts for extensive professional learning in both countries; however, less detailed curricula required the American teachers to be more creative in curriculum design, while a highly detailed national curriculum in Lithuania triggered the teachers' creativity in adapting it to the needs of their students.

By being assigned to teach at one grade level rather than learning how to teach specific students, teachers in the United States were positioned to mainly concentrate on learning about how to better teach their grade level curriculum. Four-year looping in Lithuania required teachers to respond to a wide variety of students' developmental patterns as well as to review their own and their colleagues' practices. Consequently, in their professional development, Lithuanian teachers focused on learning to teach specific students and focused on developmental elements rather than only centering on a curriculum.

The American teachers spent a lot of their instructional time administering tests, which provided information about their students' academic levels. For example, teachers used running records at least twice a year with each student to identify their reading level. Tests were designed by other institutions, acquired and approved by districts or states for the use in the classrooms. Lithuanian teachers had considerable freedom in how they assessed students' progress. They used formal and informal assessments, which in most cases were designed by them to provide their students with feedback on their progress rather than to learn about them.

In Lithuania, the professional development incentive was built into the process of teacher attestation. National goals and teacher standards served as a guideline for teachers' mandatory PD. In the US Midwest, PD was guided by general state goals for education (5 days per year required), by introduction of new curricula, and by needs and interests of teachers. The American teachers did not acknowledge any external motivation to engage in PD workshops or teacher conferences above the required minimum. After they acquired tenure, these teachers felt that they were qualified professionals in no need to seek for additional PD. They did not seem to be aware of any teacher standards or other regulations that would require them to grow professionally.

Despite major differences, there were similarities in how these groups of American and Lithuanian teachers perceived themselves as learners. In both countries, they similarly reflected on the professional value of their pre-service training, contrasting it with their learning, especially informal, at the workplace. They claimed that they learned how to teach and became comfortable teaching only after a few first years of practice. At the same time, they expressed dissatisfaction with the formal system of PD. Learning from and in practice became essential in their professional growth. Though educational policies in Lithuania and the United States positioned teachers to grow professionally in different ways (a centralized, structured, goal-oriented, and externally motivated system of PD in Lithuania and an open-ended, almost requirement-free, and flexible PD system in the United States), most of the teachers in both countries highly valued informal learning that occurred in their work place.

Specific differences that this study illuminates could reflect larger national and international tendencies, which might be essential in interpreting national educational cultures. For example, if we apply Peter Jarvis's (2000) concept of learning societies with its four types (futuristic, planned, reflexive, and market) that are defined depending on the social meaning ascribed to learning based on the analysis offered in this part, the educational infrastructure in Lithuania and the United States can be categorized as planned and market, respectively. In Lithuania, certain provisions of learning are planned and institutionalized for the realization of lifelong learning, aligning with the European Union directives. The American educational infrastructure tends to reflect the market approach (Webb et al., 2004; Whitty et al., 1998), in which knowledge production becomes an industry and the learning society turns into a learning market. In regards to teachers' professional learning, both planned and market perceptions of learning societies, unfortunately, do not seem to value informal workplace learning, which the teachers in both countries defined as an essential part of their professional growth.

I argue for the recognition and accreditation of workplace learning, learning in and from practice. However, such expanded understanding of professional leaning poses new challenges for teacher educators, educational researchers and leaders. It requires reconceptualization of teachers' professional development to recognize, acknowledge, and accredit professional knowledge, which teachers develop informally through interaction with colleagues and reflexive practices, in which every day learning becomes a reality of professional growth rather than a theoretical concept constructed by researchers.

Note

1 According to the Republic of Lithuania Law of the State Language I-779, January 31, 1995 (Lietuvos Respublikos valstybinos kalbos Istatymas Nr.I-779), all non-Lithuanian natives had to pass a Lithuanian language exam at a certain level of fluency in order to retain their jobs. For more information: http://www.minelres.lv/NationalLegislation/Lithuania/Lithuania_Language_1995_English.htm.

References

Alexander, R. (2000). *Culture and Pedagogy.* Oxford: Blackwell.

Bransford, J. D., Brown, A. L., & Cocking, R. R. (1999). *How people learn.* Washington, DC: National Academy Press.

Hufton, N. R., Elliot, J. G., & Illushin, L. (2003). Teachers' beliefs about student motivation: Similarities and differences across cultures. *Comparative Education, 39*(3), 367–389.

Jarvis, P. (2000). Globalisation, the learning society and cooperative education. *Comparative Education, 36*(3), 343–355.

Mockler, N. (2012). Teacher professional learning in a neoliberal age: Audit, professionalism and identity. *Australian Journal of Teacher Education, 38*(10).

O'Neill, O. (2002). *A question of trust: The BBC Reith lectures, 2002.* Cambridge: Cambridge University Press.

Quicke, J. (2000). A new professionalism for a collaborative culture of organizational learning in contemporary society. *Educational Management and Administration, 28*, 299–315.

Webb, R., Vulliamy, G., Hämäläinen, S., Sarja, A., Kimonen, E., & Nevalainen, R. (2004). A comparative analysis of primary teacher professionalism in England and Finland. *Comparative Education, 40*(1), 83–107.

Whitty, G., Power, S., & Halpin, D. (1998). *Devolution and choice in education.* Buckingham: Open University Press.

Final Thoughts

Overview of This Chapter

This chapter offers a part-by-part reflection, which revisits the conclusions from each part of the book to achieve the holistic understanding of all three "nesting doll" layers and to highlight questions for further investigation of informal learning in educational workplace contexts. First, the individual level of informal learning is discussed accentuating the original framework of five categories. Second, the narrative returns to the institutional level of analysis and suggests that teachers as learners develop complex relationships with their school cultures that deeply impact their informal professional learning. Third, the findings from the analysis of the national level yield a proposal for a re-conceptualization of professional development to include and accredit informal workplace learning.

In this book, I used a "nesting doll" design that contextualized the investigation of teacher informal learning in the workplace by examining discourses at three layers: individual, institutional, and district/national. I did so using an anthropological lens by scrutinizing how teachers positioned themselves as learners within these three layers of cultures (interchangeably called discourses or contexts) and how teachers shaped their professional identities as learners through interactions with these cultures. An emic perspective that highlighted the teachers' voices in regards to their participation in informal workplace learning interweaved with my interpretive and analytic voice (an etic perspective) to identify patterns in social processes associated with informal learning and the opportunities embedded in these processes. The first part outlined the contexts within which this discussion of informal learning fits, explained the design, and introduced the participants. Three following parts of the book (Parts II, III, and IV) focused on three levels of the educational system respectively: individual, institutional and national layers. By following a cultural model, I demonstrated that as a sub-culture, each layer embodied its own characteristics within a complex cultural web of relationships. Each layer provided a unique view into a larger culture and its relationship with other layers. Each part also took a different angle using discourse-analytic tools for the analysis of informal learning differently, which allowed for an in-depth discussion of features specific to each layer and, thus, shaping a multifaceted understanding of the informal learning phenomenon. The "nesting doll" design exhilarated discourse analyses that evolved from a microanalysis of teachers' reflective journals to a mega analysis of the major national trends in teacher learning.

In the ensuing part-by-part reflection, I revisit the conclusions from each part from the perspective of the holistic understanding of all three "nesting doll" layers to highlight questions for further investigation of informal learning in educational workplace contexts. First, I revisit the individual level of informal learning for which I constructed an original framework of five categories. Second, I return to the institutional level of analysis and suggest that teachers as learners develop complex relationships with their school cultures that impact their informal professional learning. Third, I reflect upon my findings from the analysis of the national level, and I propose a re-conceptualization of professional development to include and accredit informal workplace learning.

Individual Teachers as Learners

In the first part of this book, I discussed how individual teachers in the Lithuanian and American schools shaped their learning in informal settings at their workplaces. The study represented teachers' perspectives on their identities as learners as they reflected upon contexts, situations, resources, and actions that they undertook when engaging in learning. The results of this round of analysis that focused on how the teachers positioned themselves as learners in their everyday practice yielded the analytic framework that consisted of five categories: Dispositions, Focus, Sources, Processes, and Reactions. These five categories emerged from the ways teachers communicated their engagement in informal learning through their writing and in speech. While developing these categories, I also examined the dimensions of the stances of teachers' learning within each category. By plotting the qualities of the stances within each category, I positioned teachers on a continuum between opposite stances (dispositions: opportunistic—proactive; focus: self-oriented—teaching-oriented; reaction: emotional—cognitive; sources: individual—social; processes: spontaneous—deliberate).

Applying the framework of these five categories to the investigation of the teachers' reflective journal entries and interviews through the lens of discourse analysis revealed culturally specific patterns. The results demonstrated that most of the Lithuanian and some American and Russian teachers tended to display binary characteristics in each of the five categories. For example, Sigute's learning profile showed that she approached learning situations by assuming different stances with close-to-equal frequency. This finding sets the stage for further research, which might investigate relationships between informal learning opportunities and stances that teachers take toward learning. Further research of informal learning features and patterns of their manifestation in practice might help teachers, educators, and administrators determine how we could enhance teachers' learning by identifying stimulating features in everyday workplace contexts.

This microdiscourse analysis explicated several informal teacher learning patterns. Deeper observations of these patterns of relationships between some categories (specifically, dispositions–reactions–processes) suggest the possibility of predicting that those teachers, who were, for example, opportunistic in their disposition to learning, also tended to react emotionally to learning situations and engage spontaneously in a learning process. Similarly, those teachers, who took a cognitive stance in their reactions, deliberately engaged in a learning process; however, explaining relationships within or between emergent patterns was beyond the realm of this study. More research is needed to define and explain these relationships in terms of their nature. Are the patterns mentioned above context-specific? In what learning contexts are these patterns explicit? Is there a relationship between emerging learning patterns and contextualized opportunities? What patterns emerge in which contexts?

Furthermore, the diversity of teachers' informal learning, as a complex of multiple dimensions that assumed different patterns, was consistently visible across cultural patterns. For example, two American teachers (Kristi and John) demonstrated similar patterns of combined characteristics. One Russian teacher (Marija) also followed the same pattern but represented the other side of the continua on all five characteristics, thereby assuming the opposite position in the process of informal learning. Cultural affiliation seemed to play an important role in predicting what pattern of the characteristics' composite teachers might employ in their informal learning experiences. The American teachers were more likely to engage in informal learning by displaying an opportunistic disposition, self-oriented focus, and emotional reactions; engaging in the process of learning spontaneously; and using individual sources of learning. The Russian teachers, different from their American colleagues, were more likely to display a proactive disposition, teaching-oriented focus, and cognitive reactions; engage in the learning process deliberately; and use social learning sources. The Lithuanian teachers displayed all these features comparatively equally. The analysis of school and national cultures that followed in the ensuing chapters confirmed that different national educational cultures in Lithuania and the United States as well as three different kinds of school cultures, which the teachers represented, could cast some light on within-school similarities in patterns of the teachers' informal learning. More research is needed to find out how individual, school, and national educational cultures might have influenced these patterns.

The five-category framework now makes certain investigations possible in answering the following questions: how do teachers learn through casual interaction with students, colleagues, and administrators? How does a school culture relate to informal learning? How do personal, school, and national cultures influence professional teacher identity? How do teachers make choices in positioning themselves as learners in a learning situation? Pursuing these questions could provide teacher educators and administrators with additional knowledge to assist teachers in becoming life-long-learners and achieving higher quality in their professional performance.

Moreover, the five-category structure and its dimensions, which represent the diversity of teachers' informal learning as a complex of multiple stances that assume different patterns, could be developed into a typology of teachers as informal learners. This structure also serves as a framework for hypothesizing cultural patterns of teacher learning within institutional and national educational settings and paves the way for in-depth exploration of cultural similarities and differences in teacher learning within an international comparative framework.

School Cultures

The third part of this book focused on school cultures to examine workplace contexts for teacher learning and ways teachers engaged with these contexts in the process of everyday professional learning. The leading proposition of the study, that professional knowledge develops not only in the individual mind but is also cultural and intrinsic to the contexts within which individuals interact, steered this inquiry into schools as learning organizations.

To investigate the culture of schools as learning organizations, I defined culture as a social phenomenon constructed through interactions between the members and the operational contexts of an organization. Culture is reflected in common knowledge of the members who develop, share, and use it to interpret the world within and outside an organization and generate social behaviors manifested through values, attitudes, and different kinds of knowledge (Anderson-Levitt, 2002). This perception of school culture led to the exploration of how its specific characteristics (school mission, traditions, physical environment, organizational arrangements, and professional relationships) fostered opportunities for teachers' workplace learning, and how teachers in three schools related to these cultures as learners.

Analyses of the three schools' cultures and the teachers' relationships with and within them demonstrated that each school had a distinctive learning culture (Dyson & Genishi, 2005). These distinctions were visible in the content and means of formulating and publicizing each school's mission: Achievement-oriented in the American school; clear and specific goals to serve the needs of the community in the Lithuanian school; and aligning themselves with Lithuanian state traditions in the Russian school. These mission statements sent distinct messages about each school's priorities and directions for development, which accurately reflected the learning climate of the three organizations.

Traditions that could provide occasions for informal professional learning through social events existed in all the schools. Teachers could make use of these social events to develop collegial relationships that created and sustained professional learning opportunities; however, in the relatively new climate of the American school, teachers did not seem to view social events as contexts for informal learning. On the contrary, in the more established Lithuanian and Russian schools, traditions provided rich contexts for informal teacher learning. In the Russian school, traditions seemed to be the most consistent and engaging occasions for teachers' informal learning among the scarce opportunities offered there. All the elementary school teachers in the Lithuanian school had many traditions and seemed to enjoy each other's company and "inhale" ideas and practices of the colleagues together with the celebratory atmosphere of the events.

Teachers perceived and used physical spaces in their schools for informal learning differently. In the Lithuanian and the Russian schools both of which housed grades one through twelve, elementary classrooms were situated on one floor, allowing teachers for easier encounters and interactions than in the American school, which was wing-shaped and occupied two floors. In addition, different visions of classroom space seemed to assign different roles to the classroom spaces: classrooms were unique, almost personal teachers' spaces in the American school that allowed for individual expression; classrooms that were open to colleagues, always changing learning environment in the Lithuanian school were places for expression of creativity, and collaboration; and classrooms that were highly monitored by administration in the Russian school were places that were focused on implementing administrators' requirements. In addition, in the American and Russian schools, classrooms seemed to have perceived boundaries between individual teachers' spaces and other spaces at school. In the Lithuanian school, the perceived borders between classrooms and other spaces were not observable, which expanded informal learning spaces and encouraged interactions between teachers and other educators across the grades.

The schools also differed in their organizational arrangements for informal learning, with more similarities found between the Lithuanian and Russian schools. The principal of the American school created additional opportunities for informal interactions by organizing teachers' schedules to include common preparation time for the same grade level teachers. Their Lithuanian and Russian colleagues did not have intentionally planned common preparation time; during non-teaching time, they graded students' papers, prepared for the upcoming lessons, or got together for a cup of coffee or tea in the teacher's lounge (in the Lithuanian school). Some of them went to the cafeteria and talked with other teachers who happened to be there at that time.

The principals and middle managers played different roles in the American school as compared to their counterparts in the Lithuanian and Russian schools. The American principal and the head teacher (Kristi) seemed to have little impact on professional development events, except for providing administrative support. On the contrary, in both schools in Lithuania, assistant principals for elementary education and the leaders of the elementary methods committees (Marija and Ramute) were directly responsible for organizing their teachers' professional development. Lithuanian teachers reported making additional time during school, beyond organized events, to coordinate their ideas and actions in a way that was satisfactory for their professional growth and enjoyable on a personal level (e.g., before-classes gatherings in the teacher's lounge). American teachers, however, were satisfied with the scheduled social events and found no need to extend interactions beyond them, and Russian teachers thought it was essential to stay after school and work with their colleagues during their personal time.

As I mentioned earlier, I did not apply Law's (1999) framework of five organizational elements of supportive professional development culture in school, yet some of these elements emerged from my conversations with teachers and were reflected in participant observations. As such, I note them here. The teachers reported that the principal of the Lithuanian school effectively managed information/communication flow and provided them with information about professional development opportunities in a quick and informal manner; they also seemed to have developed open networking opportunities to facilitate mutual support and reflection. The principal of the American school introduced a system for shared and open planning processes for the teachers; however, following Law's framework, it was evident that two organizational elements of supportive professional development culture were not visible in the data collected for this study: the operation of clear resource allocation procedures with focused aims and targets, and the establishment of a clear evaluation strategy used as a basis for ongoing review and development.

Nevertheless, the teachers' views of the administrative arrangements in their schools reflected different leadership approaches and, thus, provided differing opportunities for teachers' professional growth ranging from close supervision and judgment (the Russian school), to accommodating teachers' professional needs (the American school), to empowering teachers to take responsibility for their work quality and professional growth (the Lithuanian school).

Professional relationships in the schools created or failed to create favorable contexts for teachers' informal learning. Distinct learning patterns that transpired in the schools reflected specific relationships that emerged from applying Hargreaves' (1999) framework of knowledge-creating schools (tinkering, transfer, research of practice and facilitation by middle managers). Professional relationships in the American school seemed to be friendly but not yet collegial. For example, tinkering with their practice, through experimentation and exploration of their practice, required transfer of knowledge between colleagues; however, social novelty and traditional professional isolation reinforced by architectural and cultural factors that increased separation prevented the teachers from sharing their professional experiences and dilemmas. Instead, the teachers in the American school engaged in co-tinkering while co-planning and observing their grade-level colleagues' practices by picking up and transferring newly developed understandings into their practice. In the Russian school, the teachers engaged in individual tinkering; however, due to the limited opportunities for interactions, they rarely engaged in knowledge transfer. Though the teachers participated in curriculum development and piloting of new approaches, they did so only with colleagues they trusted. The teachers varied in their use of principal-provided support and opportunities for informal learning. Some teachers extended their learning opportunities beyond the borders of the school; others took advantage of the school's organizational arrangements and initiated collaborative learning between teachers of different grades; yet the others confined their professional learning to collaboration only with their grade level teachers.

In the Lithuanian school, teachers practiced tinkering individually by playing and experimenting with new ideas. They engaged in knowledge transfer through observations and discussions of their colleagues' teaching, participation in formal professional development events and exchanging ideas after that; however, their vigorous learning community appeared to cultivate professional (self)-perfection, excluding those who did not match their high standards (as it happened with a substitute teacher), rather than helping newcomers find their ways to contribute to the team. The American and Russian schools engaged in self-assessment and internal audit. In contrast, the Lithuanian school measured their professional achievements differently: they developed close relationships with the University that invited them to teach there and work with their student-teachers in their classrooms. The teachers in all three schools engaged both in collaborative practices (more in the Lithuanian and the American schools) and assumed individualistic stances toward learning (more in the Russian and the American schools); however, it was not evident in the data whether the teachers favored collaboration over isolation or whether the degree of collaboration was related to the opportunities for informal learning provided by the schools.

National Educational Cultures

Part IV discussed different ways in which Lithuanian and American education systems organized teachers' formal and informal professional learning. Comparative analysis highlighted patterns within the contexts of pre- and in-service professional learning that emerged from analyzing national/state educational documents. This national sketch of teacher learning affordances and opportunities (the discussion was not aimed at an in-depth analysis of national systems) foregrounded the teachers' accounts of their engagement in formal and informal professional learning.

In Lithuania, state requirements positioned and motivated teachers externally and internally to seek higher levels of professionalism defined by the levels of attestation. Open competition for teachers between state-run teacher training institutions and non-governmental organizations that offered alternative teacher training seemed to be able to bring PD closer to teachers' interests than in the American Midwestern state. Multiple PD offerings in Lithuania allowed for more choices for teachers to experience training with innovative content and methods of delivery that met their needs. In the Midwestern US school, such relationships were determined by minimal local requirements, and mostly left for the teachers to define. In addition, because of the highly decentralized system, the quality of opportunities for effective learning varied significantly from state to state and from district to district (Bransford et al., 1999), which the participating teachers have experienced and brought up in our discussions.

In Lithuania, the PD incentive was built into the process of teacher attestation. National goals and teacher standards for professional progress served as specific guidelines for teachers' mandatory professional development. In the Midwest, professional development was guided by general state goals for education (5 days per year required), by introduction of new curricula, and, occasionally, by the needs and interests of teachers; however, the American teachers did not acknowledge any external motivation to engage in PD or teacher conferences above the required minimum. After they acquired tenure, these teachers felt that they had enough education to be considered qualified professionals. Even though the standards and other regulations that required teachers to grow professionally were present, the teachers did not seem to be aware of them. This situation might have changed since the states and school districts across the nation responded to the federal legislation by adopting evaluative value-added measurement systems for teachers and principals (e.g., Alger, 2012; Auguste et al., 2010; Danielson, 2013; Kane & Staiger, 2012; Marzano et al., 2012; Rentner & Kober, 2012). These systems emerged as a response to a political call for a higher accountability for teachers with a focus on improved educator effectiveness demonstrated in student achievement. They triggered an opposition movement among educators, including over a dozen lawsuits. In response to this educators' outcry, Every Student Succeeds Act (ESSA) adopted by the federal government in 2015, tried to rectify the situation by withdrawing the federal government's control over states' teacher evaluation systems and permitting more local control. As a result, the number of the states still using value-added models dropped to 29%. Other states either stopped using them and switched to local control or use them only formatively (Close et al., 2019).

Teacher identities as learners also appeared to differ in Lithuania and in the American Midwestern schools. First, teachers perceived their work differently: most of the American teachers in this study regarded teaching as a regular job, while the Lithuanian teachers considered it a vocation. Second, curricula and assessment reforms created contexts for extensive professional learning in both countries; however, less detailed curricula required American teachers to be more creative in designing the layout of the content, while a highly detailed national curriculum in Lithuania triggered teachers' creativity in adapting it to the needs of their students. Third, teachers in the United States, who taught at one grade level rather than looping across a few grade levels and teaching the same students as they progressed through several grade levels, were positioned to focus on learning about how to better teach their grade level curriculum. Four-year looping in Lithuania allowed teachers to get to know their students very well and, thus, enabled them to respond to a wide variety of their students' developmental patterns as well as share their experiences with their colleagues. Consequently, in their professional development, Lithuanian teachers focused on learning how to teach specific students rather than a curriculum. In order to learn about their students' academic needs, American teachers spent a lot of their instructional time administering tests. At the end of the school year, they seemed to know almost all of their students well enough; however, they had to hand them over to a colleague teaching the next grade. On the other hand, Lithuanian teachers had considerable freedom in how they assessed their students' progress. They used written and oral assessments, in many cases they designed themselves, to provide their students with formative feedback on their progress. The Midwestern teachers had to implement state and federal required tests as a measure of the school improvement.

The analysis of teachers' interviews revealed similarities in how these groups of American and Lithuanian teachers perceived themselves as learners. In both countries, they similarly reflected on the professional value of their pre-service training, rating it low and contrasting it with their learning, especially informal, in the workplace. The participating teachers claimed that they learned how to teach, and became comfortable with teaching after only a few years of practice. At the same time, they expressed dissatisfaction with their formal systems of professional development. According to their accounts, learning in and from practice became essential for their professional growth. Though educational policies in Lithuania and the United States positioned teachers to grow professionally in different ways (a centralized, structured, goal-oriented, and externally motivated system of PD in Lithuania and an open-ended, almost requirement-free and flexible PD system in the United States), most of the teachers in both countries highly valued the informal learning that occurred in their workplace.

These specific similarities and differences that transpired in this exploratory study might point to larger national and cross-national tendencies, which could help interpreting national educational cultures. For example, the application of Peter Jarvis' (2000) concept of learning societies—with its four interpretations of social meaning ascribed to learning (futuristic, planned, reflexive, and market)—categorizes the educational infrastructure in Lithuania and the United States as planned and market, respectively. In Lithuania, certain provisions of learning were planned and institutionalized for realization of lifelong learning to align with the European Union aspirations in this area. The American educational infrastructure tended to reflect the market approach (Webb et al., 2004; Whitty et al., 1998), in which knowledge production became an industry and the learning society turned into a learning market. Regrettably for teachers' professional learning, neither planned nor market perceptions of learning societies accommodate and accredit workplace informal learning, which the teachers in both countries define as an essential part of their professional growth.

From the perspective of the teachers participating in this research, teacher education and accreditation systems would improve the quality of teaching and of teachers' professional development if they formally recognized informal workplace learning as an important component of professional growth. Policies that would do so would acknowledge, value, and reward the professional knowledge teachers develop informally through interaction with colleagues and their reflexive practices in the workplace.

Informal Learning and Learners Revisited

In this study, I did not intend to solve the problem of drawing clear boundaries between formal and informal learning. Whether such boundaries are possible or warranted has yet to be determined. Yet this study illuminates distinctions between formal and informal learning in natural contexts as a topic for further research and discussion. I encountered the problem of distinguishing between the two while analyzing data, when I assigned codes to learning situations that the participating teachers reported. For example, when describing his work for a class that he took toward his higher degree in education (which I categorized as formal learning), John reflected that he had discussed some ideas from that work with his colleagues during co-planning (that I qualified as informal learning), which could have led to transformation of his initial understandings. In this case, a formal learning experience extended to include informal learning. In another example, when teachers in the American school engaged in co-planning during the time specifically scheduled for this activity, it was even more problematic to specify whether their new understandings were the result of informal or formal interactions, inevitable from their participation in a planned event.

Further exploration is needed of formal situations that involve informal learning and of informal situations that draw on formal learning experiences. To overcome this dilemma in my data analysis, I stayed close to the definition of informal teachers' learning as learning that occurs in settings that are not initially designed and organized for teachers' learning. In addition, I limited my investigation to workplace learning, at the same time admitting that teachers acquire professional knowledge informally in many other ways (e.g., watching TV, reading fiction, playing with their children, window-shopping, going to museums and galleries).

In this book, I described teachers as agents of learning, as embodied and social learners (Hodkinson et al., 2004). I also defined learning as a cultural practice, which differs from a "classic" psychological definition of learning (any permanent change that is not the result of maturation). In learning seen as a cultural practice, the distinction between change and no change is not evident and clear. As Hodkinson and his colleagues notice, such learning

> ...entails reinforcement and deepening (of understanding, of beliefs, of practices, of skills). Such learning may be passive or active on the part of the learner, at least in the sense that a learner may deliberately strive to learn or learn simply by being there and taking part. Either way, learning is essentially a process of participation and construction (or reconstruction), not the transfer of knowledge or skills into the learner as vessel.
>
> (p. 14)

As a socially constructed cultural practice, learning involves different meanings assigned by participants who bring their values and understandings to the process of learning, often implicitly contributing to the cultural reconstruction. I found that when the idea of learning for personal growth is substituted by attainment of credentials necessary to perform the job, and when teachers' performance is judged by the students' outcomes in high stakes testing, what counts as learning often excludes informal learning. Even though teachers strive to grow as professionals, meanings that educational authorities (federal, state, district) bring to bear on teacher professional development have direct implications for what can be learned and how. Thus, informal learning that provides teachers with possibilities for personalizing their learning experiences and making them relevant to their everyday practice could be enhanced if it is supported by federal, state, and district policies as well as organizational arrangements of school administration. It could be a challenging task because as Lave (1996) argued, "There are enormous differences in what and how learners come to shape (or be shaped into) their identities with respect to different practices". Thus, she sets the goal for research "to explore each practice to understand what is being learned, and how" (pp. 161–162).

The nature of the study (exploratory) limited me to selecting a few subcultures for a deeper exploration, leaving out other parts of the cultural web for future examination. For example, I collected survey data from all elementary teachers in the focal schools to provide additional support for claims that I made about school cultures. Though it seemed to be an important piece of data that could have strengthened validity of school culture cases, I set it aside, choosing the path of deeper engagement with rich and ample interview and observation records.

I also intentionally left out such important foci as, for example, the district-level analysis, which could have provided insights on how national policies are mediated and "translated" for schools to implement. District policies found their presence only as the participants in the interviews mentioned them. Shifting an angle of analysis to compare different grade-level teaching cultures (e.g., preschool, elementary, middle-, and high-school teachers) and distinct professional cultures in general (e.g., teachers, doctors, engineers, actors) could cast light on scarcely researched aspects of informal learning by drawing on different bodies of literature and bringing other perspectives to bear on informal professional learning. It might also be worthwhile to compare how school cultures within one country that serve different communities (e.g., Native American, African American, Latino, Arab American or inner city, suburban, small-town schools) create opportunities for teachers' informal learning and how teachers respond to these opportunities.

In sum, this analysis of 11 teachers in the context of three school cultures and two national cultures in relation to teachers' informal learning illuminated differences that appear to have a great deal to do with the priorities of each school's culture and with certain positioning of teachers-as-learners' identities by the national educational cultures. In addition, the study revealed that school cultures' characteristics were in accord with the national culture that was shaped by federal/district policies, national politics and social/cultural features all of which influenced the ways teachers enacted their identities as learners.

This study has shown the importance of the relationships between a school and a nation's socio-political and historical–cultural contexts. Those relationships, as viewed in three cross-national and cross-developmental cases, appeared to shape the ways in which informal teacher learning was regarded, valued, and acted upon by educators.

This study aimed at a holistic approach to informal learning as it occurs in the workplace by situating it within three embedded cultural contexts. While this perspective and the methodologies it yielded have proven useful, other approaches might provide additional insights. More research is needed to investigate relationships between local and federal policies and examine their influence on the recognition and the uptake of informal workplace teacher learning. Here are some of the questions that need answers: What are the relationships between principals' leadership styles/models/policies and school-based opportunities for informal learning?

How do school sub-cultures (grade-level, administrative, subject matter, and other groups) construct and support informal learning opportunities? How do cultures of schools that successfully serve multiple societal groups (i.e., well-respected, high-status schools) encourage and support their teachers' informal learning in specific ways that differ from other schools (given that all three schools discussed in this book fall under the "high-status" category)?

The perspective of this study and the employed methodologies offer three prismatic views of a single but complex phenomenon—informal workplace learning. Earlier described as a "nesting doll" approach, each of the three prisms represents a unique aspect of informal leaning. The study's focus on individual cultures defined teachers as agents in the process of professional learning and growth. The institutional focus placed teachers in their immediate professional contexts—their schools—and illuminated how individual features and national tendencies play out within school cultures to create opportunities for teachers' informal learning. Its national/state focus provided an analysis of teachers' points of view of informal learning in relationship to broader educational policy. As much as these multidimensional layers informed the discussion of informal learning, generalizations across schools and across countries from this small sample would be imprudent and irresponsible. Nevertheless, engaging in prismatic analyses of socio-cultural contexts opens an expansive space for research and discussion of informal learning as a complex phenomenon.

References

Alger, V. E. (2012). *Teacher selection and evaluation in Nebraska* [Report]. Retrieved from https://www.platteinstitute.org/Library/docLib/20120109_Teacher_Selection_and_Evaluation_in_Nebraska.pdf

Anderson-Levitt, K. M. (2002). *Teaching cultures: Knowledge for teaching first grade in France and the United States.* Cresskill, NJ: Hampton Press, Inc.

Auguste, B. G., Kihn, P., & Miller, M. (2010). *Closing the talent gap: Attracting and retaining top-third graduates to careers in teaching: An international and market research-based perspective.* McKinsey.

Bransford, J. D., Brown, A. L., & Cocking, R. R. (1999). *How people learn.* Washington, DC: National Academy Press.

Close, K., Amrein-Beardsley, A., & Collins, C. (2019). Mapping America's teacher evaluation plans under ESSA. *Phi Delta Kappan, 101*(2), 22–26.

Danielson, C. (2013). *The framework for teaching evaluation instrument, 2013 instructionally focused edition.* Retrieved January, 17, 2021.

Dyson, A. H., & Genishi, C. (2005). *On the case: The approaches to language and literacy research.* New York: Teachers College Press.

Hargreaves, D. H. (1999). The knowledge-creating school. *British Journal of Educational Studies, 47*(2), 122–144.

Hodkinson, P., Biesta, G., & James, D. (2004). *Towards a cultural theory of collegebased learning* [Paper]. *The annual conference of the British Educational Research Association*, Manchester.

Jarvis, P. (2000). Globalisation, the learning society and cooperative education. *Comparative Education*, *36*(3), 343–355.

Kane, T. J., & Staiger, D. O. (2012). *Gathering feedback for teaching: Combining high-quality observations with student surveys and achievement gains* [Research paper]. MET Project. Bill & Melinda Gates Foundation.

Lave, J. (1996). Teaching, as learning, in practice. *Mind, Culture and Society*, *3*(3), 149164.

Law, S. (1999). Leadership for learning; the changing culture of professional development in schools. *Journal of Educational Administration*, *37*(1), 66–76.

Marzano, R., Toth, M., & Schooling, P. (2012). *Examining the role of teacher evaluation in student achievement: Contemporary research base for the Marzano Causal Teacher Evaluation Model.* Retrieved from the Learning Sciences Marzano Center website: http://www.marzanocenter.com/files/MC_White_Paper_20120424.pdf

Rentner, D. S., & Kober, N. (2012). After the stimulus money ends: The status of state K-12 education funding and reforms. *Center on Education Policy.*

Webb, R., Vulliamy, G., Hämäläinen, S., Sarja, A., Kimonen, E., & Nevalainen, R. (2004). A comparative analysis of primary teacher professionalism in England and Finland. *Comparative Education*, *40*(1), 83–107.

Whitty, G., Power, S., & Halpin, D. (1998). *Devolution and choice in education.* Buckingham: Open University Press.

Index

Page numbers in *Italics* refer to figure numbers; **bold** refer to table numbers and page numbers followed by 'n' refer to notes numbers.

Made in the USA
Las Vegas, NV
30 October 2024

8fb05d0e-6c50-4e63-8547-28ed1ffa384fR01